ACROSS THE SEA ACROSS THE PLAINS

THE EPIC ACCOUNT OF THE

WILLIE & MARTIN HANDCART COMPANIES

FROM EUROPE TO ZION

ACROSS THE SEA ACROSS THE PLAINS

THE EPIC ACCOUNT OF THE WILLIE & MARTIN HANDCART COMPANIES FROM EUROPE TO ZION

SHELLI SIMMONS

CFI
AN IMPRINT OF CEDAR FORT, INC.
SPRINGVILLE, UTAH

ISBN 13: 978-1-4621-1017-9

Published by CFI an imprint of Cedar Fort, Inc.
2373 W. 700 S., Springville, UT 84663
Distributed by Cedar Fort, Inc. www.cedarfort.com

LIBRARY OF CONGRESS CATALOGING-IN-PUBLICATION DATA

Simmons, Shelli, 1968- author.
Across the sea, across the plains : the epic account of the Willie and Martin Handcart Companies from Europe to Zion / Shelli Simmons.
pages cm
Includes bibliographical references.
ISBN 978-1-4621-1017-9
1. James G. Willie Emigrating Company. 2. Edward Martin Emigrating Company. 3. Mormon pioneers--History--19th century. 4. Mormon handcart companies. 5. Overland journeys to the Pacific. I. Title.

F593.S54 2012
978'.020882893--dc23

2012002119

Cover design by Angela D. Olsen
Cover design © 2012 by Lyle Mortimer
Edited and typeset by Melissa J. Caldwell

Printed in the United States of America

10 9 8 7 6 5 4 3 2 1

Printed on acid-free paper

To my son Justin
and all whom I have
loved and lost

I have a desire to leave a record of those scenes and events, thru which I have passed, that my children, down to my latest posterity may read what their ancestors were willing to suffer, and did suffer, patiently for the Gospel's sake. And I wish them to understand, too, that what I now word is the history of hundreds of others, both men, women and children, who have passed through many like scenes for a similar cause, at the same time we did. I also desire them to know that it was in obedience to the commandments of the true and living God, and with the assurance of an eternal reward—an exaltation to eternal life in His kingdom—that we suffered these things. I hope, too, that it will inspire my posterity with fortitude to stand firm and faithful to the truth, and be willing to suffer, and sacrifice all things they may be required to pass thru for the Kingdom of God's sake.†

Elizabeth Horrocks Jackson
Martin Company

CONTENTS

ACKNOWLEDGMENTS

First and foremost, I express gratitude for my Savior Jesus Christ. I also express gratitude for all of the named and unnamed members of the Willie and Martin Handcart Companies, the missionaries who sacrificed so much to bring the gospel to them, as well as the rescuers who risked their lives to bring them into the Salt Lake Valley. I wish I could have included all of their remarkable stories in this account.

To my family, words cannot express the love I have in my heart for you! Thank you for your love, patience, and understanding during the countless hours I spent at the computer and in research for this project.

To Cedar Fort Publishing, I will always be grateful for your belief in this project and your assistance in making this dream a reality. Special thanks to my editor, Melissa Caldwell, for sharing your proficiency and expertise—your suggestions were invaluable. To Angela Eschler, thank you for your graciousness in offering your advice and your professional skills—your help on this project was immeasurable. To Kelly Pugh for your talent and skill in creating the paintings that bring *Across the Sea, Across the Plains* to life. A link to these paintings can be viewed online at www.AcrosstheSeaAcrossthePlains.com.

To my cherished friends Anita Stanley, Alicia Cerva, and Lori Brooksby—the experiences we shared during our service together inspired this project. I express sincere gratitude to Lori Brooksby, Gayla Perkins, Becky Gray, Anita Stanley, and Loretta Grundvig for your assistance in reading and critiquing the manuscript. To a dear friend, Lisa Richards—thank you for your thoughtfulness for the past twenty years. It means more than you will ever realize.

Finally, to you, the reader, I pray you will be touched, as I have, by this account.

I wish to go on record concerning the magnitude of what our forebears accomplished and what this means to us. It is a story with which most of you are familiar, but it is worth another telling. It is a story so large in scope, so fraught with human suffering and the workings of faith, that it will never grow old or stale. Whether you are among the posterity of the pioneers or whether you were baptized only yesterday, each is the beneficiary of their great undertaking. What a wonderful thing it is to have behind us a great and noble body of progenitors! What a marvelous thing to be the recipients of a magnificent heritage that speaks of the guiding hand of the Lord, of the listening ear of His prophets, of the total dedication of a vast congregation of Saints who loved this cause more than life itself.[‡]

—President Gordon B. Hinckley

AUTHOR'S NOTE

The information contained herein is largely compiled from personal journal accounts of missionaries called to proclaim the great and marvelous work of the restoration of the gospel of Jesus Christ to the European nations and of those souls who were converted to the gospel as a result of the missionaries' labors. Together, many of these faithful men, women, and children would later become members of the Willie and Martin Handcart Companies of 1856. Their journal accounts and recollections of their experiences are priceless treasures that document what was required of the early Saints in order to establish the gospel upon the earth in the latter days.

Of these early Saints, President Gordon B. Hinckley stated: "Legion are the stories of those who were there and who suffered almost unto death and who carried all of their lives the scars of that dreadful experience. It was a tragedy without parallel in the western migration of our people. When all is said and done, no one can imagine, no one can appreciate or understand how desperate were their circumstances."[1]

While it is true the accounts contained herein are wrought with human suffering, if you look deeper, you will see much more. You will see a special and select group of people who left behind a great and lasting legacy of faith, courage, selflessness, charity, love, and compassion in order to fulfill the mighty purposes of God. These Saints were willing to give their all, even their lives, for the gospel of Jesus Christ, which they loved. Their journal accounts document their trials, adversity, and challenges, which began long before they started pulling handcarts in Iowa and continued long after they arrived in the Salt Lake Valley.

In regard to our pioneer ancestors, President Gordon B. Hinckley stated:

> It is good to look to the past to gain appreciation for the present and perspective for the future. It is good to look upon the virtues of those who have gone before, to gain strength for whatever lies ahead. It is good to reflect upon the work of those who labored so hard and gained so little in this world, but out of whose dreams and early plans, so well nurtured, has come a great harvest of which we are the beneficiaries. Their tremendous example can become a compelling motivation for us all, for each of us is a pioneer in his own life, often in his own family, and many of us pioneer daily in trying to establish a gospel foothold in distant parts of the world.[2]

As we reflect upon the work of those who labored so hard and gained so little in the world, we do so with great reverence, for we truly have become the great beneficiaries of their strength, courage, love, compassion, and devotion. Their experiences, though of a much different nature, are directly applicable to us today, and they can serve as a great source of comfort, instruction, inspiration, and guidance, and can become a compelling motivation for us as we carry forth this work in our day.

In March 1856, as the Saints of the European nations were about to embark upon (in the words penned by eleven-year-old Mary James) "the most remarkable journey recorded in the annals of history," the following was written in the *Millennial Star*:

> Before the Lord can do these mighty works, the Saints have to exercise a faith in Him which will lead them to undertake greater things than crossing the plains on foot, with hand-carts, and plenty of provisions. It is full reliance in God and His servants, that the Saints must attain to, before they can be proper instruments for the accomplishment of His mighty purposes. The Lord has declared that He will have a tried people. How is this to be accomplished, if not by

> testing their energies, and purifying them in the furnace of affliction, until every frail reed on which they lean for support is broken—every earthly hope swept away, and they realize in the fullness of their souls, that none but the Lord can deliver them.[3]

This statement from the *Millennial Star* is just as applicable to us in our day: before the Lord can perform His mighty works, we have to exercise a faith in Him, which will lead us to undertake greater things than crossing the plains on foot, with handcarts. We must fully rely on God and His servants before we can be proper instruments in accomplishing His mighty purposes. The Lord has declared that He will have a tried people. How is this to be accomplished, if not by testing *our* energies, and purifying *our* hearts in the furnace of affliction, until every frail reed on which *we* lean for support is broken—every earthly hope swept away, and we realize in the fullness of *our* souls, that none but the Lord can deliver us.

Like Wallace Stegner once said of an unlikely band of pioneers immigrating to America in 1856, they lacked the rudimentary skills that make frontiersmen. They had never pitched a tent, slept on the ground, cooked outdoors, or built a campfire. They looked more like the population of the poor farm on a picnic than like pioneers about to embark upon a thousand-mile handcart journey. But as it turned out, they had some of the stuff that makes heroes.[4] Like this unlikely band of pioneers, we too look, to the world, like an unlikely band of pioneers without the skills needed to carry forth the mighty purposes of the Lord in the last days. But, as it turns out, we are the ones who have been held in reserve to come forth at this time to "be an influence for good in helping to build the kingdom of God and prepare the world for the Second Coming of the Savior."[5]

1

OPENING THE DOOR OF SALVATION

THE EUROPEAN GATHERING

KIRTLAND, OHIO
JUNE 4–JUNE 13, 1837

On Sunday, June 4, 1837, while Heber C. Kimball was seated in the Kirtland Temple, the Prophet Joseph Smith approached him and quietly spoke words that forever changed his life: "Brother Heber, the Spirit of the Lord has whispered to me: 'Let my servant Heber go to England and proclaim my Gospel, and open the door of salvation to that nation.'" Though overwhelmed with this weighty responsibility, Heber was ready and prepared to accept the call. He had known in his heart that one day he would be required to perform such a work.[1]

Heber's mission call to England came during grave and difficult times in the history of the Church. Much dishonesty, hypocrisy, jealousy, and contention existed within the hearts of many Saints in Kirtland. Further exasperating these conditions were the economical difficulties created by a financial panic felt throughout the United States. In the words of Brigham Young: "This was a crisis when earth and hell seemed leagued to overthrow the Prophet and church of God. The knees of many of the strongest men in the church faltered." Although many prominent men once loyal to the prophet "fell away and became enemies and apostates," the meek and humble stood firm and steadfast in the midst of so much uncertainty.[2]

Heber and his family were among the meek and humble who remained faithful during such trying times. The decision to accept the call to serve a mission to England weighed heavily upon Heber's shoulders. He knew he would be leaving his family in almost destitute circumstances, yet he had faith and complete trust in the Lord, and in his heart he strongly felt "that the cause of truth, the Gospel of Christ, outweighed every other consideration." Heber felt a great sense of responsibility and overwhelming feelings of inadequacy, feeling as if he was "a man of stammering tongue, and altogether unfit for such a work." He questioned how he could preach in the land "which is so famed throughout Christendom for learning, knowledge and piety; the nursery of religion; and to a people whose intelligence is proverbial!" Heber was aware of his personal weaknesses, yet he demonstrated faith, like unto the great biblical prophet Enoch (Moses 6:31), as he understood the will of Heavenly Father "that the fulness of my gospel might be proclaimed by the weak and the simple unto the ends of the world" (D&C 1:23–24). With little time to prepare, Heber sought solace in the attic of the Kirtland temple, praying daily for protection and power to fulfill his mission honorably. He was blessed with a great determination to go on his mission and believed wholeheartedly that "God would support and endow him with every qualification he would need." Several members of the Quorum of the Twelve Apostles, of which Heber was a member, opposed him going on this mission, stating Heber was a fool to go at the call of a fallen prophet.[3]

Heber recorded the following words from the blessing he received while being set apart by the First Presidency to preside over the England mission: "That God would make me mighty in that nation in winning souls unto Him; angels should accompany me and bear me up, that my feet should never slip; that I should be mightily blessed and prove a source of salvation to thousands, not only in England but America."[4]

On June 13, 1837, just nine days from the time Heber received his call, with faith and courage unmeasured, he bade farewell to family and friends and, without purse or scrip, started for England. What is penned by the hand of Robert B. Thompson of the events he witnessed at Heber C. Kimball's home just prior to Kimball's departure is deeply personal and telling of the emotions felt by the Kimball family at the time. Robert wrote of coming upon the scene quite by accident, but he felt riveted to remain to witness the event. Heber was praying, petitioning God to

> grant him a prosperous voyage across the mighty ocean, and make him useful wherever his lot should be cast, and that He who "careth for sparrows" and "feedeth the young ravens when they cry," would supply the wants of his companion and little ones in his absence. He then like the patriarchs, and by virtue of that office, laid his hands upon them, individually, leaving a father's blessing upon, and commending them to the care and protection of God, while he should be engaged in preaching the gospel in distant lands. While thus engaged, his voice was almost lost in the sobs of those around, who tried in vain to suppress them. The idea of losing a protector and a father was indeed painful. He proceeded, but his heart was too much affected to do so regularly; his emotions were great, yea, unutterable; and he was obliged to stop at intervals, while the big tears started down his cheeks—an index to the feelings which reigned in his bosom. I was not stoic enough to refrain, but in spite of myself I wept, and mingled my tears with theirs; at the same time, I felt thankful that I had the privilege of contemplating such a scene. Nothing, thought I, could induce that man to tear himself from so affectionate a group, from his partner and children who are so dear to him—nothing but a sense of duty and love to God, and attachment to his cause.[5]

England
July 1837–April 1838

On Thursday, July 20, 1837, immediately after the ship Garrick anchored in Liverpool, England, a small boat came alongside to transport the passengers ashore. Missionaries from The Church of Jesus Christ of Latter-day Saints were among the first on board. Before the small boat reached the pier, Heber C. Kimball jumped ashore. Heber noted the following: "My feelings at that time, were peculiar, particularly, when I realized the object, importance, and extent of my mission, and the work to which I had been appointed, and in which I was shortly to be engaged. . . . I was led to cry mightily to the Lord for wisdom and for that comfort and support which I so much needed. At the same time I thought, that if I could have been relieved from the responsibility which rested upon me, by fighting Goliath on as unequal terms as David did, I should have felt myself happy."[6]

The arrival of the missionaries in Liverpool, England, was truly a time to rejoice. They were brought to this land bearing the glorious message of the restoration of the gospel of Jesus Christ upon the earth. The deliverance of this message would mark the end of a famine in that land, "not a famine of bread, nor a thirst for water, but [a famine] of hearing the words of the Lord" (Amos 8:11).

Having arrived with nothing but the kindness and mercy of God to support and sustain them, the missionaries remained in Liverpool for two days. Those two days were spent in council and petitioning the Lord for guidance and direction on how to proceed in establishing the Church in the great nation of England. Impressed upon their minds was the direction to begin their mission in Preston, a large manufacturing town in Lancashire, located thirty-one miles to the northeast of Liverpool.[7]

On Saturday, July 22, 1837, the missionaries traveled by coach to Preston. Upon their arrival, they found the streets of Preston alive with the excitement of a national election. Music was playing, flags and banners were flying, and thousands were parading up and down the streets in support of the various political candidates. The missionaries watched in awe, since they had never before witnessed such a scene. In front of them a large flag was unfurled over their heads on which was printed "Truth will Prevail." At the sight of these words, their hearts rejoiced exceedingly, and they cried aloud, "Amen, thanks be unto God, truth will prevail." After unloading their trunks and getting settled, Joseph Fielding traveled to the home of his brother, Reverend James Fielding, who resided in that area.[8]

For some time, Joseph Fielding, along with his sisters Mary and Mercy, had been corresponding with their brother, sharing their testimonies of the restoration of the gospel. Little did they realize what an important role this correspondence would play in preparing the way and making ready the minds of many to accept the restored gospel of Jesus Christ. Reverend James Fielding had been reading the letters to his congregation and had invited them to pray to God asking Him to send His servants. "Their faith shook the heavens, and in dreams and visions many were shown the very men whom the Lord was about to send into their midst. Heber C. Kimball, especially, on his arrival in Preston was recognized by persons who had never until then beheld him in the flesh." The missionaries were kindly received by the Reverend and were invited to attend Sunday morning services in a small chapel located on Vauxhall Road.[9]

During Sunday morning's service with the Reverend and his congregation, the elders prayed fervently to the Lord that the way would be opened for them to preach to the congregation. Their prayers were heard and answered. At the close of the morning service, Reverend Fielding, without any prior request from the missionaries, gave notice that an elder of the Latter-day Saints would preach at his pulpit that afternoon. Upon returning to the Vauxhall Chapel that afternoon, the missionaries preached and bore powerful testimony and were asked to return in the evening to preach again. At the close of Sunday's evening meeting, notice was given that the elders would again preach on Wednesday evening.[10]

Following the services held on Wednesday, July 26, nine members of the congregation offered themselves for baptism. This angered the Reverend Fielding, and he forbade the elders from baptizing members of his congregation. The missionaries informed the Reverend that members of his congregation were of age and could act for themselves; the baptisms were scheduled for Sunday morning. From that time forward, the Reverend James Fielding opposed the very messages he had previously encouraged his congregation to pray to receive.[11]

On Sunday, July 30, 1837, the morning the first baptisms were to take place, the powers of the adversary combined in attempts to thwart the work from progressing. Isaac Russell was the first to feel the effects of the adversary, and he called out for Heber to rush to his aid. Heber immediately arose, and he and Orson Hyde laid their hands upon his head. While thus engaged, Heber felt as if he was struck with great force, and he was knocked senseless to the floor. The account continues in Heber's words:

> The first thing I recollected was being supported by Elders Hyde and Richards, who were praying for me. . . . then assisted me to get on the bed, but my agony was so great I could not endure it, and I arose, bowed my knees and prayed. I then arose and sat up on the bed, when a vision was opened to our minds and we could distinctly see the evil spirits. . . . They came towards us like armies rushing to battle. They appeared to be men of full stature, possessing every form and feature of men in the flesh, who were angry and desperate; and I shall never forget the vindictive malignity depicted on their countenances as they looked me in the eye; and any attempt to paint the scene which then presented itself, or portray their malice and enmity, would be vain. I perspired exceedingly, my clothes becoming as wet as if I had been taken out of the river. I felt excessive pain, and was in the greatest distress for some time. I cannot even look back on the scene without feelings of horror; yet by it I learned the power of the adversary, his enmity against the servants of God, and got some understanding of the invisible world. We distinctly heard those spirits talk and express their wrath and hellish designs against us. However, the Lord delivered us from them, and blessed us exceedingly that day.[12]

In a conversation following his return to the United States, Heber C. Kimball shared this experience with the Prophet Joseph Smith and expressed great concern regarding his personal worthiness. In response, the Prophet replied: "No, Brother Heber, at that time you were nigh unto the Lord; there was only a veil between you and Him, but you could not see Him. When I heard of it, it gave me great joy, for I then knew that the work of God had taken root in that land. . . . The nearer a person approaches the Lord, a greater power will be manifested by the adversary to prevent the accomplishment of His purposes."[13]

In spite of the events experienced by missionaries hours earlier, at approximately nine o'clock in the morning, Heber C. Kimball baptized nine members of Reverend Fielding's congregation, on the eighth day after their arrival in Preston. "The circumstance of baptizing in the open air being somewhat novel, a concourse of between seven and nine thousand persons assembled on the banks of the river to witness the ceremony. It was the first time baptism by immersion was administered openly."[14]

PUCELL FAMILY

Two days later, on August 1, 1837, Margaret Perren Pucell was baptized. Her husband, Samuel, was baptized seven days later on August 8. It is recorded that the Pucells gave the first sixpence to the missionaries. They "were among the first members of the Preston branch of the church, Lancashire, England, organized there in July, 1837, by President Heber C. Kimball and others. . . . Sister Pucell at one time, hearing that some of the six or eight associate elders of President Kimball hadn't anything to eat one day, took one of her skirts and pawned it for enough to buy a loaf of bread, a few ounces of tea and sugar and half a pound of butter, which she took to the elders, begging them to accept the donation." The Pucell family would work and save for nineteen years before the way would be opened to immigrate to the Salt Lake Valley with the Martin Handcart Company.[15]

MCBRIDE FAMILY

Also on August 1, Robert McBride was baptized at the hands of Orson Hyde. Because of opposition from her family, Heber C. Kimball would not baptize Robert's wife, Margaret, until January 4, 1838. Robert's son Peter wrote: "From that time, our home was open to the elders where services were held, the sacrament administered and many missionaries found a haven of rest. Mother held open house, always had something ready to serve hungry elders and a good bed for them to rest in." Like the Pucell family, the McBrides worked and saved for nineteen years before they were able to emigrate with the Martin Handcart Company.[16]

In England, the work began rolling forward with great momentum. Requests for the elders to preach rang frequently in their ears; they labored both day and night to satisfy the desire to hear the news of the restoration of the gospel of Jesus Christ. Heber C. Kimball noted: "Consequently, our lungs were very sore and our bodies considerably wore down with fatigue."[17]

In Heber's words, "Thus mightily ran the word of God and prospered. . . . During this state of things, our enemies were not idle, but heaped abuse upon us with an unsparing hand, and issued torrents of lies after us, which, however, I am thankful to say, did not sweep us away."[18]

The missionaries soon began visiting cities north of Preston. Great interest and excitement arose with their arrival, and many influential men suspended operation of their factories to allow their workmen the privilege of hearing from the missionaries. Heber noted: "We could scarcely tear ourselves away from them and when we did so, they wept like little children, such a desire to hear the gospel, I never saw equalled before. The Saints will be able to gather some idea from this circumstance, of the great and extensive calls for the Elders of Israel in that land, where there are so many thousands, thirsting for the streams of knowledge, and the privileges and blessings of the gospel."[19]

On one occasion, Heber felt impressed to preach in an area where he had been informed that for the past thirty years, efforts from several ministers of different denominations had proved futile because of the hardness of their hearts. This did not discourage Heber, for he knew the gospel of Jesus Christ could reach even the hardest of hearts. Accordingly, he went and obtained a large barn where the crowds gathered in excess. Heber preached with great power and conviction. The spirit present was undeniable and, in the words of Heber, "people who were represented as being so hard and obdurate, were melted down into tenderness and love, and such a feeling was produced as I never saw before, and the effect seemed to be general." Heber baptized twenty-five people and was engaged in that duty until after midnight.[20]

Heber had similar results in many other areas as well. He related:

> These towns seemed to be affected from one end to the other, parents called their children together, spoke to them of the subjects which I had preached, and warned them against swearing and all other evil practices and instructed them in their duty, &c. &c. Such a scene I presume was never witnessed in this place before—the hearts of the people appeared to be broken and the next morning they were all in tears thinking they should see my face no more. When I left them my feelings were such as I cannot describe, as I walked down the street followed by numbers, the doors were crowded by the inmates of the houses to bid us a last farewell, who could only give vent to their grief in sobs and broken accents. While contemplating this scene we were induced to take off our hats, for we felt as if the place was holy ground—the Spirit of the Lord rested down upon us,

> and I was constrained to bless that whole region of country, we were followed by a great number, a considerable distance from the villages who could hardly separate themselves from us. My heart was like unto theirs, and I thought my head was a fountain of tears, for I wept for several miles after I bid them adieu.[21]

When Heber returned to America, he shared his tender feelings regarding this experience with the Prophet Joseph Smith. Joseph responded by testifying to Heber that the ground they walked was indeed holy, "that some of the ancient prophets had traveled in that region and dedicated the land," further sharing blessings to fall upon Heber and his missionary companions.[22]

As winter came, England experienced extraordinarily harsh weather. "In consequence of the inclemency of the weather, several manufacturing establishments were shut up, and several thousand workmen as well as women and children were thrown out of employment, whose sufferings during that time were severe." Many became destitute and perished from starvation. Heber C. Kimball penned: "Such sufferings I never witnessed in my life before and the scenes which I daily beheld while in that country was ready to chill the blood in my veins: the streets were crowded with men, women and children, who solicited alms from the passengers as they walked along. Numbers of those poor wretches were without shoes or stockings and scarcely any covering to screen them from the inclemency of the weather."[23]

During this time of great difficulty, missionaries were richly blessed. Heber wrote: "I have had to go into the water to administer the ordinance of baptism six or seven times in a day, and frequently after having come out of the water and changed my clothes, I have had to return back again before I reached my home; this too when the weather was extremely cold, the ice being from twelve to fourteen inches thick, which continued so about twelve weeks, during which time I think there were but ten days, in which we were not in the water; 'the harvest was indeed plenteous but the laborers were few.'"[24]

Heber's account continues:

> We were continually employed and hardly gave 'sleep to our eyes or slumber to our eyelids,' and some nights we would hardly

> close them. The task was almost more than we could endure, but realizing the circumstances of this people, their love of the truth, their humility and unfeigned charity, caused us to use all diligence and make good use of every moment of time, for truly our bowels yearned over them. Notwithstanding our unwearied and unceasing labors, we could not fill the calls we had from day to day, for the work kept spreading, the prospect of usefulness grew brighter and brighter, and the field opened larger and larger, while the cries from the North, from the South, from the East and from the West of come over and help us, were more and more frequently sounding in our ears.[25]

As the time drew near for the missionaries to return home to America, their focus was not only on preaching the restored gospel and baptizing, but also in organizing the established branches. One day previous to their departure on April 9, 1838, a general conference of the Church was held in the Temperance Hall in Preston, where over six hundred of the Saints gathered. The missionaries truly had cause to rejoice; some two thousand Saints had embraced the gospel and entered the waters of baptism over the last eight months. Heber C. Kimball himself converted about one thousand five hundred. Joseph Fielding was appointed to preside over the Church along with his counselors, Willard Richards and William Clayton.[26]

Heber C. Kimball recorded:

> Some persons may be disposed to accuse me of weakness on this occasion, but if any should do so, I would say that I do not envy any man's feelings, who could witness such a scene, with all its associations, and the finer feelings of his heart strings not to be touched on such an occasion; indeed it would have been almost an impossibility for us to have left this dear and affectionate people, had we not had the most implicit confidence in the brethren who were appointed to preside over them in our absence; but knowing their faith and virtuous conversation, and that they had the confidence of the church, we felt confident that the affairs of the church would be conducted in righteousness; consequently we left them under different feelings than we otherwise could, had they had no shepherd.[27]

Ohio, Missouri, and Illinois
May 1838–April 1839

Kirtland, Ohio

The missionaries arrived in Kirtland in May 1838, having been absent a little over eleven months. They found the city in great turmoil, with apostasy raging in the hearts of many who held positions of leadership and great trust. These men denounced Joseph Smith as a prophet and united together in their efforts to overthrow the Church. Thereafter, Kirtland was no longer safe for any Saint. Throughout the spring and summer of 1838, the Saints fled from their homes to the wilderness area in Caldwell County, Missouri, a distance of nearly eighteen hundred miles.[28]

Missouri

In Missouri, the Saints soon found that greater trials and tribulations were nigh at hand. "The fall and winter of 1838 was one of the darkest periods in Church history. Mobocracy on one hand, and apostasy on the other, dealt the cause of God cruel blows, such as no human work could hope to withstand." The influx of Saints arriving in Missouri caused alarm and feelings of great animosity among the Missourians, who had already driven the Mormons from Jackson County by force five years earlier in 1833. Conditions began to deteriorate rapidly, and once again the hearts of the Saints began to fail. Consequently, many of them dissented. The dissenters harassed the Saints with lawsuits and condemned Church leaders, yet amid all of the trouble and strife, apostasy, and mobocracy, the Prophet Joseph Smith remained resolute in moving the work forward.[29]

From this time forward, the Saints in Missouri suffered terribly; they were persecuted relentlessly and exposed to all manner atrocities, many even unto death. Heber C. Kimball records: "The enemies of righteousness were determined to overthrow the Saints, and regardless of all laws, (which was trampled upon with impunity,) they made every preparation, and used every means in their power to accomplish their unhallowed designs. The Saints, tenacious of their liberties, and sacred rights, resisted these unlawful designs, and with courage worthy of them, they guarded their families and their homes, from the aggressions of the mob, but not without the loss of several lives." Heber's account continues: "Yes, the blood of the Saints has stained the soil of Missouri, for which the King of Kings and Lord of Hosts will recompense upon her, the punishment of her crimes."[30]

Governor Lilburn W. Boggs, having received numerous exaggerated and false reports regarding the Mormons, felt they were in open and avowed defiance of the laws, initiating hostilities, and making war upon the people of Missouri. On Saturday, October 27, 1838, the governor issued an "extermination order" directing the militia in part: "Your orders are therefore, to hasten your operations and endeavor to reach Richmond in Ray county, with all possible speed. . . . The Mormons must be treated as enemies, and must be exterminated, or driven from the State, if necessary for the public peace. . . . Their outrages are beyond all description."[31]

Three days later, on October 30, a mob of about 240 armed men on horseback approached a community of Saints living near Jacob Haun's mill. Upon seeing the mob, the women and children fled into the woods and the men sought to defend themselves in the blacksmith shop.

> David Evans, seeing their superiority of numbers, swung his hat and cried for peace. This was not heeded, and they continued to advance, and their leader Mr. Comstock, fired a gun, which was followed by a solemn pause of ten or twelve seconds, when, all at once they discharged about 100 rifles, aiming at a blacksmith's shop, into which our friends had fled for safety; and then charged up to the shop, the cracks of which between the logs were sufficiently large to enable them to aim directly at the bodies of those who had there fled for refuge from the fire of their murderers.

The mob was ruthless and brutal, shooting mercilessly at everyone in sight. "The slaughter of these not satisfying the mob they then proceeded to rob and plunder. The scene that presented itself after the massacre to the widows and orphans of the killed is beyond description. It was truly a time of weeping, of mourning and of lamentation." President Brigham Young "was also among the number. He also fled, and although the balls flew around him like hail, he was not wounded." The attack left seventeen dead and many wounded.[32]

On the following day, thousands of men, determined to execute the governor's extermination order, surrounded the city of Far West. Joseph Smith was betrayed into the hands of the militia by men who were once trusted and loyal associates. The militia demanded Joseph give himself up or every man, woman, and child would be massacred. Joseph, along with several others, was held before an illegal court martial and sentenced to die by firing squad. However, General Alexander Doniphan of the Missouri militia refused to carry out the execution order. The men remained prisoners and were later taken to Liberty Jail.[33]

During this time it was recorded that an unprecedented amount of snow fell. The men were gathered together and were commanded to deliver up their weapons of war. They were not allowed to return to their families, and the following day were brought up at the point of bayonet and forced to sign deeds of trust transferring all their property. They had no choice but to comply with the orders. "The mob then commenced plundering the citizens of their bedding, clothing, money, wearing apparel, and everything of value they could lay their hands upon; and also attempting to violate the chastity of the women in sight of their husbands, pretending they were hunting for prisoners and firearms." Truly these were "times that tried men's souls. . . . Apostles, Presidents, and Elders fell from the faith and joined hands with the robbers and murderers of their brethren."[34]

Twelve-year-old Arza Hinckley recalled:

> They came in and marched our brethren up to a table in the center of them and at the point of a gun demanded that they leave the Church or sign away their property to pay the expenses of being mobbed, and leave the state forthwith or be shot down. I, as one of the boys, used to be allowed to pass the guard to bring in the cows at night. Some of us were allowed to stay until spring. For want of mills to grind our corn in, we had to take tin pans, punch holes in them from the inside to make rough, boil our corn to soften it and rub it on the pan to make meal of it. Flour was out of the question.

When Arza was five years old, his father passed away, his mother remarried, and Arza went to live with his new grandfather, who shortly thereafter joined the church. From a young age Arza developed a great love for the Book of Mormon, noting: "I used to read the Book of Mormon, pray and cry." Arza was baptized at the age of nine and thereafter "devoted his life spiritually, temporally, mentally, physically and financially to it. He was always ready at duty's call, no matter what the sacrifice necessary." Arza would go on to serve in the Mormon Battalion as well as in the rescue efforts of the Martin Handcart Company.[35]

While imprisoned in Liberty Jail, the Prophet Joseph received reports of the Saints' sufferings as they continued to be persecuted. Joseph's heart weighed upon him heavily and led him to cry out: "O God, where art thou? And where is the pavilion that covereth thy hiding place? How long shall thy hand be stayed, and thine eye, yea thy pure eye, behold from the eternal heavens the wrongs of thy people and of thy servants, and thine ear be penetrated with their cries? Yea, O Lord, how long shall they suffer these wrongs and unlawful oppressions, before thine heart shall be softened toward them, and thy bowels be moved with compassion toward them?" (D&C 121:1–3).

The Lord in his tender mercy replied to the cry from Joseph's heart in part:

> My son, peace be unto thy soul: thine adversity and thine afflictions shall be but a small moment; And then, if thou endure it well, God shall exalt thee on high; thou shalt triumph over all thy foes. . . . Know thou, my son, that all these things shall give thee experience, and shall be for thy good. The Son of Man hath descended below them all. Art thou greater than he? Therefore, hold on thy way, and the priesthood shall remain with thee; for their bounds are set, they cannot pass. Thy days are known, and thy years shall not be numbered less; therefore, fear not what man can do, for God shall be with you forever and ever. (D&C 122:7–8; 122:7–9)

With the Prophet imprisoned, the responsibility to organize a large-scale migration rested upon the shoulders of Brigham Young. Some ten thousand to twelve thousand Latter-day Saints fled from Missouri to western Illinois under harsh winter conditions. John Taylor recorded:

> We had just before this been driven from our homes by a ruthless mob, who, with the fury of demons, had burned our houses,

> laid waste our fields, destroyed our property, butchered many of our brethren, and, inspired by a demonic influence, not satisfied with this, they followed us with unrelenting fury and a brutality that would have sickened the most savage barbarian until the governor's exterminating order was literally fulfilled. . . . My heart recoils when I reflect upon the scenes we then passed through. . . . I have witnessed thousands of our brethren and sisters, together with their helpless offspring, driven from their homes during the inclement season of an American winter, robbed of their all, and wandering as fugitives, wending their way to a strange land, houseless, homeless, and friendless, except what friendship they experienced from the hands of the people of the state of Illinois, pitching their tents by the way, or laying under the canopy of Heaven, until with fatigue and cold, and privations, many of them sickened and died."[36]

Nauvoo, Illinois

The Prophet Joseph Smith remained imprisoned in Liberty Jail until he, along with several others, were allowed to escape in April 1839. Shortly thereafter, Joseph established a new gathering place for the Saints in Nauvoo, Illinois, and Montrose, Iowa, as well as in numerous neighboring locations surrounding Nauvoo.[37]

Despite the horrific scenes that the Saints endured, the work continued to roll forward regardless of the unrelenting efforts to thwart the progression. With specific instruction from the Lord, the Twelve Apostles were called to return to the temple site in Far West, Missouri, on April 26, 1839, and from there depart for a mission to England (D&C 118:4–5). Because of the great persecution, many did not think it wise for the Twelve to attempt such a journey at the risk of their lives. The Twelve responded with one voice, "The Lord God had spoken, and it was for us to obey. It was the Lord's business to take care of His servants, and we would fulfill the commandment, or die trying." On this beautiful, clear, moonlit night, as the apostles rode into Far West, "it seemed as though the Lord, having a foreknowledge of what would take place, had given the revelation in this manner to see whether the Apostles would obey it at the risk of their lives."[38]

Wilford Woodruff recorded:

> Inasmuch as the devil had been in a measure thwarted by the Twelve going to Far West, and returning without harm, it seemed as though the destroyer was determined to make some other attempt upon us to hinder us from performing our missions; for it seemed that as soon as any one of the Apostles began to prepare for starting, he was smitten with chills and fever or sickness of some kind. Nearly all the quorum of the Twelve or their families began to be sick, so it still required the exercise of a good deal of faith and perseverance to start off on a mission.[39]

Regarding the difficult and trying circumstances the Apostles found themselves, John Taylor penned:

> It may be asked by some, how was it that you were so afflicted when you were engaged in the work of the Lord? To this I would answer, I have seen diseases of all kinds healed by the laying on of hands according to the ordinance of God. I have seen men raised from the jaws of death, and through the instrumentality of those men that were thus afflicted; but we could not get faith either to heal ourselves or our brethren. We had already endured privations and afflictions from the hands of our persecutors that were sufficient to take away our lives, and the disease was the natural effect produced by our hardships; and again Satan wished to hinder and prevent us from fulfilling the word of the Lord. If this is not satisfactory to the skeptical, I would ask. Why Satan was allowed to afflict Job? Why Paul was obliged to leave Philetus at Miletum sick, who was sick, nigh unto death, for the work's sake? Why Timothy was not healed of his infirmities, but had to take a little wine for his stomach's sake, and for his often infirmities? Or why, when Paul besought the Lord to remove the thorn in the flesh, he would not?[40]

ENGLAND
DECEMBER 1839–APRIL 1841

In December 1839, Wilford Woodruff and John Taylor were among the first apostles to sail for England. Following their arrival in Liverpool, they proceeded to Preston, arriving on January 13, 1840. The Apostles found the Church struggling in its infancy yet progressing under the presidency of Joseph Fielding, Willard Richards, and William Clayton.[41]

Griffiths Family

On Tuesday, February 4, 1840, just twelve days after their arrival in Liverpool, John Taylor and Joseph Fielding baptized their first converts and established a small branch of about thirty Saints. Among those first converts were John and Margaret Griffiths, baptized by John Taylor. John was later called by Wilford Woodruff and Heber C. Kimball to preside over the Wollwich Branch in London. John's daughter Margaret recorded how diligently he served in this position: "he would work all day from six to six and then he would go preaching and he had so far to go. . . . he had to walk, and it would be sometimes twelve and one o'clock before he would get home. Well, when I got about eight years old I would go with him for company and to help him sing. . . . I was a little missionary for I traveled with him for years and walked many, many miles." The Griffith family would continue to serve diligently until the time of their emigration sixteen years later, in 1856, with the Martin Handcart Company.[42]

After being impressed that the Lord had a great work for him to perform in the south, Wilford Woodruff and a recent convert named William Benbow traveled to Herefordshire, where they called upon William's brother John Benbow, a wealthy farmer. Wilford was kindly received, and arrangements were made for him to preach to a small congregation the following day. Members of the congregation had broken off from the Methodists and called themselves the United Brethren. On the evening of March 6, 1840, Wilford Woodruff preached to a large number and several offered themselves up for baptism. Wilford spent most of following day clearing out a pool where the baptisms could be performed. John and Jane Benbow along with four preachers of the United Brethren were the first to be baptized.[43]

Rowley Family

Wilford Woodruff experienced unparalleled success in this area, daily baptizing members of the United Brethren whom embraced the gospel with all their hearts. Eventually, all but one of the six hundred members would join the Church. Ann Jewell Rowley writes the following of her conversion to the gospel and later experiences:

> We were members of a religious body called the "United Brethren." There was more than 600 of us who had broken off with the "Wesleyan Faith." We were continually praying for light and truth. Before our first child was born, we were privileged to hear a man named Wilford Woodruff proclaim a new gospel message. We really went to hear this man because we were curious and because we had heard that the Church of England had sent a constable to arrest him, but this man had converted him instead. Then the church sent two spies who were commissioned to sit in on the meetings and report back. They too were converted, so the church dared not send anyone else. We all wanted to hear this astonishing man. We had only to hear him once and William and I knew with all our hearts that he was offering us a priceless treasure. We accepted his offer and were baptized into the "Church of Jesus Christ of Latter-day Saints."

Ann's account continued: "Our lovely and spacious home was always open to the missionaries and we delighted in holding meetings there." One evening, while Wilford Woodruff and other missionaries and members gathered in the Rowley home, an angry mob gathered outside. William decided he would go outside and ask these neighbors, who he had known all of his life, to listen to reason. As he opened the door, he was seized by the mob and beaten severely. This was just the beginning of the trials the Rowley family would experience before they reached the Salt Lake Valley in 1856 with the Willie Handcart Company.[44]

On April 15, 1840, Brigham Young was sustained as President of the Quorum of the Twelve Apostles in a general conference held at the Temperance Hall. There were now eight members of the Twelve in the British Isles. They included Brigham Young, Heber C. Kimball, Parley P. Pratt, Orson Pratt, John Taylor, Wilford Woodruff, George A. Smith, and Willard Richards. Church membership at that time was recorded as 1,671. During the conference, the subject of emigration was discussed and recent converts John Benbow, Thomas Kington (formerly the superintendent of the United Brethren), and Edward Ockey contributed considerable amounts of money toward emigration assistance and printing the Book of Mormon and hymnbooks. Mr. Benbow also transferred ownership of the Gadfield Elm Chapel to the Church.[45]

Emigration Begins
June 6, 1840

Emigration of the British Saints began with forty-one Saints less than one month after the call to gather had been issued. These Saints took their passage for America on board the ship *Britannia*, which set sail from Liverpool on June 6, 1840, and arrived in New York on July 20, 1840. Thereafter, thousands immigrated to America.[46]

As a result of the large immigration numbers, great effort went into organizing the process. Experienced missionaries were called to serve as immigration officials, who established a shipping agency to oversee travel arrangements. Applications for emigration were gathered, monies were collected, ships were chartered, passenger confirmations were obtained, and last-minute substitutes were found when necessary. Homes in Liverpool were purchased to house members waiting for departure, and immigration officials were assigned to meet emigrants at arrival and departure points, give counsel and direction, and also travel with the emigrants to their destination. Once in America, railroad tickets were purchased, and arrangements were also made for emigrants to travel by steamship. Officials handled the purchase of food, supplies, and equipment to complete the journey. The immigration of thousands of Saints was a work of extraordinary magnitude that required attention to every detail and the united efforts of all involved to ensure its success. Over the years, the emigration system established by the elders of the Church "grew to such proportions and perfection that Samuel W. Richards was invited by the British government, before a committee of the House of Commons, to expound the splendid emigration system which the 'Mormons' had constructed."[47]

In England, although the Apostles enjoyed continued success, opposition remained their constant companion. On one occasion, a hostile mob assembled and surrounded a home in which Wilford Woodruff was to preach. In spite of the threats of physical violence against them, following the sermon, some desired baptism. The small group walked down to a pond and was soon surrounded by the mob armed with stones. Wilford offers further detail of the account in his own words: "If they had faith enough to be baptized, I had faith enough to administer the ordinance unto them; we repaired to the pool, which was surrounded by the mob armed with stones, I walked into the water with my mind stayed on God and baptized five persons while they were pelting my body with stones, one of which hit me on the head and came very near to knocking me down, however I received no lasting injury."[48]

Similar situations were repeated on many occasions. As Saints began to assemble for a meeting held at the home of Thomas Kington in Dymock, the beat of pails, kettles, pans, and sticks were heard through the streets, and soon a mob surrounded the home. Wilford Woodruff wrote:

> We closed our window shutters and doors in the room where we were, and I opened the meeting by singing and prayer, and as soon as I commenced, they armed themselves with stones, brick-bats, eggs, and everything they could lay their hands upon, and began to throw them upon the house like a shower of hail for nearly an hour, they dashed in the windows, scattered stones, brick and glass through the rooms, broke the tile on the roof, and continued to commit such depredations until I closed the meeting. . . . Some of the brethren went themselves and took the names of the leaders and returned into the house amid a shower of stones and brick-bats, though without injury; the saints soon went home, the mob dispersed, we cleared the house of stones, brick-bats, and glass, and lay down and had a good night's rest.[49]

In a letter to his wife, Heber C. Kimball described the great opposition facing the missionaries. Mobs collected to break up meetings and newspapers were being filled with all kinds of lies; he also described that many who accepted the gospel were turned out of their work because of their beliefs, and countless were going hungry for the want of food. Heber penned: "Times grow worse and worse in this country; the people are driven almost to desperation; the times appear sad and gloomy. . . . Lies, Slanders, Misrepresentations, &c., in all their varied forms, have been heralded forth from the press and pulpit, and have come in upon the world like a flood of water out of the mouth of the dragon, to stop the progress of truth, but all in vain" as the gospel continued to move forward in an unprecedented manner.[50]

Early in 1841, the Prophet Joseph Smith wrote to the Twelve and instructed them to return to Nauvoo in the spring. As the time for their departure drew near, general conference was held on April 6, 1841. Membership was recorded at 5,814, an increase of more than 4,000 since the April 1840 conference. Not included in that total were nearly 800 Saints who had immigrated to America during the year.[51]

The Prophet Joseph Smith recorded the following about the Twelve's historic mission:

> Perhaps no men ever undertook such an important mission under such peculiarly distressing and unpropitious circumstances. . . . However, notwithstanding their afflictions and trials, the Lord always interposed in their behalf, and did not suffer them to sink in the arms of death. Some way or other was made for their escape—friends rose up when they most needed them, and relieved their necessities; and thus they were enabled to pursue their journey and rejoice in the Holy One of Israel. They, truly, "went forth weeping, bearing precious seed," but have "returned with rejoicing, bearing their sheaves with them."[52]

2

"NO UNHALLOWED HAND CAN STOP THE WORK FROM PROGRESSING"

FROM NAUVOO TO THE SALT LAKE VALLEY

NAUVOO, ILLINIOS
APRIL 1841–JANUARY 1846

During the absence of the Twelve, the malaria-infested swampland of Nauvoo had given way to a beautiful city consisting of hundreds of houses, shops, factories, and mills. The population grew rapidly and flourished with the emigration of the foreign Saints. Peace and tranquility was enjoyed for only a short time while the Saints worked tirelessly and selflessly toward the completion of the Nauvoo Temple.[1]

Shortly thereafter, persecutions started once again, mobs began to combine, and calumny continued to defame, as many people united their efforts to persecute and exterminate the Saints.

> A spirit of vindictive hatred and persecution was exhibited among the people, which was manifested in the most bitter and acrimonious language, as well as by acts of hostility and violence, frequently threatening the destruction of the citizens of Nauvoo and vicinity, and utter annihilation of the "Mormons" and "Mormonism," and in some instances breaking out in the most violent acts of ruffianly barbarity. Persons were kidnapped, whipped, persecuted, and falsely accused of various crimes; their cattle and houses injured, destroyed, or stolen; vexatious prosecutions were instituted to harass

> and annoy. . . . The anti-"Mormons" had public meetings, which were very numerously attended, where they passed resolutions of the most violent and inflammatory kind, threatening to drive, expel and exterminate the "Mormons" from the state, at the same time accusing them of every evil in the vocabulary of crime.[2]

Early in the morning on June 24, 1844, as the Prophet Joseph Smith prepared to surrender himself to authorities in Carthage, a crowd gathered outside the Mansion House with entreaties not to give himself up because they believed he would be murdered. Surrounded by trusted and close friends, Joseph bid farewell to Nauvoo. Dan Jones records:

> He stood erect like a beacon among roaring breakers,—his gigantic mind grasping still higher; the fire flashed in his eye; with hand uplifted on high he spoke "My friends, nay dearer still my brethren, I love you, I love the City of Nauvoo too well to save my life at your expense,—if I go not to them they will come and act out the horrid Missouri scenes in Nauvoo;—I may prevent it, I fear not death, my work is well nigh done, keep the faith and I will die for Nauvoo.' So said the Prophet as he mounted his steed, and together with his brother Hyrum and some 30 or 40 more who chose to follow, they ascended the hill; when near the sacred spot—The Temple, he paused, he looked with admiration first on that, then on the City ere it receded from view in the flats below, and remarked, this is the loveliest place and the best people under the heavens, little do they know the trials that await them.

Within four miles of Carthage, they were met by a company of horsemen. Joseph counseled the men traveling with him to stand down: "Let all their vengeance be wreaked upon my head, I am going like a lamb to the slaughter with a conscience void of offence."[3]

While in Carthage, Dan Jones overheard the mob leaders saying they did not expect to prove anything against the Prophet, but they had numerous accusations against him and as one failed, they would try another to keep him detained there. Dan confronted the mob and requested of them to desist from their cruel persecutions. Their response was "they had worked too hard to get old Joe to Carthage to let him get out of it alive, and pointing to his pistols said, 'The balls are in there that will decide his case.'" After being informed of the threats, Joseph replied: "They are going to take me to prison without a guard; you will not leave me, will you?" Dan's response was rather he had come to die with Joseph. An arrest warrant, authorizing the Prophet's detention, was signed, and without a hearing, Joseph and Hyrum were escorted to Carthage Jail. John Taylor, Willard Richards, and Dan Jones, among others, accompanied the prisoners.[4]

DAN JONES

Dan Jones, a native of Wales, immigrated to America shortly after marrying in 1837. He and his wife took up residence in St. Louis, Missouri, where Dan operated a steamer on the Mississippi River. It was during this time Dan became acquainted with rumors about the Mormons. Through careful investigation, he perceived the rumors to be false. By accident, Dan found a letter written by Emma Smith to a friend while she was visiting her husband in the Missouri prison. Dan wrote: "I shall never forget the feelings which that segment of a letter caused me to have. I perceived clearly that not only did its author believe the New Testament, the same as I—professing the apostolic faith, and rejoicing in the midst of her tribulations at being worthy to suffer all that for a testimony of Jesus and the gospel—but also it contained better counsel, more wisdom, and showed a more gospel-like and godly spirit than anything I had ever read!" Dan was baptized in the frigid waters of the Mississippi in January 1843. Dan first met Joseph Smith in Nauvoo while working as the captain of the *Maid of Iowa*. He was transporting three hundred converts from Great Britain. Joseph invited Dan on a tour of Nauvoo and introduced him to his family. A strong and loyal friendship soon developed, and Dan spent the next few years devoted to protecting the Prophet.[5]

While in Carthage with Joseph and Hyrum, Dan assisted with raising the money required for bail. Bail was refused when they were charged with treason, a non-bailable offense. Dan went to Governor Ford to appeal for the release of the prisoners. His appeal fell upon deaf ears, and Dan returned to the jail. On June 25, 1844, Joseph spent the afternoon dictating to his scribe, Willard Richards, while Stephen Markham and Dan Jones worked to repair the door to the room of the jail. Dan noted: "Most of my forenoon's work consisted in hewing, with my penknife, a warped door to get it on the latch, and in preparing to fortify against a night attack." Willard Richards, John Taylor, and Dan Jones remained the night with Joseph and Hyrum Smith. Together they prayed and read from the Book of Mormon, and Joseph bore his testimony to the guards.[6]

While lying on the ground of the Carthage Jail the following evening, Joseph turned to Dan Jones, who was next to him, and whispered "Are you afraid to die?" Dan replied, "Has that time come, think you? Engaged in such a cause I do not think that death would have many terrors." Joseph then uttered his last prophecy: "You will yet see Wales and fulfill the mission appointed you ere you die." At about midnight, men were heard moving up the stairway. The Prophet called out, "Come on, ye assassins, we are ready for you, and would so willingly die now as at daylight." Hearing this, they retired again, and consulted, advanced, and retreated alternately, evidently failing to agree, until the morning light chased them away.[7]

Cyrus H. Wheelock

The following morning, on June 27, 1844, Cyrus H. Wheelock came to visit the Prophet. Cyrus was born in 1813 in New York and was baptized in 1839 at age twenty-six. He spent many of his first years in the Church on missions, with his first mission just shortly after his baptism. Like Dan Jones, Cyrus was devoted to protecting the Prophet. Just before Cyrus left the jail, sensing the danger, he gave the Prophet a pistol. Cyrus left the jail along with Dan Jones. Dan was asked by the Prophet to inquire about the shooting the night before. While out, Dan overheard a soldier boasting of plans to kill the Prophet, so he immediately went to Governor Ford to appeal for protection. Again his appeal fell upon deaf ears. Neither Dan nor Cyrus was permitted to return inside the jail. Later that evening, Joseph and his devoted brother Hyrum were ruthlessly murdered by a large mob, as witnessed by Willard Richards, who escaped unharmed, and John Taylor, who had been shot five times. Thereafter, both Dan Jones and Cyrus H. Wheelock would remain faithful and devoted members of the Church and would play important roles in the 1856 emigration season.[8]

The years following Joseph's martyrdom grew increasingly hostile for the Saints. In September 1845, as conditions became grave, Brigham Young was left with no choice but to announce that the Saints would leave Illinois in the spring 1846. They worked tirelessly to complete the temple and prepare for their journey west, but ultimately mobs forced them from their homes during the harsh winter. Harvey H. Cluff recalled: "The martyrdom of these men of God cast a gloom over the people so intense at the time, that those who were children then still remember with bowed silvered locks the terrible feelings which they experienced at the time. No cyclone or dark cloud of persecution inflicted upon the Saints in the past seemed so black and fatal. Forced into the wilderness among savages, was supposed by the enemy, to prove the final destruction of the Church of Jesus Christ of Latter-day Saints." Harvey later played an instrumental role in the rescue of the Willie Handcart Company in 1856.[9]

Exodus West
February 1846–September 1848

The first wagons departed Nauvoo on February 4, 1846. Ten days later, a snowstorm brought eight inches of snow and frigid temperatures to the refugees camped along the banks of the Mississippi. Within a week, the river froze, enabling the Saints to cross. The next four months brought unrelenting snow- and rainstorms, wind, swollen creeks, and mud, which, at times, completely hindered their progress and brought unimaginable suffering. In April, conditions became so treacherous that horses sank to their bellies in mud, wagons had to be double teamed, and travel was reduced to less than a half a mile per day. The Saints reached Council Bluffs on the bank of the Missouri River on June 14, 1846, having taken over 130 days to travel 300 miles. These truly were trying times because the faith and fortitude of the Saints were severely tested.[10]

Mormon Battalion

It was during these difficult times that the Quorum of the Twelve Apostles named Jesse C. Little to petition the federal government for assistance of the Saints' westward migration. Just days before Jesse's arrival in Washington DC, the United States declared war on Mexico. With the assistance of Thomas L. Kane, Jesse called on President James K. Polk and petitioned for assistance. This petition convinced the president to allow a few hundred Mormons to serve in the war, but he gave instructions that no Mormons should be enrolled in the US Army before they reached the West Coast. An order was drafted from the war department, which "unintentionally nullified" the directive by President Polk. The order "appeared to approve the immediate enlistment of a battalion of Mormon infantry to serve in the Army of the West."[11]

Seventeen days later, on July 1, 1846, a request came to Brigham Young from the American government for five hundred men to assist in the war with Mexico. Of this request, James Ferguson wrote:

> Though unjust, insulting, and cruel, it was a call from our native or adopted country. The common rights of man, bequeathed him by God and nature, were assailed. Though its benefits had been denied us, the Constitution was still sacred and dear to us, and a death-blow was aimed at its principles. With hell raging in mad fury behind, and the threatening statutes based on perfidious treaties before us, our camps exposed and defenseless, the past, with all its loud wrongs, was buried deep in our tortured memories. The flag—that flag which in whatever country, or on whatever ocean, I see it now, no matter how crushed and desolate my circumstances, gleams, like the sunbeam through the black storm, full of hope and promise of a future tranquility—that flag, bespattered and still dripping with the blood of our murdered Prophets, was unfurled once more. The call was answered, and five hundred bleeding hearts were offered for immolation to defend its honour. And he, our President, against whom the most envenomed darts of our enemies had been hurled—Brigham Young . . . was the first to lead the answer to the call. "Your demand," he said, "shall be complied with, though it be a Battalion of our Elders."

Nonetheless, as stated in the circular read to the Mormons that day, this enlistment allowed an advance party to pave the way for the rest of the Saints, entirely at the expense of the United States. President Brigham Young addressed the Saints, stating that "he wished the brethren to make a distinction between this action of the general government, and their former oppressions in Missouri and

Illinois," and remarked: "The question might be asked, Is it prudent for us to enlist to defend our country? If we answer in the affirmative, all are ready to go." President Young further stated that the outfit of five hundred men would cost them nothing and the pay for their enlistment would bring much-needed financial assistance to the Saints, who once again found themselves in dire conditions and destitute circumstances. This request from the government not only offered a financial benefit but also gave permission for the Saints to settle for a time on Indian lands.[12]

EDWARD MARTIN

On July 16, the Mormon Battalion was mustered into service at Council Bluffs for a period of twelve months. Among those valiant men was Edward Martin, who answered the call to serve. Edward and his wife, Alice Clayton, were living in Nauvoo at the time of the martyrdom. Edward was one of the first in England to hear the missionaries preach about the restoration of the gospel of Jesus Christ. Orson Hyde baptized him on October 14, 1837, in the River Ribble. Edward and Alice were married in 1840 and were among the first Saints to emigrate to America in 1841. Upon their arrival, they gathered with the Saints in Nauvoo and built a home near the temple site. They were sealed on January 29, 1846, in the Nauvoo Temple and were among those expelled by the mobs from the beautiful city of Nauvoo, leaving behind the grave of their daughter Lucy Ann. Two days prior to his departure with the Mormon Battalion, Edward buried his son Edward John, who was born in Nauvoo. Edward left behind his pregnant wife and three-year-old daughter, Mary Ellen, and would not return for eighteen months. Also volunteering in the Mormon Battalion were Levi Savage, Redick N. Allred, Daniel Tyler, Ephraim Hanks, and Arza Hinckley—all who would play a significant role in the emigration and rescue efforts of the Willie and Martin Handcart Companies in 1856.[13]

Two days following the departure of the Battalion, Brigham Young revealed that the destination of the Saints would not be California but the Great Basin in the top of the mountains. In 1842 the Prophet Joseph Smith "prophesied that the Saints would continue to suffer much affliction" that some will "live to go and assist in making settlements and build cities and see the Saints become a mighty people in the midst of the Rocky Mountains." Due to the loss of so many men to the war efforts and the lateness in the season, emigration was halted and Winter Quarters was established in Florence, Nebraska.[14]

JAMES G. WILLIE

At the age of 21, James Gray Willie left his native England to seek his fortune in America, believing it to be the land of opportunity. Six years later, while in Connecticut, James heard the gospel preached for the first time and was baptized a month later in January 1842. In spring 1843, he was asked to serve a mission to Vermont. In October 1845, President Brigham Young sent an epistle to all Church members to inform them of the universal removal of the Church to the West. James and Elizabeth Ann Pettit, whom James met while in New York, traveled west in the same wagon company. When they arrived in Nauvoo, they found the Saints had been driven out. Those who remained had infirmities or were without sufficient means to leave. James and Elizabeth married on June 13, 1846, in Nauvoo and remained for two weeks before going on to Winter Quarters, arriving just after the Mormon Battalion left for California.[15]

MOSES & HARVEY CLUFF

On Thursday, September 10, 1846, a mob of nearly eight hundred men laid siege upon the almost desolate Nauvoo, attacking the poor and infirm Saints who remained. Homes were looted, the Nauvoo Temple was desecrated, and many Saints were beaten and forced to leave without sufficient provisions or clothing. The Cluff family was among those remaining in Nauvoo. Moses Cluff witnessed the desecration of the Nauvoo Temple. The temple was enveloped in flames, and he beheld the "motley crowd jeering and making all kind[s] of jests and he listened to the profanity of the wicked crowd until his blood ran cold." Cluff family history records: "Depraved indeed must the person be who would rejoice in witnessing the destruction of an edifice reared by a poor, yet an industrious people, in a wild and unsettled country, whether it be done by Mormons, Catholics or Methodists." Moses and Harvey Cluff were among the Saints who endured the unspeakable hardships from Kirtland, Ohio, to Nauvoo, Illinois. Their father was a workman for the Kirtland and Nauvoo temples. On one of the many occasions that Joseph Smith was forced into hiding, he found temporary quarters at the Cluff home, where he was housed and cared for. Moses had the responsibility to carry food and drink to the Prophet. Moses, along with his brother Harvey, would later be called upon to take part in the emigration season and subsequent rescue of the Willie and Martin Handcart Companies in 1856.[16]

During this time, Brigham Young sent forth the following call to rescue the Nauvoo Saints who sought refuge near Montrose, Iowa. "Let the fire of the covenant which you made in the House of The Lord, burn in your hearts, like flame unquenchable, till you, by yourselves or delegates . . . can rise up with his team and go straightway, and bring a load of the poor from Nauvoo. This is a day of action and not of argument." The James G. Willie family history records James as being among those to answer the call to rescue the suffering Saints.[17]

The winter of 1846 was harsh, as some twelve thousand Saints were scattered across the Midwest. These Saints suffered greatly because they lacked sufficient provisions and the proper shelter to protect them from the elements. By the end of the winter, over seven hundred Saints had lost their lives due to the effects of privation, exposure to the elements, and sickness.[18]

James G. Willie and his wife, Elizabeth, left with the first companies to depart from Winter Quarters, on June 19, 1847. They traveled to the Salt Lake Valley in the Jedediah M. Grant Company. Once in the Salt Lake Valley, these first settlers continued to endure great hardships because many were without sufficient food, clothing, and shelter. The spring of 1848 brought a devastating late frost and a drought that injured crops. Food was rationed to about a half pound of flour for each person. Their diet was supplemented with "crows, thistle tops, bark, roots, and sego lily bulbs." To add to the difficulties, "great swarms of crickets descended from the foothills and began devouring what remained." For two weeks, the Saints, armed with sticks, shovels, and brooms, fought to save what was left of the crops. Miraculously, seagulls "flew in and began to devour the insects." It was under these unforgiving conditions that the Salt Lake Valley was established in the midst of the Rocky Mountains.[19]

Release of the Mormon Battalion

On Friday, July 16, 1847, at Fort Moor, California, Edward Martin was released from the Mormon Battalion and began his journey back to his family. The 2,100-mile march of the Battalion was truly epic and historical. It is recorded as one of the longest continuous marches in US military history. Though the battalion fought no battles and their contributions were inconsequential to the outcome of the Mexican War, they were nonetheless heroic in nature. In addition to leaving their families in destitute circumstances to serve their country that had previously ignored their plea for relief from persistent and deadly mob violence, the Battalion was ordered to march with a group of Missourians who were members of the very mobs who had driven them from their homes. True to their disdain for the Mormons, the Missourians were cruel and treated them terribly. [20]

The Battalion's main responsibility was to establish a wagon road through the Southwest. Upon completion of the road, in San Diego, California, the Battalion whitewashed homes, dug wells, and built a gristmill. In Los Angeles, they built Fort Moore for the US Army and received their release. The Battalion was noted as being devoted and loyal, and their conduct won the Church much goodwill in the eyes of their commanding officers. The following was written by Lieutenant-Colonel Philip St. George Cooke: "The Lieutenant-Colonel, commanding, congratulates the Battalion on their safe arrival on the shore of the Pacific Ocean, and the conclusion of the march of over two thousand miles. History may be searched in vain for an equal march of infantry. With crowbar and pick and ax in hand we have worked our way over mountain and hewed a passage through a chasm of living rock more narrow than our wagons. Thus marching half naked and half fed, and living upon wild animals, we have discovered and made a road of great value to our country." Of the Battalion members, Brigham Young stated to Heber C. Kimball: "These men were the salvation of this church." The sacrifices made by these valiant men transformed them into frontiersmen and prepared many for even greater trials, challenges, and responsibilities that they would face in the coming years.[21]

Edward Martin reached Winter Quarters, Nebraska, on Friday, December 10, 1847, after traveling by foot over six thousand miles since leaving Nauvoo. During his nearly eighteen-month absence, his wife, Alice, gave birth to a son, Edward H., who lived only five short months. Edward wrote: "The suffering and privations we had to pass through I say nothing about but suffice to say we did it for Christ and the Gospel's sake and that is sufficient." The Martins remained in Winter Quarters until June 1848, when they traveled to the Salt Lake Valley with the Heber C. Kimball Company. Along the way, Alice gave birth to a daughter, Eliza Susanna, whom they buried two weeks after their arrival in the Salt Lake Valley in September 1848.[22]

FRANKLIN D. RICHARDS

Franklin D. Richards was born in Massachusetts on April 2, 1821. He was the fourth of nine children and was the nephew of the apostle Willard Richards, who was miraculously unharmed in Carthage Jail during Joseph's and Hyrum's martyrdom. Franklin spent his youth being educated, working on the farm, and helping his father in the carpentry trade. At age ten, he went to work in order to lighten the financial burden of his father, who struggled to support his large family. Although his educational opportunities were limited, Franklin loved to learn. He loved to read and committed whole chapters of scripture to memory. Because of his love of learning, a few women in the community raised enough money for him to attend one of the New England colleges. Franklin, however, felt a great responsibility and duty to aid his father with the family's finances and denied himself the opportunity to attend college. In 1836, at age fifteen, Franklin heard the gospel preached by Brigham and Joseph Young and was baptized by his father two years later in June 1838. At age seventeen, he and his cousin set out on a 1,300-mile journey to join the Saints in Missouri. When Franklin arrived in Far West, he learned of his brother George's brutal death, which occurred at Haun's Mill just weeks prior to his arrival.[23]

During 1840–45, Franklin served five missions. Franklin was married in December 1842 and moved to Nauvoo. In the spring of

1844, Franklin was called to serve a mission to England. While in New York, he received word of Joseph's martyrdom and returned to Nauvoo before journeying to Europe. Shortly after arriving in Nauvoo, Franklin was sent on a mission to Michigan to gather means to complete the Nauvoo Temple. Upon his return, he toiled daily in the temple to aid in its completion. During his exodus west, Franklin's seventeen-year-old brother volunteered to serve in the Mormon Battalion, became ill in Colorado, and died. While in Winter Quarters, Franklin was again called to serve a mission in Europe. Franklin left his pregnant wife in a terribly destitute situation and once again headed to Europe.[24]

"Twenty days after leaving Sugar Creek, [Franklin's wife] gave birth to a son, her second child. . . . The babe had barely opened its eyes upon this world when it was summoned to the spirit land. The picture of this homeless pilgrim mother, lying helpless in her wagon on the broad, lonely prairie, her dead babe on her breast, and her husband a thousand miles away, was pitiful enough to melt a heart of stone." While Jane's life trembled in the balance, their oldest child became gravely ill and died. In this poverty-stricken condition, Jane was left alone to grieve the deaths of her two children and her brother-in-law. Brigham Young said this of Jane, "It shall be said of you, that you have come up through much tribulation."[25]

In spite of the monumental trials and challenges of the Saints in America, the work continued forward. The opposition could not stop the work from progressing, for this truly was a great and marvelous work! "The Standard of Truth has been erected; no unhallowed hand can stop the work from progressing; persecutions may rage, mobs may combine, armies may assemble, calumny may defame, but the truth of God will go forth boldly, nobly, and independent, till it has penetrated every continent, visited every clime, swept every country, and sounded in every ear, till the purposes of God shall be accomplished, and the Great Jehovah shall say the work is done."[26]

On Wednesday, October 14, 1846, Franklin D. Richards, Parley P. Pratt, Samuel W. Richards, Moses Martin, and Cyrus H. Wheelock arrived in Liverpool, where Franklin was given charge over all the branches in Scotland. Franklin spent only three months in Scotland before he was called to serve as a counselor to Orson

Spencer in the British mission presidency. Orson's health was poor, and for much of the time, he was confined to his room. The responsibilities of the presidency fell upon Franklin, who continued his service in the British mission until 1848, when he was called upon to bring over the first group of Saints from the British Isles bound directly for the Rocky Mountains.[27]

Franklin D. Richards and his counselors, Cyrus H. Wheelock and Andrew Cahoon, sailed on the ship *Carnatic* on February 20, 1848. The weather was ferocious on this voyage. Storms tossed the ship violently, and at times it seemed as if they would be buried in the depths of the sea. Under these circumstances, Franklin called upon God with great faith and rebuked the elements, commanding the furious winds and waves to cease their violence and to be still. "The tempest immediately subsided." The company, consisting of 120 Saints, arrived safely in Winter Quarters just prior to the departure of President Brigham Young and his vanguard company bound for the Salt Lake Valley.[28]

After an absence of a year and nine months, Franklin D. Richards and his wife immediately made preparations to travel to the Salt Lake Valley with the Willard Richards Company, leaving Winter Quarters on July 5, 1848. The journey through rugged, mountainous, rocky canyons was treacherous and filled with great difficulties. As a result of being the last company to travel that season, a majority of the feed along the trail had been consumed, leaving the cattle greatly reduced. In addition, a number of cattle died from drinking alkali water. The company had no choice but to yoke up the yearlings and milch cows. Before reaching the Salt Lake Valley on October 19, 1848, they also encountered several snowstorms.[29]

PERPETUAL EMIGRATION FUND

In February 1849, Franklin D. Richards was ordained an apostle. During his seven-month stay in the Salt Lake Valley, he was part of a committee that helped organize the Perpetual Emigration Fund. It was originally designed to assist those who remained in Winter Quarters to the Salt Lake Valley. Franklin helped raise the first five thousand dollars donated to the fund.[30]

In 1850, Franklin was again called to serve a mission to England.

Franklin arrived in Liverpool on March 29, 1850, having made his journey "during the most unfavorable portion of the year, through hundreds of miles of snow on the vast plains, deep and almost impassable mud through a portion of the United States, as well as squalls, gales, and hurricanes on the sea." Upon his arrival in England, he served as counselor in the British mission presidency until he was called to succeed Orson Pratt as president of the mission in January 1851.[31]

As the fire of emigration continued to burn brightly in the European Saints' hearts, thousands were willing to part with "all their effects, and toddle off with a few things in a pocket-handkerchief," wrote William H. Kimball. Because of the economical conditions that existed at the time, in spite of their best efforts to work hard and save, many would never have means sufficient to emigrate. The sheer magnitude of the poverty deeply affected the missionaries, and the cries for deliverance rang loudly in their ears. By 1852, the way was opened through the approval of using the Perpetual Emigration Fund to help the European Saints.[32]

For the European Saints, the Perpetual Emigration Fund was "designed to deliver the honest poor, the pauper, if you please, from the thralldom of ages, from localities where poverty is a crime and beggary an offence against the law, where every avenue to rise in the scale of being to any degree of respectable joyous existence is forever closed, and place them in a land where honest labor and industry meet a suitable reward, where the higher walks of life are open to the humblest and poorest, and where they can lay a foundation for indissolubly uniting themselves and their children in the progressive scale of human existence." Funds were allocated from tithes and other contributions, and those who used the funds were expected to pay back their debt after they arrived in the Salt Lake Valley. Franklin D. Richards sent the first company of 251 Saints from England in January and February 1852. Four months later, in May 1852, Franklin returned to Salt Lake City.[33]

On August 28, 1852, a special conference was held, during which many were called to serve missions abroad. Among those called to England were Edward Martin, James G. Willie, Daniel Spencer, John Van Cott, Mellen Atwood, Chauncey G. Webb,

David Grant, John A. Hunt, William Clayton, William Woodward, Daniel D. McArthur, and Spicer Crandell. Dan Jones was called to serve in Wales; Moses Clough to Berlin, Prussia; Jesse Haven to South Africa; and Reddick N. Allred to the Sandwich Isles. These men served up to four years and would play a significant role in the 1856 immigration season.[34]

In Europe, the work continued to roll forward with great majesty and power. The gospel of Jesus Christ moved in an unprecedented manner throughout England, Scotland, Wales, Denmark, Ireland, the Isle of Man, Australia, and the East Indies. Parley P. Pratt records: "This has been done in the midst of a flood of opposition unparalleled in the history of man. Lies, Slanders, Misrepresentations, &c., in all their varied forms, have been heralded forth from the press and pulpit, and have come in upon the world like a flood of water out of the mouth of the dragon, to stop the progress of truth, but all in vain."[35]

3

HE WILL REMEMBER THE ISLES OF THE SEA

ENGLAND, SCOTLAND, WALES, DENMARK

ENGLAND 1842–1856

LINFORD FAMILY

In Gravely, Cambridgeshire, England, John and Maria Linford were converted to the gospel through the efforts of Joseph Fielding in December 1842. Shortly after, John served as president of several branches. John was a successful owner of a shoemaking business, but when his membership in the Church was discovered, customers and family members vowed to starve him by withholding their business. His son James wrote:

> During those hard times, Father kept open house for the Elders as usual, and they never knew the straightened circumstances we were in; neither did anyone else. My noble mother stood by my father without a murmur in this hour of trial. It was a dark outlook for a husband and father as financial ruin and starvation stared him in the face. We thanked the Lord for turning away the trial. . . . From the time Father became a member of the Church in 1842 until he emigrated, 1856, he kept open house for the Elders, paid donations to help buy glass for the Nauvoo Temple, contributed to the tithing fund, and also contributed to the support of the local branch. Our house was used for religious meetings, three being held each Sunday.

John, Maria, and three of their boys would emigrate in 1856 through the blessings of the Perpetual Emigration Fund with the Willie Handcart Company. Their oldest son James would remain behind to serve a mission.[1]

ROWLEY FAMILY

On February 14, 1848, Ann Jewell Rowley's husband, William, passed away. Ann and her husband were among the congregation of United Brethren converted to the Church by Wilford Woodruff in 1840. Ann was now a widow with seven children under the age of twelve, with the youngest being just six months old, and two step-children from William's first marriage. Ann writes of her struggles after the loss of her husband:

> I was very grateful for the gospel of Jesus Christ and the comfort it gave me. I knew that our parting was only temporary and that viewed from the eternities, this was but a fleeting moment. I also knew that no matter how fleeting a moment it was, I had to make the best of it. I had a very real job to do. The children had to be fed and clothed, but the big task and the one I must accomplish, is to get us all to Zion. I must be among the people of my faith and I must get the Temple work done for us. Each person that could earn money at all, was required to work. The next seven years were hard. This was the period of time when England was exploiting 'Child Labor', just prior to their industrial revolution. Many big industries would hire them for next to nothing. Samuel was only 7 and John 9, but they worked in a brick yard tramping mud, to be used for bricks. I would help the little fellows across a narrow dangerous bridge, to go to work at daylight and at night I would meet them and help them home. The girls, even 11 year old Elizabeth, worked late in the night making kid gloves, doing mock frocking and other needlework. We did this in our home. Then at the end of the week, I would take them to market, where they were sold to the gentry. Our savings were meager.

Despite these challenges, Ann and her children worked tirelessly, remaining resolute in their determination to go to Zion. Through the blessing of the Perpetual Emigration Fund, they would journey to Zion with the Willie Handcart Company in 1856.[2]

Emily & Julia Hill

From a young age, Emily Hill was concerned with spiritual matters. She records:

> When but a mere child I was much concerned about my eternal salvation and felt that I would make any sacrifice to obtain it. I asked all kinds of questions of my mother and sisters; seeking how to be saved, but could get no satisfaction from them nor from the religious body (Wesleyans) to which they belonged. Hungry and thirsty for truth, I searched the scriptures, invariably turning to the lives of ancient apostles or to the beautiful writings of the Prophet Isaiah. . . . Truly I was waiting for something, I knew not what, that came to me sooner than I expected.[3]

In 1848, when Emily was about twelve years old, her cousin, Miriam Slade, came to visit. Miriam, with great conviction, shared with Emily her testimony of the gospel of Jesus Christ as restored by Joseph Smith upon the earth. Emily listened and felt its truthfulness. In stark contrast, Emily's family was greatly amused by the testimony. Miriam invited the family to a meeting with the elders in a nearby village. Because of the distance, Emily's brothers chose not to attend, and her sisters "considered themselves altogether too respectable to attend an outdoor meeting of such a primitive sect." With the approval of her father, Emily attended the meeting with Miriam.[4]

Emily's testimony of her experience that day in a small village in Chatford is moving: "Never, never shall I forget that day, surely it was the turning point of my whole life. A few devoted worshippers of truth met together in a small house, to bear their testimony to one another and to worship God! . . . 'The way' was open before me, and simple and young as I was I instinctively knew that 'I could not err therein.' . . . It was indeed as though I had been brought 'out of darkness into marvelous light', and I could not shut my eyes against it."[5]

Later that evening, Emily and Miriam attended an outdoor meeting where a crowd ridiculed those in attendance. "Though naturally sensitive to ridicule, I did not care the least for the sneers of the crowd but joined in the songs of the Saints as well as I could, for in my childish way I wanted it understood that I was not ashamed to count one with the peculiar people called Latter-Day Saints." Emily's account continues: "Many a time since, when 'offences' have come in my way, over which with mortal weakness I have almost stumbled, the testimony of that eventful day has been to me a precious recollection which nothing could obliterate. I was so overjoyed at finding what I had so long desired, and so eager to convince my friends that I could hardly wait to get home." Upon returning home, Emily bore testimony that she knew the Church was true and declared she would join when she was old enough. This declaration alarmed Emily's parents, and thereafter they watched her closely. Emily longed for the day when she would be old enough to act for herself. Sometime later, missionaries made their way to the Hill home and bore such a powerful testimony that Emily's older sister Julia was converted. Both Emily and Julia were determined, regardless of the cost or the sacrifice, that they would be true to the knowledge they held in their hearts of the restored gospel of Jesus Christ.[6]

Although both were continually denied the privilege of joining the Saints on a few rare occasions they were blessed with the opportunity. They were most grateful to partake of the sacrament and contribute their own money to the Church. On one of those rare occasions, the elders blessed Emily with the promise that she "should write in prose and in verse and thereby comfort the hearts of thousands." Emily was eventually permitted to move in with Julia, who had moved to another town to work as a milliner's apprentice. Emily pens: "There for the first time I enjoyed religious freedom and there also I took my lessons of hard times; preparing me for greater hardships in store."[7]

Julia was baptized on March 18, 1852, at age nineteen. Seven days later on March 25, Emily was baptized at age sixteen. They both worked until they earned enough money to emigrate, despite their parents' objections. Eight years after they first heard the gospel, they would join with the Saints on board the *Thornton* and travel with the assistance of the Perpetual Emigration Fund to the Salt Lake Valley with the Willie Handcart Company.[8]

LOADER FAMILY

In 1850, James and Amy Britnell Loader were living in a small village in Oxfordshire, England. James worked as a gardener for a wealthy English nobleman and had been employed there for thirty years. James and Amy were blessed with a home situated on the estate, and although they had a large family of thirteen children, they lived comfortably. They belonged to the Church of England and brought their children up in strict observance of that religion. Everything would change for the Loader family when missionaries from The Church of Jesus Christ of Latter-day Saints contacted them. Missionaries John Jaques, John Dalling, and John Archer played an important role in the conversion of the Loaders, and they later married into the family.[9]

Between 1850 and 1854, all but four members of the Loader family were baptized. Upon learning of their membership in the Church, Nobleman Sir Henry Lambert gave James a year to renounce his new religion. James would not, and in consequence, he was dismissed from his employment and evicted from his home. His daughter, Patience, who was working in London at a hotel, suffered similar consequences. Her employer told her she must leave because he feared she would persuade others to believe also. Patience left the hotel but not before she shared the gospel with Sarah and Susan Mancell, who were baptized shortly thereafter. Patience soon found employment working for eighty-two-year-old General William Turner and his invalid wife, who lived in London. Patience took charge of everything and became like a daughter to them. After the passing of the general's wife, Patience remained to take care of the general until he died. The general put his affairs in order and assured Patience she would be well provided for and would never have the need to work another day as long as she lived. Patience developed a great love for the general. His heart broke when Patience told him she would be leaving to emigrate with her family to America. The fire of the gospel burned deep in Patience, and she gave up a life of ease and comfort for the gospel that she so dearly loved.[10]

In 1855, several members of the Loader family sailed to America on board the ship *John J. Boyd*. A terrible voyage, it lasted sixty-six days, and many people died. Among the deaths was Patience's niece, one-year-old Zilpah Loader, daughter of John and Harriet Loader. Of the storms endured, Patience records an experience she had one evening during a horrific storm:

> [O]ne night when we had a bad storm we could not sleep as we had to hold on to the berth to keep from being thrown out . . . My poor mother was fretting and thought we would all be lost and drown in the sea. . . . Just when the ship was tossing and rolling the worst, I opened my eyes. We was all in darkness: but in a moment the curtains opened and a beautiful lovely figure stood there. Oh such a lovely countenance I had never seen before in all my life . . . he spake the words to me as I looked at him. He said, 'Fear not, you shall be taken there all safe.' . . . I called to my dear father and mother in the next berth. I told them what I had seen and . . . my father and mother believed in what I said and we all felt encouraged and felt to rely on this promise that our ship would take us all through safe to New York.

The Loader family arrived safely in New York and soon was working to earn the means necessary to continue their travels to the Salt Lake Valley.[11]

Griffiths Family

In 1853, Margaret Griffiths passed away during childbirth, leaving her husband, John, a widower with five children. John and Margaret were among the first baptized by John Taylor in 1840. Wilford Woodruff and Heber C. Kimball called John to preside over a branch in London in 1841. John was instrumental in this position as well as in numerous other branches, faithfully serving until Heber C. Kimball sent word for him to emigrate in 1856. By then, he had married Elizabeth Webb. John left behind the graves of his first wife, Margaret, and five of his eleven children and traveled with the Martin Handcart Company to the Salt Lake Valley with four of his children. John's oldest son, Thomas, had emigrated three years earlier.[12]

Scotland
1839–1856

Elders Alexander Wright and Samuel Mulliner arrived in Glasgow, Scotland, in December 1839 and decided to begin their work in Edinburgh, the home of Samuel's parents. While Samuel remained in Edinburgh, Alexander, although afflicted with small pox, was determined to carry the gospel forward to his family. He walked one hundred miles across Scotland through winter storms to reach the small village of Marnock. Upon his arrival, Alexander confined himself to prevent the spread of the disease and finally, on January 12, 1840, shared the gospel message with his family. Samuel baptized the first Scottish Saints on January 14, 1840, in the icy waters of the River Clyde.[13]

While in Glasgow and Paisley, Scotland, missionary Reuben Headlock found:

> The spirit of inquiry was very general in this place and the adjoining villages. Many came to hear. Some of the preachers said we were not worth minding when we first began to preach, but soon their hearers began to leave them; they then began to sound the tocsin of war; the people were exhorted not to come and hear us. A master in a cotton mill threatened to turn out of his employment any of his workpeople who went to hear us, but the truth fastened on the hearts of the people with such power that many were determined to sacrifice all things for the sake of it.[14]

In May 1840, Orson Pratt climbed a hill above the Edinburgh Castle to dedicate Scotland for missionary labor and ask the Lord to bless the Church with two hundred converts.

By the time Orson departed from Edinburgh, his prayers were answered and he left over two hundred Saints under the care of George D. Watt, the first convert baptized in the River Ribble in 1837 by Heber C. Kimball. Thereafter, although progress remained slow, thousands joined the Church.[15]

Caldwell Family

Margaret Ann McFall was born August 13, 1816, in Ireland. She and her family lived there for only a short time before moving to Scotland. At age eighteen, Margaret married William Caldwell. Six years later, in October 1840, she joined the Church. Before their youngest daughter, Agnes, was born in February 1847, William left for Canada.

> He went with the idea of finding a place suitable for his family. The boat he was on was sunk. . . . He was neither on the list of

> missing persons or on the list of those saved. I set to work immediately trying to keep my family together; I was so busy, and with my inability to write, I lost connections with his family. I felt the Lord would bless me with wisdom and knowledge in raising my family. We all pitched in and went to work. I could cook and do dressmaking, and I took in roomers and boarders, saving what little money I could for moving my family to Utah.

Margaret, along with her five children, spent the next nine years working and saving for their journey to the Salt Lake Valley. In 1856 through the blessings of the Perpetual Emigration Fund, the Caldwells made preparations to immigrate to America. Shortly before they were to leave, William Jr. "did a very foolish thing; he with his companions joined the Scottish Army. No matter how hard we all tried we could not bring about his release. As we had already made all arrangements for our passage, there was nothing to do but leave him. He was surely a sorry boy, to be left behind. Christina McNeil, a young girl who had been working for me, was glad to use his ticket and accompany our little family on our great adventure."[16]

CHRISTINA MCNEIL

At age seventeen, Christina McNeil accepted the gospel message and was baptized in Scotland in October 1849. As a result, Christina was told to leave her house and never return. Christina spent the next seven years on her own. Many of those years were spent working in a boarding house for Margaret Ann Caldwell. Christina's mother occasionally visited her, and Margaret described her as "a drunkard and only came to see her daughter when she needed money." Christina worked and saved what she could and was blessed to emigrate in 1856 with the Caldwell family in the Willie Handcart Company.[17]

EUPHEMIA MITCHELL

Just a few short weeks after Euphemia Mitchell turned eighteen, on a cold winter morning on November 30, 1851, she woke up at 3:00 a.m. and snuck out of the house so that she could be baptized. "All of us children slept in the same room with our mother and I knew it would be very difficult for me to get up and out of the room without waking Mother. I prayed and prayed that if it be right that I be baptized that I would be able to wake up on time. I did wake up that morning and dressed and was baptized where the ice had to be broken." The baptism was held at this time to avoid any harassment from those who opposed the Church. Euphemia first heard about the Church from a friend, May Bain. She attended her first meeting when she was sixteen years old. Her widowed mother did not want her to join the Church, so when she discovered Euphemia's membership, she told Euphemia she "was not welcome at home anymore."[18]

Bain & Smith Family

At age twenty-three, Euphemia was invited to emigrate to America with her friend, twenty-two-year-old Marjorie "May" Bain, who emigrated with the assistance of the Perpetual Emigration Fund in the Willie Handcart Company. May's mother, Marjorie McEwan Bain Smith, had been divorced from her father George Bain and was widowed by Alexander Smith. Also emigrating were May's half-sisters, Jane, Mary, Elizabeth "Betsey," and her half-brother Alexander. May's brother, Robert Bain, who served as a traveling elder in England, emigrated two years prior. In order to save enough money to emigrate, May, her mother, and her sisters "worked at [their] looms by day, [their] fancy work by night, and saved the proceeds."[19]

Kirkwood Family

Thomas and Margaret Campbell Kirkwood also accepted the gospel of Jesus Christ. Thomas and Margaret had six children, but in August 1848, they lost their sixteen-year-old daughter, Margaret. Four years later, in February 1852, they lost nine-year-old Catherine. Margaret suffered yet another devastating loss that same year when her husband passed away in December. She was widowed with four sons to care for; adding to the difficulty of the situation, her son Thomas was crippled. Through the blessings of the Perpetual Emigration Fund, the Kirkwoods emigrated to the Salt Lake Valley in 1856 with the Willie Handcart Company.[20]

ANDREW SMITH & JOSEPH MCKAY

On January 29, 1852, Andrew Smith was baptized in Scotland, a month before his fifteenth birthday. From a young age, Andrew learned the value of hard work by herding cows, mining coal, and later working in the cotton mill and Paisley shawl factory. One night while Andrew and his brother John were visiting Jane and Francis McKay, Andrew shared with Jane his experience of hearing some missionaries preach and bore testimony of the truthfulness of their message. Jane expressed interest in hearing these young men preach. Without her parents' knowledge, she and Andrew agreed to meet later that evening. Jane's sisters helped her out of their bedroom window, onto the roof of a shed, and onto the ground to meet Andrew waiting outside. Jane's older sister, Mary, accompanied them as well.[21]

Jane and Mary were well-versed in the Bible and were able to ask intelligent questions of the missionaries. During this meeting, they too felt a confirming witness of the truthfulness of what was being taught. When Jane and Mary returned home, they shared what they had heard with their sisters Frances and Martha. Jane's parents eventually learned what their girls had been up to. Her mother, Martha Blair, was unhappy to learn of their association with the Mormon elders because she had heard so many bad things about them. However, Jane's father, Joseph, felt there was something lacking in his Bible study and was eager to go with Jane to the next meeting. All of the McKay family except one son was baptized, and for the next eight years, they worked to accomplish their dream of joining the Saints in Utah. In 1856 Jane's father and Andrew Smith immigrated with the Willie Handcart Company to prepare the way for the McKay family.[22]

WALES
1840–1856

Henry Royle and Frederick Cooke were the first official missionaries to arrive in northern Wales in 1840. The missionaries were met with immediate success and in October reported having a branch of thirty-two members. Membership increased to one hundred during the next few months. Thereafter, local priests began to oppose, slander, and falsify the character of the missionaries, even following them around in attempts to disturb their meetings. Missionaries reported: "They call us robbers and infidels, declaring that we rob other churches. If the opposition continues to increase, as it has done for some time past, we shall perhaps loose our heads soon; but the Lord is with us, and I do not fear them." By April general conference in 1841, membership was recorded at 170.[23]

Missionaries also arrived in 1840 in southeastern Wales, where progress remained slow. Dan Jones, a native of Wales, and his wife arrived in Wales in January of 1845 in fulfillment of Joseph's prophesy to Dan while in the Carthage Jail: "You will yet see Wales and fulfill the mission appointed you before you die." Nearly a year after his arrival in Wales, at a special general conference, Dan reported five members attending. The Wales mission recorded total membership at 493. During this conference, Wilford Woodruff appointed Dan to preside over the Church in Wales, because Dan was the only missionary who could speak, read, write, and publish in Welsh.[24]

While in Wales, Dan experienced grave difficulties, which his experiences in Nauvoo had prepared him for.

> The scenes here are very like the continental rabbles of Missouri, &c., and still raging worse and hotter daily. You need not be surprised should you hear of Carthage tragedies in Wales, ere long. The whole towns and works hereabouts, containing over 60,000 people, are actually drunken with infatuation, and rage for or against Mormonism. This is all the topic, and reverends, out of the pulpits, have actually declared that we should be treated as Joe Smith was. . . . The last two Sundays our hall was surrounded with hundreds of such characters, even in broad daylight, gnashing their teeth, and threatening everything, besides throwing stones through the windows. . . . It is dangerous for me to go among them now, for some declare that they consider it God's service to rid themselves of me!

In spite of the opposition, by the time Dan completed his mission in January 1849, Church membership was at 3,603. In 1849, Dan Jones prepared to lead 249 converts to America on board the ship *Buena Vista*. He needed bodyguards to watch him round the clock. "The life of our dear Brother Captain Jones was in such danger that his house was attacked almost every night for weeks before his leaving Merthyr, so that his godly life was not safe in sleeping except between guards from among his brethren; and there were scoundrels so inhuman who had been paid to kill him as he left, so that he had to leave secretly the day before."

Dan wrote:

> And is it a fact or just a dream that I have escaped on the water from the midst of my Welsh brothers with my life by the skin of my teeth? If so, why? If not, why all the persecution, the slander, and the false accusations I suffered for years from the press and the pulpits? Why did my residence have to be guarded for weeks? Why was my life safe only among guards? Why did I have to flee in secret before the time? Why was I not able to bid farewell to my dear wife and my baby? It was doubtless not for transgression in the world; for once, twice, yes, even three times I challenged any man to prove me guilty of transgression. Oh, it must be admitted, it cannot be hidden, that religious persecution is what caused it all; there must be strength in my religion, if nothing else but that could prove it, for it to have been able to excite the old passion of every false religion to persecute it. Persecution does not originate from God; neither does the religion which persecutes come from Him.[25]

DENMARK
1849–1856

The gospel of Jesus Christ was not preached in Denmark until the adoption of a constitution in 1849, which guaranteed freedom of speech, press, and religion. At a general conference held October 6, 1849, in Salt Lake City, Erastus Snow, Peter Olsen Hansen, John Erik Forsgren, and George Parker Dykes were the first missionaries called to serve in Scandinavia. They arrived in Copenhagen in May and June 1850. The first baptisms took place on August 12, 1850, with a branch of about fifty being organized a month later.[26]

Bodil Mortensen

Bodil Mortensen was born in 1845 on the island of Maribo, Denmark. Bodil's oldest sister, Anne Margrette, first accepted the gospel in her family. This decision was met with disapproval from her parents, but in time, they too investigated and joined the Church in 1852. The family had a great desire to gather with the Saints in the Salt Lake Valley, but they were too poor to emigrate together. Consequently, Anne Margrette emigrated in 1855; Bodil emigrated in 1856 with family friends Jens and Elsie Nielson; and Bodil's parents along with her brother and sister emigrated in 1857.[27]

Jens & Elsie Nielson

At age fourteen, Elsie Rasmussen began working as a farm hand. While thus employed, she became acquainted with Jens Nielson. Jens and Elsie fell in love, married in 1850, and moved to a coastal city on the mainland of Denmark, where they were blessed with financial prosperity. Jens recalls: "I had very little money to start with, but the Lord blessed me on my right hand and on my left and I was very successful and prospects in temporal concern were very bright. I was looked upon as a respectable neighbor and many times invited to the higher class of society."

Their rise in social status was short-lived, as Jens describes:

> In the fall of 1852, two Mormon elders came to our neighborhood. I knew nothing of the Mormons except very bad reports. They had the privilege of holding a meeting close to my home. I thought I would go there for curiosity sake. As soon as I saw those men's faces, I knew they were not the men as represented to be, and I told my friends so before I heard them speak. Before the meeting was out, I knew the testimony they bore was of God. We bought some few of their tracts and studied them for a few weeks and were perfectly satisfied the work was of God.[28]

On March 29, 1854, Jens and Elsie were baptized and thereafter endured much persecution. On one occasion, Jens was attacked by an angry mob of his countrymen. When Jens appealed to the magistrate of the law, he presented his clothes, which had been torn to rags, as evidence and explained the injuries suffered at the hands of the mob. The magistrate told Jens there was no law in Denmark to protect the Mormons. Jens writes: "From that time on all my former friends turned against me and spoke all kinds of evil against me, and that falsely. All my possessions had no power over me then, my only desire was to sell out and come to Zion. That same year I partly made a bargain with a man for my home but before the bargain was closed, the president of the conference paid me a visit." During the visit, Jens was given counsel to serve a mission: "That counsel came right in contact with my natural feelings, but the Spirit whispered [to] me I must obey, for 'obedience is better than sacrifice.' Then I was ordained a priest and sent out to preach."[29]

While serving his mission, Jens recalls an experience where "a mob threw two of the elders into a pond of filthy water declaring they would baptize them. Whenever the elders struggled to the bank and tried to get out, they were struck by some of the jeering crowd on the bank and pushed rudely back into the water. This torment continued till the elders were almost worn out with chill and exhaustion." John Van Cott, president of the Scandinavian mission, wrote the following regarding the persecution endured in Denmark at this time:

> In many places the brethren are hunted as though they were wild beasts, and those who would be glad and willing to take our brethren in, that are out upon missions, and contribute to their necessities, dare not do it in many instances, owing to the stringent laws which exist, and a determination on the part of some to enforce them . . . In Denmark there is more liberty, yet in many places there is considerable persecution. Meetings have been broken up in several places, and many of the brethren that have been out on missions know what it is to be arrested and imprisoned, with the privilege of living on bread and water. There have been over 20 arrested here in the Copenhagen Conference, during the time that I have been here. Some have been imprisoned for weeks, others transported to their native town, or permanent dwelling place. Some of the same have been sent back to their appointed fields of labour, and measures have been taken so that they cannot be moved lawfully without they are charged by proper authority.

While on his mission, Jens baptized some twelve or fifteen persons and was later called to preside over the branch where he lived. "I was very successful in my mission, after which I received an honorable release to go to Zion. I sold my place, got my money, and paid all my obligations." Jens and Elsie would emigrate in 1856 with their five-year-old son, Niels, and family friend, Bodil Mortensen. Although they had money from the sale of their property and possessions to travel comfortably by wagon, they chose to selflessly part with their means and travel with the Willie Handcart Company, thus making it possible for many others to gather to Zion.[30]

Mortensen Family

In the small town of Harbolle, on the island of Moen in Denmark, Peder and Helena, or "Lena," Mortensen resided, raising their nine children. Peder grew up as an only child and inherited his wealth and property from his parents. He was well educated and musical. As a youth, he injured himself and was left crippled. He used crutches with great difficulty and suffered from severe rheumatism. In spite of this, he was a hard worker, was skilled in farming and shoemaking, and was a cooper. Lena also came from a wealthy family. She was described as a jovial, strong, resolute, and resourceful woman. The family was religious in nature and belonged to the Lutheran Church. Peder often prayed to the Lord "to send some of His servants who were divinely called and had authority to officiate in the ordinances of the Gospel of Jesus Christ that they could become His disciples in very deed."[31]

In the spring of 1855, missionaries Soren P. Guhl and Mark Scoby arrived in Harbolle to share the message of the restoration of the gospel of Jesus Christ. In attendance at one of their meetings were two of Peder's sons, twenty-seven-year-old Morten and twenty-two-year-old Anders. Morten was studying to become a Lutheran minister and attended the meeting out of curiosity, expecting to confound the missionaries. He left the meeting with the overwhelming feeling that he had found the very religion they had been praying for. When sharing this news with the family, his father's response was one of skepticism: "There is so much evil spoken of these Mormon Elders everywhere, surely they cannot be true followers of Christ." The family attended the next meeting, and they were very impressed. Morten was baptized in May 1855 by Elder Soren P. Guhl and would be followed by the rest of the family.[32]

Following their baptism, the Mortensen family was shunned, ridiculed, and persecuted on a daily basis. They were no longer respected or accepted in their community. On one occasion "an angry mob converged on their home to do them harm, but the family was saved by the sudden collapse of the mob's leader as he stood at their gate." In Copenhagen, while the family was making final plans to emigrate, Morten was asked to stay in Denmark and serve a mission. The decision weighed heavily upon the family because of the physical condition of Peder and of daughter Ann Kirstine, "Steena," who was crippled with a bad knee. Morten agreed to serve a mission, and the family received a promise from the mission president that the entire family would reach the Saints in Zion well and safe. Although the Mortensens had the financial ability to travel to the Salt Lake Valley in the comfort of a wagon company, they too selflessly parted with their means and traveled in the Willie Handcart Company, thus blessing the lives of many. Their son, Morten, would emigrate in 1859 after serving an honorable three-year mission.[33]

4

SPECIAL GATHERING

PERPETUAL EMIGRATION FUND & HANDCART PLAN

PERPETUAL EMIGRATION FUND

In 1854, Franklin D. Richards was again called to preside over the entire European mission. He arrived in Liverpool on June 4, 1854, and found the Saints in great poverty with virtually no way of alleviating their oppression. The Perpetual Emigration Fund could not meet the needs of the thousands who petitioned for assistance. William H. Kimball wrote home to his father, Heber C. Kimball: "I feel to weep and mourn and lament, when I behold the poverty of the people; they are starving to death, and there are scores and hundreds of my brethren in the poor-houses of the country." The letter petitioned all to work toward increasing available funds to assist the Saints in such great need. Brigham Young offered up property worth 60,000 dollars and issued the call for others to do the same. The object of this was "to sell this property to such of the brethren in this country as have the money to pay for it, and then use the money to emigrate the poor the coming year."[1]

In the fall of 1855 Brigham Young sent forth a directive to Franklin D. Richards to "help on those in Britain who have been in the Church from the introduction of the Gospel on those lands; old members, many of whom have remained poor and unable to get away, or through infirmity are remaining, comparatively unnoticed in the Branches . . . God requires us to help these out, and bring them to Zion, where they can be taken care of, and not suffered to want for the necessaries of life; hunt them out . . . that none of these old members be suffered to remain, who are longing for deliverance."[2]

In England, Franklin D. Richards called upon the pastors and presidents to

> gather out the aged, the infirm, and the destitute, those who for years have struggled on true to their God and their brethren, and who have continually, with a free and liberal spirit, administered to the Elders, and used the little that the Lord has given them to build up His kingdom . . . and diligently search out all those brethren and sisters who joined the Church in an early day, say from ten to eighteen years ago, and who have been faithful in the cause of truth. . . . We wish the Elders to be diligent in searching out more particularly those who have patiently and perhaps silently endured all things for the Gospel's sake. It is the Lord's poor that we are so emphatically called upon to help, and length of service, faithfulness, age, and destitution should be the special, prominent reasons for bestowing favour and blessings of the gathering.[3]

As the gathering of the poor, longtime members of the Church began in Britain, economic conditions worsened in the Salt Lake Valley. Brigham Young was almost forced to suspend emigration assistance for the 1856 season because of the lack of donations to the fund brought on by a drought, the inability of the immigrating Saints to repay their debt to the fund, and a rise in immigration costs. Brigham Young stated: "Unless we receive aid, either by donations or the payment of debts owing to the Company, we shall be obliged to measurably suspend operations the ensuing year. We have already extended relief to the utmost limit, and have almost entirely absorbed every available resource of the Church to aid in this matter."[4]

Handcart Plan

In a letter dated October 31, 1855, Brigham Young wrote:

> Times continue close with us in regard to money matters. So much unexpected indebtedness, all so suddenly falling due, and scarcely any money to be found, crowds us pretty hard; but, by

> the help of the Lord and our brethren, we expect to be able to get through with it, but must hereafter keep our P. E. Fund operations within the resources of the Company's funds. We do not expect to purchase a wagon, or yoke of oxen, for them another year, but adhere strictly to our former suggestion of walking them through across the plains, with hand-carts, &c., as previously stated.

The handcart plan had been considered by Brigham Young as early as 1852, with experienced men appointed to investigate its feasibility.[5]

Upon careful review, although the committee greatly preferred traveling by wagon, they concluded there were many benefits to traveling by handcart. It was determined that the labor of dealing with both ox and horse teams was close to, if not equal to, the labor of pushing or pulling a handcart. The committee felt the same amount of labor could be more usefully and efficiently employed in propelling a handcart with much less time, labor, and annoyance. They further determined that this new system, if carefully managed under the strictest regulations, could be done with much less expense and with comparatively little increase of hardship. It would open the way for those who could not otherwise afford to travel under the traditional system of immigration. In their opinion, it was better for the Saints to travel among friends in this manner than to endure the conditions that existed in Europe at the time. It was not recommended that those with sufficient means travel by handcart.[6]

The conclusions were carefully considered, and it was determined to go forward with the recommendations of the committee. Many considered this a direct answer to their prayers to help them join with the Saints in the Salt Lake Valley.[7]

5

SHEPHERDS OF THE FLOCK

1856 EMIGRATION SEASON

AUGUST 1855–MAY 1856

In a letter dated August 31, 1855, Brigham Young wrote Franklin D. Richards and requested that he, John Jaques, Daniel D. Spencer, James Linforth, and his son Joseph A. Young emigrate the following season. Also, forty-two missionaries that had served upward of four years were notified of their release and given permission to emigrate. For nearly ten years, Franklin D. Richards served in Britain with Cyrus H. Wheelock, who faithfully served by his side. During the last two years of their service, some eight thousand Saints left their native soil to live in the Salt Lake Valley, and nearly double that number were baptized.[1]

JOHN JAQUES

John Jaques was born January 7, 1827, in England. At age seven, he attended grammar school and became a "bright and diligent student." Along with school, he worked in his father's gardens. He remembers collecting manure as a young boy to be sold to other farmers: "I had a wheelbarrow and used to go out along the road, gather up all I could and put it in a heap by the roadside until I had a cart load, and then I would sell it to the farmers. A good cart load of horse manure brought four shillings. That was a little fortune for a boy." At age thirteen, John went to work as an apprentice for a cabinetmaker and was contractually bound for seven years. When the owner's business failed, John's father procured another apprenticeship for him with a cabinetmaker and upholsterer. He worked twelve hours a day, receiving only room and board. John described working for corrupt men and often finding himself as the butt of ridicule for his highest regard of truth and virtue: "No matter the circumstance, though they be actually in some degree compromising, no matter who is the tempter nor what is the temptation, your virtue is worth more than them all, it is the pearl of great price. It is beyond all price. It should be perfectly invincible. No offer involved it is worth a moment's consideration. The unfailing motto should be, 'Never surrender.'" During his teen years, he attended a Baptist church and became interested in religion. John became acquainted with the "Mormon church" through a journeyman the cabinetmaker employed and was baptized in 1845 at age eighteen. His parents were greatly opposed to his conversion. His father wrote,

> I do not think you are acting as you ought, neither to your master nor to me or you would not be led away in this manner. Remember your master has right to make you attend a different place than you do on a Sabbath, and I wished you at first with your Master's consent to attend the Wesleyan Chapel. As to your leaders, maybe they do not teach you as you do not obey one of the great commands in Scripture—honor and obey your parents and also your Master. You need not send me any more such trash as that you sent. I think if any man had studied the Bible, yea, even a school boy might see they are wrong. If I though you want money to buy such stuff I would not send you a farthing—but man when I see you.

John served a mission at age twenty, and while there, he met, and later married, Zilpah Loader. In 1852, he was appointed as an assistant editor of the *Millennial Star*.[2]

With the request to emigrate, John sent word to his in-laws, the Loader family, requesting they prepare to travel with the handcart companies. The Loaders were already in New York, working toward traveling to the Salt Lake Valley with the wagon companies. The response from the Loader family to John's request was not what he expected. Patience Loader responded to the request by expressing that traveling to the valley with the handcart companies would be physically impossible:

> If we girls were strong boys then I think it might be done, but father is the only man in our family. I don't feel myself that I can go like this. If, by staying here for a little time, we can get means to go by a wagon, it will be far preferable. Mother, I am sure, can never go that way. She says herself that she cannot do it, and I don't think any of us can. Why, we understood that the hand-carts were the last resource! Mother says that she must have a revelation before she can see this right. Why, we shall have to sell nearly all our clothes! And what shall we do for things to wear when we get to the Valley? Seventeen pounds weight each is but very little.[3]

John Jaques was in complete disbelief that the family would, in his mind, possess such a lack of faith. In turn, he wrote a letter exhorting the Loaders to reconsider, mentioning their reasons for not wanting to immigrate were trifling reasons: "I would rather you had sent me word that you all were in want of bread, and anxious to get to Zion, than that you were doing comfortably, and forgetting the Lord and Zion, and falling in love with Babylon again." Patience requested that John and his family stop in New York for a time until means could be acquired to continue to the Salt Lake Valley in comfortable outfits, and John responded: "I won't stop in New York if my wife has to clothe me in sheep-skins, or goat-skins, or buck-skins, or buffalo-skins, when I get to Zion. I shall be happier in them there than if I and my family were clothed in purple and fine linen, and silks and satins, and the best broadcloth in Babylon."

John's response continued:

> There are hundreds in England who have begged and prayed with tears for your privilege of going to Zion, but have been unable to get it. And now you slight it! It is most grievous? . . . You talk of staying a little while in New York or St. Louis, till you can buy a wagon? . . . How can you expect the Lord to give you means to buy a wagon, when He has provided you a cart? . . . Perhaps when you can buy a wagon, if you ever have the means, you will want to wait a little longer, till the railroad is made. . . . I can but exhort you to repent of your faint-heartedness, repent of your trifling with the salvation of the Lord, and be ready to go with us, with a cheerful heart, trusting in God, and not in your own strength, when we come, and all will be

> well—you will rejoice in the Lord more than ever before, and thank His holy name that you did not stay in New York. Remember, this is the most critical period of your life. It is the turning point, to decide your destiny. . . . Greater consequences to yourself, your children, and your ancestors hang on your decision than you can well imagine, for it will carry an influence for good or evil into eternity.

In the letter, John specifically reprimanded Patience: "Patience seems very much afraid that she will not have clothes enough when she gets to Zion. Well, if she sets more store upon fine clothes than upon the counsel of the Lord and the blessings of living in Zion, I can say she is different to me. The fact is, she has too many clothes—they are a trouble to her, and she seems willing to hazard her salvation for them."

John went on to attempt to put the journey in perspective: "You have looked upon the journey all in a lump. Recollect that you will only have to perform one day's travel at a time. . . . You have also thought of performing the journey in your own strength, forgetting that you should put your trust in the Lord, who strengthens even the weak according to their day. You know that when He calls His Saints to do any thing, if they will rely upon Him and do the best they can, He will fit the back to the burden, and make everything bend to the accomplishment of His purposes." The letters of correspondence between John Jaques and Patience Loader were published in the *Millennial Star* for all to read.[4]

In New York, while Patience was in President John Taylor's office one afternoon, President Taylor asked her when she was going to Utah. She mentioned the family had planned on working in New York for a year to save up enough money to purchase a nice outfit, but instead had been ordered by Franklin D. Richards to leave New York at once and travel to the valley with the handcart companies. Patience asked President Taylor if he would like to have his girls pull a handcart across the plains. He said no and then said: "But Patience I cannot say anything about the matter as you are under the council of President Richards you will have to go according to councils, but at the same time I don't think you will be able to go any further than Council Bluffs this season. You will be too late starting." Council Bluffs, he informed, was 275 miles from Iowa City. "And when you get there you will find out how you feel if you can stand the journey or not but my opinion is that you will have to stay there until next spring." When Patience returned home, she shared with her family the conversation she had with President Taylor and later wrote in her journal of her feelings at the time:

> My poor mother still held in the same mind she did not feel that she could ever undertake that long journey by handcarts and we girls all felt the same as Mother and as for myself, I think I felt the worst out of all the family. I could not see it right at all to want us to do such a humiliating thing to be I said harnessed up like cattle and pull a handcart loaded up with our bedding, cooking utensils, and our food and clothing and have to go through different towns to be looked at and made fun of as I knew we would be it was very hurtful to my feelings. Yes, I will say and to my pride in my young days such way of traveling was very humiliating to my feelings and I did not think it was necessary.

One day T. B. H. Stenhouse came from the President's office informing the Loader family that their names were in the *Millennial Star* and that Brother Loader was thought to be apostatizing from the Church. This was a pivotal moment for the Loaders. They could have chosen to react to the published letters with anger and offense, but instead they all gave notice to quit work and immediately made themselves ready for the journey with the handcart companies. James Loader said to his wife: "I cannot stand that to be accused of apostasy. I will show them better; Mother I am going to Utah. I will pull the handcart if I die on the road." The Loaders traveled to the Salt Lake Valley with the Martin Handcart Company.[5]

From November 1855 to June 1856, 4,395 Saints said good-bye to family, friends, and their native homeland to follow their hearts and gather with the Saints in the Salt Lake Valley. Of those emigrating this season, half were assisted by the Perpetual Emigration Fund. Available funds were

> appropriated to aid those who have proven themselves worthy by long-continued faithfulness in the Church, whether they can raise any means of their own or not. These must be brought, so long as we can act within the means of the Company, no matter if they have a sixpence in the world. It should be a source of great consolation to

> the poor Saints, that while the world despise and persecute them, the Lord has them in remembrance, and has chosen them out of the world as vessels of honour unto Himself, and is permitting them to pass through the fiery furnace of affliction, that they may come out like the gold seven times purified.[6]

Among the emigrants were diligent and faithful missionaries, most having served upward of four years. These missionaries were notified that although released from their present fields of labor, their responsibilities were far from over. They were asked to devote all of their efforts into seeing the Saints arrived safely into the Salt Lake Valley. President Franklin D. Richards counseled:

> You cannot crown your mission with a labour more befitting your calling, or more consonant with the spirit of the Gospel you have been preaching, than to consider it your duty and privilege to assist the poor in gathering home. To toil along with hand-carts through a journey of 1,000 miles over the "desert plain," and rugged mountains, through streams and canyons, will be no easy task, even for those who are accustomed to the fatigues and hardships of mountain life, and the Saints who are willing to do it, with their aged and little ones, for the Gospel's sake, the Lord will make the objects of His special care and blessing. None of the emigrating Saints have ever crossed the plains who have had greater demands on the shepherds of the flock, than those who will travel in the hand-cart companies the coming season.[7]

The immigration season of 1856 placed difficult and heavy demands on the returning missionaries now called to serve as "emigration officials." They were overwhelmed with this season's emigration for several reasons, including the revision of immigration laws, along with the adoption of a more northern and healthier route through the States, and the implementation of the handcart system. Adding to the demands were the difficulties in acquiring ships. Fewer ships were going to the more northern American ports and a great number of them were being used in transporting men home from the recently ended Crimean War. This scarcity resulted in an increase in the price of passage. Officials noted: "We cannot expect to know the scarcity or plentitude of ships any great length of time before securing one, as this depends upon the fluctuations of commerce, and also upon winds, which at winter and spring seasons sometimes blow adversely for weeks together."[8]

Of the eight ships acquired by the immigration officials that season, the *Thornton* and *Horizon* were late in leaving Liverpool. Franklin D. Richards counseled: "As the Emigration will be somewhat late this season in getting off from Liverpool, Pastors and Presidents are especially requested to counsel the Saints and aid them in the disposition of their effects, that they may not be left destitute, or be thrown out of their homes longer before their embarkation than is necessary. Let your careful attention be given to this subject, that the poor may make the wisest use of their limited means. We hope to give each shipload about three weeks' notice of their embarkation."[9]

6

ACROSS THE MIGHTY WATERS

EMIGRANTS ON BOARD THE SHIPS *THORNTON* AND *HORIZON*

THORNTON EMIGRANTS LIVERPOOL, ENGLAND TO NEW YORK, NEW YORK MAY 4–JUNE 14, 1856

The 764 passengers aboard the *Thornton* set sail from Liverpool, England, on May 4, and after a rough forty-one-day passage, they arrived in New York on June 14, one week later than anticipated. Thirty-one-year-old Anna F. Tait, of Scotland, recorded, "I believe there has never before been a company with so many old and young, halt, blind, and lame, from so many nations, crossed the sea." Labor aboard the ship was hard, and storms sometimes raged all day. During strong gales and heavy squalls the turbulent ocean water bashed over the bow and spilled onto the hatchway and into the lower decks in torrents. With few exceptions, all would feel the effects of seasickness. During the voyage, winds were intensely cold and piercing. Large mountainous icebergs towering in the sky were spotted, and the ships successfully maneuvered around them. In stark contrast to the strong gales and heavy squalls, there were days on end when little progress was made because of the lack of wind and dense fog, which became extremely dangerous, necessitating a bell being rung every minute to prevent collisions. Because of contrary winds experienced throughout the voyage, it was deemed advisable to ration the water until more favorable conditions prevailed. Water rationing lasted for sixteen days. Ocean travel was difficult not only because of the adverse weather conditions but also because of the cramped quarters and the constant and dangerous threat of disease outbreaks.[1]

James Family

William and Jane Hayne James were passengers on the *Thornton* with their eight children. In 1854, when missionaries came to their village in England, Jane was impressed by their message. Their eleven-year-old daughter, Mary Ann, recalled of her mother, Jane: "The apostasy and restoration, unthought of before, appealed to her and she was led to prayer. The answer came and she was ready to leave all we had, and with an almost invalid husband and eight children, brave the journey to an unknown land and a wilderness." The fire of emigration burned brightly in Jane's heart, and she wanted to emigrate right away, while William wanted to wait until his health improved. Jane felt they should go before their children left home, and it was decided that they would indeed emigrate. William was a farm laborer, but because of his poor health, it was necessary for Jane and their older daughters to work to help provide for the family. Jane's mother died when Jane was an infant, so she was raised by her grandmother. Her childhood was spent in poverty, with no opportunity to attend school. As soon as she was old enough, she began making her own living, which she continued to do for the remainder of her life. On Tuesday, June 10, approximately 120 miles off the coast of New York, as the *Thornton* was surrounded by thick fog, the James family was called upon to make the first of many great sacrifices on their journey to the Salt Lake Valley. Mary Ann recorded: "During this voyage, my parents were called upon to part with their baby. Death claimed our little Jane and we were obliged to place the precious bundle in a watery grave. Mother's heart strings were torn, but the brave little mother that she was felt not to murmur against the will of Him who gave."[2]

In spite of the many challenges on board the ship, great order prevailed, and spirits remained high under the direction of forty-one-year-old James G. Willie, a returning missionary from England. The *Thornton*'s captain complimented the Saints on their cleanliness and for their ready compliance with his requests, wishing them prosperity in all their future works. He also mentioned that he would remember the Saints with the warmest feelings as long as he lived and asked God to bless them.[3]

On Saturday, June 14, 1856, with clear and favorable skies, a doctor boarded the *Thornton* and gave passengers a certificate of good health. The luggage was passed without inspection. Thirty-one-year-old Anna F. Tait, of Scotland, recorded, "Our names were called over, and we had to state where we were going, what money we had, and other particulars, which were entered into a book, and we then passed into the house." The house was known as Castle Garden, and it was used as a processing station and emigrant hotel offering many conveniences, such as running water, baths, and cooking facilities.[4]

Cunningham Family

Fifteen-year-old George Cunningham, who joined the Church in Scotland, was emigrating with his parents, James and Elizabeth Nicolsen Cunningham, and his siblings, seventeen-year-old Catherine, twelve-year-old Elizabeth, and nine-year-old Margaret. His family was among the first to be baptized in their district. From the tender age of seven, George helped sustain his family by working in a coal mine: "I labored there for six years, often working twelve or fourteen hours a day, sometimes not seeing the light of heaven for a whole week, only on Sunday. . . . No one knows the dangers and privations experienced there, only those who have gone through the same." George knew much of hard work and sacrifice and felt so blessed to be among those emigrating in 1856: "I well can remember the first step that I made on American soil. I had been taught to believe that it was the land of promise, blessed above all other lands, and although only a small boy of fifteen years of age, I felt like thanking God for the blessings I then enjoyed."[5]

The following day, on Sunday, June 15, the Saints busily made preparations to continue their journey. Sixty-two-year-old Peder Madsen of Denmark recorded: "We strolled on the balcony until we got permission to go into the city. . . . A large part of the company went into the city to make purchases of the necessary items." Peder joined the Church in 1852 and emigrated with his thirty-six-year-old daughter, Petrea, and 160 other Danish Saints. Peter was also the clerk of this group and faithfully served in this capacity until his death in Echo Canyon, within a few days of reaching the valley.[6]

HORIZON EMIGRANTS LIVERPOOL, ENGLAND TO BOSTON, MASSACHUSETTS MAY 25—JUNE 30, 1856

PUCELL FAMILY

The 856 passengers on board the *Horizon* departed Liverpool on May 25 and anchored in the Massachusetts Bay in Boston thirty-five days later on June 30. They landed sixteen days after the arrival of the *Thornton* in New York. "The company consisted in large part of persons who had been 'Mormons' for many years, some of the oldest members of that body in Britain, poor but faithful, and they were specially reserved for this company, to be brought out under the auspices of the Perpetual Emigration Fund company. In an address to the company on board, Cyrus H. Wheelock remarked that among the passengers were the persons who had given the first sixpence to the 'Mormon' elders when they first went to England, and the names of those persons were Samuel Pucell and family." Among those emigrating with Samuel and his wife, Margaret, were their children: twenty-four-year-old Ann, fourteen-year-old Margaret, and ten-year-old Ellen "Nellie." Samuel's oldest son, twenty-five-year-old William, and his wife, twenty-five-year-old Eliza, also emigrated with their three-month-old son, Robert.[7]

MCBRIDE FAMILY

Before leaving Liverpool, England, on board the *Horizon*, Robert and Margaret McBride, with their five children, visited Margaret's parents, who did not treat them kindly. Margaret's father told them he never wanted to see or hear from them again and should they write letters, they would be burned before they were read. He expressed hopes they would all be swallowed up in the ocean before they landed upon the cursed American shore because they had brought disgrace to the family name by joining such a church. Robert and Margaret were among the first to accept the gospel in England. Orson Hyde baptized Robert in 1837, and Heber C. Kimball baptized Margaret in January 1838.[8]

Mellor Family

James and Mary Ann Payne Mellor heard the gospel preached from some of the first missionaries in England. They were baptized in April 1844. Louisa writes: "It was not long after father and mother accepted the Gospel that they found their friends and loved ones turning away from them." James worked as a wool comber and in the factory dyeing yarn. The Mellors were poor, and their children had little opportunity to attend school. In 1856, through the blessing of the Perpetual Emigration Fund, the Mellors could emigrate. Just prior to *Horizon*'s departure on May 23, 1856, Mary Ann went into premature labor, delivering twins, her eleventh and twelfth children. The twins lived for seven hours and passed away together. James and Mary Ann had previously lost two young daughters. The family agonized over the decision whether to abandon their emigration for that year. At the request of Mary Ann, James finally agreed to leave and took five of their seven children on board the ship with him. Sixteen-year-old Louisa remained behind in the hospital to care for Mary Ann and Emma, one of the two-year-old twins. Louisa described her sixteenth birthday as follows on May 23, 1856: "A sad one it was for me, as I was left with a sick mother and a little sister 2½ years old, as my father had to take the rest of the family and go aboard."[9]

Bad weather delayed the departure of the *Horizon* for two days. With this delay, James was allowed to disembark and visit his wife. At his arrival at the hospital, he found Mary Ann determined to go on board the ship. Doctors strongly opposed her leaving the hospital and predicted she would die on board the ship. She was carried on a stretcher and taken to the ship on a steamer. Upon learning of her condition, the captain commented she would soon be feeding the fish. Elders George Goddard and Cyrus H. Wheelock administered to Mary Ann, declaring that her mission on earth was not yet finished and promising her that she would make it to Utah.[10]

Passengers on board the *Horizon* had similar, though not quite as difficult, experiences crossing the mighty ocean waters as those traveling on the *Thornton*. John Jaques described the seasickness that plagued many as follows: "Sea-sickness changed our countenances to a pitiful, pallid hue . . . such a worshipping of buckets and tins, and unmentionable pans, I shall not attempt to describe. For my part, I paid the most devoted attention to the slop-pail about every half hour." Seasickness aside, the children made themselves happy "both above deck and below deck. Marbles, skipping ropes, and all the available paraphernalia of childhood's games are called into request. The older boys amuse themselves by tugging at the ropes with the sailors. So merrily we live together." John Jaques also noted: "Some of the passengers never recovered their usual vigor while at sea, but remained in a debilitated state until they set their feet on dry land again. On the other hand, some, who were remarkably hearty at sea, began to lose vigor as soon as they landed in America."[11]

Among the births noted on board the ship was Nancy "Horizon" Wilson, the daughter of James and Elizabeth Ollerton Wilson. James and Elizabeth were traveling with Elizabeth's parents, John and Alice Dandy Ollerton, and her siblings, nineteen-year-old Alice, fifteen-year-old Jane Ann, and six-year-old Sarah. The Ollertons were among the first baptized in Preston, England; John was baptized on November 6, 1837, and Alice on February 8, 1838. Little Nancy "Horizon" lived only twenty-three days before she passed away and was buried at sea.[12]

Thirty-eight-year-old Edward Martin, a returning missionary from England, was called to preside over the Saints traveling on the *Horizon*. Jesse Haven and George P. Waugh were his counselors. As noted by John Jaques, all were "busy as bees" throughout the voyage. Captain Martin spent his time on board the ship tirelessly ministering to the needs of the Saints.[13]

Jesse Haven

Forty-two-year-old Jesse Haven, serving as a counselor to Edward Martin, was born in Massachusetts in 1814. He was baptized in 1838 at age twenty-four and was ordained an elder by his cousin Brigham Young. Jesse had endured great persecutions and mob violence in Far West and Nauvoo and suffered many difficulties in Winter Quarters before he was called, in 1848, to serve his second mission, leaving his wife in destitute circumstances. At the completion of the mission, Jesse and his wife journeyed in 1850 to the Salt Lake Valley, where he remained for two years before being called to serve a mission to South Africa in a special conference in 1852. Upon arrival in South Africa, Jesse served as the mission president. Within a week, mobs—upward of five hundred people—gathered to harass the missionaries, anti-Mormon articles began appearing in local newspapers, and ministers encouraged their congregations to not admit the missionaries into their homes and to refuse requests for even a morsel of food. During these trying times, the missionaries frequently fasted and prayed for the Lord to open the hearts of the people. Their prayers were answered two months after their arrival with the baptism of their first convert. By the time the missionaries left in December 1855, over 170 people had been baptized, and six branches had been organized. As the time grew near for the missionaries to depart, those who desired to leave with them found it impossible because ship owners and agents agreed to not allow Mormons to emigrate. Through the blessings of God, a wealthy and respected convert purchased the ship *Unity,* and in November 1855, two Mormon elders and fifteen Saints sailed to Liverpool and continued on to America on board the *Caravan.* Jesse Haven left South Africa a month later and labored in Scotland until May 1856.[15]

George P. Waugh

Sixty-eight-year-old George P. Waugh, also serving as a counselor to Edward Martin, was affectionately known to those on board the *Horizon* as "Father Waugh." Father Waugh was returning from a three-year mission to Scotland and was described as "one of the most devoted Scottish worthies that ever came to Utah." He spent his time on board the ship ministering to the sick and afflicted. He continued this dedicated service to the Saints until the day he died, just two days prior to reaching the Salt Lake Valley.[16]

When the Saints on board the ship *Horizon* neared the shores of America, twenty-two-year-old Samuel Openshaw, of England, recorded his feelings: "Beautiful day and a propitious wind brought us in sight of Yankee Land which is the first land that we have seen since we left sight of Ireland and truly it was beautiful as we entered into the Bay of Boston, to behold the rise and decline of hills beyond interceding with green grass, cattle grazing, bedect beautiful houses, rocks rising out of the water as if to resist the force of the waves. It was truly sublime to us to gaze upon it. Our hearts were cheered to behold our destined port." The Openshaws were among the first to join the Church, in 1840.[17]

On June 30, the steamer *Huron* towed the *Horizon* to Constitution Wharf in Boston harbor. Of his arrival, forty-five-year-old Joseph Beecroft noted: "I feel grateful to my Father in Heaven for his goodness in sparing our lives to see the land of Zion, the land of the free and home of the brave. The land of Joseph's, choice above all lands. . . . The sights that presented themselves on all sides baffles all description. Such was their grandeur, splendor, and sublimity. . . . The shades of night soon followed. . . . Thus ended one of the most important days that ever dawned in my history." Joseph's account continues: "I now felt joy to spring up because I had got to land and thought of those who had kissed the very ground when they first touched the shore. I felt on free soil for the gospel has made me free and I will live under its banner while I live and in death I will sail under it into another world, and in the resurrection I will be a more than conqueror under its ample folds and life giving principles through the spirit of God."[18]

7

UNLIKELY BAND OF PIONEERS

A People of Immeasurable Faith and Courage

New York and Boston
June–July 1856

The emigrants in both New York and Boston came upon many locals who were curious about the "Mormons." Several articles had been written about them in the local newspapers, including one from the *New York Herald*:

> Great Arrival of Mormons. . . . They come from all parts of England, from the extreme north to the isle of Jersey, and consist of farmers, mechanics and laborers. Among the mechanics are weavers, carpenters, boot and shoemakers, joiners, miners, potters, &c. The Swedes are mostly farmers, with a few blacksmiths. Our reporter, who visited Castle Garden yesterday, was told by one of the Elders who came out with them, that they were mostly old converts, of ten or fifteen years standing, and were brought out at the expense of the Mormon Emigration fund. A good many, however, he stated, came out on their own expense. Some of them intend stopping here, but the majority are going direct to Utah. They are mostly families, and appear to belong to the better class of emigrants.[1]

Wallace Stegner described the emigrants of 1856 as follows:

> In all its history, the American West never saw a more unlikely band of pioneers. . . . Looking for the brown and resolute and

> weather-seasoned among them, you would have seen instead starved cheeks, pale skins, bad teeth, thin chests, all the stigmata of unhealthy work and inadequate diet. There were more women than men, more children under fifteen than either. One in every ten was past fifty, the oldest a woman of seventy-eight; there were widows and widowers with six or seven children. They looked more like the population of the poor farm on a picnic than like pioneers about to cross plains. Most of them, until they were herded from their crowded immigrant ship and loaded into the cars and rushed to the end of the Rock Island Line and dumped here at the brink of the West, had never pitched a tent, slept on the ground, cooked outdoors, built a campfire. They had not even the rudimentary skills that make frontiersmen. But as it turned out, they had some of the stuff that makes heroes.[2]

Although the Saints were unaccustomed to life on the frontier and truly did not possess the rudimentary skills that made frontiersmen, they were no strangers to the extreme difficulties life had to offer them. They were Saints who were proven, tried, and tested in the furnace of affliction, Saints who remained faithful and stalwart regardless of the trials that came their way. This adversity strengthened their character and made them the individuals they were, a people of immeasurable faith and courage who were willing to sacrifice anything for the gospel's sake. Their prior adversities helped mold, shape, and prepare them for what was to come. Though a majority of them were poor according to worldly standards, they were not poor in spirit! They were tough and courageous, and they were dedicated members of the Church truly possessing the attributes of heroes.

TENANT FAMILY

The journey to the Salt Lake Valley in 1856 brought various economic classes of immigrants together. Although roughly half were traveling with the assistance of the Perpetual Emigration Fund that season, others were wealthy and chose to selflessly give of their means to assist those in need. Joseph Beecroft describes his experience in traveling with Thomas Tenant, a wealthy farmer who purchased one of Brigham Young's properties for the amount of 25,000 dollars; the money was then donated by Brigham Young to the Perpetual

Emigration Fund, thus providing the way for many to travel to America during 1856. He was credited for providing the single greatest contribution to financing that emigration season. Joseph wrote: "Before we changed carriages and when we got into the other carriages we had Mr. Tenant for our nearest neighbor. He had his wife, her mother, and his child. What had Mormonism done? Such a spectacle was scarcely ever witnessed as to see one who has been so rich, so high in life, to come to be huddled together with the poorest of the poor and see how patiently he endures all things is truly wonderful." In Iowa, Thomas and his wife, Jane Ayerton Tenant; their one-year-old son, Thomas; and Jane's mother and brother were placed in the Hodgett Wagon Company. Neither Thomas nor his mother-in-law would reach the Salt Lake Valley. Thomas was buried at Fort Laramie, and his mother-in-law at Willow Springs.[3]

Bleak Family

James and Elizabeth Bleak also gave of their means to assist others. James was born in 1829 in England. He was the only child of six to grow to adulthood, his four siblings having died in infancy. When James was fourteen, his father died. Just two years later, his mother died, leaving James and his seven-year-old brother, John, orphans. Both James and John went to live with a relative, and within two years, John died. Completely alone, James turned his focus to his studies and became well educated, learning the silver and goldsmith trades and becoming an expert silversmith. In 1849, at age twenty, James married. Two years later, he was invited to a meeting where the father of his friend Joseph Thompson was speaking. Following the meeting, Joseph's father felt impressed that something was wrong with James and asked if he could give him a blessing. James describes: "When I came to the meeting, I could scarcely see anything. Around the gaslights on the streets were halos or rainbow colors, but when I left the building all of that was gone and my vision was clear and bright. I had been healed by the power of God. I have never suffered with that trouble to my eyes since. This miracle and the sermon I had listened to convinced me that your father was a servant of God. So I continued to attend the services and after a thorough investigation of the principles of the gospel, I applied for baptism, and your father baptized and confirmed me a member of the Church." James' wife, Elizabeth, also joined the Church. At age twenty-four, James was called as president over a London branch. In 1856, James was released, and he and Elizabeth made plans to come to America, sending money to the mission office in Liverpool for a wagon and ox team. Members with the means to travel by wagon were counseled that they would receive great blessings if they had faith to travel to the valley with the handcart companies, giving the difference to those without sufficient means. Although James had much concern for his wife and young children, he put his faith in the Lord and chose to travel by handcart. Prior to their departure, James was blessed that on this journey "he shall see the angel of death laying waste on his right and on his left, on his front and on his rearward, yet he and his family shall gather to Zion in safety, and not one of them shall fall by the way." The Bleak family would travel to the Salt Lake Valley in the Martin Handcart Company.[4]

WEBSTER FAMILY

Francis Webster was born on February 8, 1830, in England. He was the son of a poor farmer and suffered from such ill health, his parents had little hope he would live a long life. Despite his health, he was a hard worker. Francis lived at home until he was between fifteen and sixteen years old. In March 1848, he heard the missionaries preach a few times, desired to join the Church, and was baptized on April 17, 1848. He left a month later for Australia to make his fortune. Before leaving, he met Ann Elizabeth Parsons, who promised to wait for him until she was twenty-one. Francis returned to England four years later with sixteen hundred dollars in gold dust and was rebaptized by James Bleak. True to her word, Ann waited for Francis, and they were married on December 5, 1855. They decided to make their journey to the Salt Lake Valley in 1856 and, with the money Francis made while abroad, they planned on traveling in comfort with plenty of supplies in a wagon company. But ultimately they decided to assist the poor members and travel by handcart, even though Ann was pregnant. The Websters traveled to the valley in the Martin Company.[5]

8

EMBARKING UPON A MOST REMARKABLE JOURNEY

From New York and Boston to Iowa

THORNTON EMIGRANTS FROM NEW YORK TO IOWA JUNE–JULY 1856

From New York, the emigrants from the *Thornton*, under the direction of James G. Willie, traveled 1,200 miles by railway and steamship to Iowa City. Peder Madsen records:

> We left Castle Garden and were taken by barge to the steamship. Our belongings were weighed and transferred to the ship which took us from New York at 7 o'clock. . . . At 11 o'clock our belongings were transferred to the cars we boarded. I must add that these cars . . . were fitted with seats for two persons on each side, so that there was an aisle in the middle straight through the car where one could walk. It was two feet wide. The passenger entrances were at the ends but on the side so that one could board even if it was moving. There were seats for 86 persons, a stove in the middle of the car, and a toilet at the end.[1]

Many from this company noted the rough and unkind treatment they received from the railway authorities in Toledo, Ohio, and in Chicago, Illinois. When the company was detained at Pond Creek City because a railroad bridge was in need of repair, the emigrants slept overnight in the cramped railroad cars. The following morning, a large warehouse was procured to house them until the bridge was repaired. Many of the locals gathered outside the warehouse in attempts to attack the Saints. Authorities were notified, and the police arrived to disperse the rowdy crowd. The Willie Company arrived in Iowa City on June 26 amid a torrential rainstorm. The company obtained a large engine shed, where they found shelter and waited out the storm. The following day they walked about two and a half miles to the staging grounds in Iowa.[2]

HORIZON EMIGRANTS FROM BOSTON TO IOWA

From Boston, the emigrants from the *Horizon,* under the direction of Edward Martin, also traveled by railway and steamship to Iowa City. They passed through country described as beautiful and delightful with extensive woodlands, fruit trees, and vines along the railway, which held their constant attention and admiration. The weather was extremely hot, much different than the emigrants were accustomed to, with temperatures soaring between 96 and 100 degrees.[3]

Twenty-year-old John William Southwell recorded:

> At this pier nothing but cattle cars could be obtained and into these we were loaded, bag and baggage. In those we rode to Albany, state of New York. Here we laid over two days and two nights. Here we were permitted to change to a third class accommodation. The seats were two inch plank with no back. In this miserable way we were conveyed to Cleveland, Ohio, at very slow pace. The country along the track was studded with fine orchards, bearing fine apples and all kinds of fruit. The fruit was so tempting that at the rate of travel, the young men would jump from the train, fill their pockets, and overtake the slow moving institution. However slow, it brought us into Cleveland on the morning of the greatest day in America. Not realizing the meaning of all this parading and firing of firecrackers and artillery, an elder of the church explained it all to our satisfaction. Since that day, however, the 4th of July is as precious to a Latter-day Saint as to any American born citizen who lives under the flag flying stars and stripes, the red, white, and blue.[4]

Similar to the Willie Company, the Martin Company also experienced rough and unkind treatment. John Jaques noted: "Toledo was the place were the railroad employees were the most discourteous, uncivil, and harsh in conduct towards the company. Scarcely had the train arrived at the depot there, when the energetic but vulgar salutation was hurled at the emigrants . . ." John William Southwell describes another incident in further detail:

> While waiting in that city for change of cars a great rainstorm continued two days. We and our luggage were exposed to the weather, the company having no sheds to protect. A large barn was secured and all were transferred to it until the storm abated. A few had secured rooms for their accommodation but the great majority were huddled together in the barn. Like Missouri and other places the people of the town despised the Mormons and after the Saints had retired for the night, a mob of bullies including some females gathered around the barn and kept up for hours such a howling and bombarding with stones and bats it equaled any Indian powwow I have ever listened to on the frontiers. Finally the presidency of the company found a person who it seemed had some authority, who persuaded the mob to desist and go to their homes. However, it left the people in a state of terrible excitement. Not a person closed an eye that night in sleep.[5]

Members of the Martin Company arrived in Iowa City on July 8, thirteen days after the Willie Company, also during a terrible storm.[6]

IOWA

For those emigrating during the 1856 season, travel by railroad and steamship ended in Iowa City. The remainder of their more than one-thousand-mile journey would be made with wagons and handcarts. John Taylor, who at the time was presiding over the Eastern States mission, documented the earliest preparations of establishing a more northern and healthy route to the Salt Lake Valley:

> I have been anticipating, according to the statements made, in the general epistle of the first Presidency, that some person or persons might be sent from the Valley to superintend the emigration in the West. In the absence of such persons, I have felt it a duty incumbent upon me to make all preliminary arrangements for the furtherance of the interests of the emigration . . . I feel deeply solicitous for the welfare of the traveling Saints, and more especially am I anxious that everything shall be conducted properly, with due care and safety,

> and as far as may be practicable, for the comfort of those who may be going by handcarts. It is a new project, and will require our greatest attention and vigilance. I have, according to instructions received from President Young, had the Northern route surveyed, and entered into preliminary arrangements for camp grounds at Iowa City.[7]

Daniel Spencer

Approximately two and a half miles from the railroad terminal ending in Iowa City, immigration officials prepared at the staging grounds for outfitting the companies. This would prove to be a monumental task overseen by sixty-two-year-old Daniel Spencer, appointed by Franklin D. Richards. In 1840, Daniel met some elders and witnessed the persecution heaped upon them. He resolved to investigate the cause of the enmity and unchristian-like manifestations, and for two weeks he closed his establishment and "there alone with his God he weighed in the balances of his clear head and conscientious heart the divine message and found it not wanting. One day, when his son was with him in his study, he suddenly burst into a flood of tears, and exclaimed: 'My God, the thing is true, and as an honest man I must embrace it; but it will cost me all I have got on earth.'" People were astonished that a man of Daniel Spencer's social standing and character believed in such a religion. The conversion and conduct of Daniel Spencer carried a deep and weighty conviction among many good families in the region, which, in a few months, resulted in the establishment of a flourishing branch of the Church. In 1841, he was called to serve a mission to Canada and Massachusetts.

Following his missions, while in Nauvoo, Daniel served as a member of the city council and as mayor. Daniel belonged to a group of men selected by Joseph Smith to explore the Rocky Mountains. This expedition was interrupted by Joseph's martyrdom. Daniel was asked to lead one of the first wagon companies to arrive in the Salt Lake Valley in 1847. In 1852, during a special conference, he was called to serve a mission to England and, upon his release in 1856, was appointed to oversee outfitting the handcart and wagon companies in Iowa City. The following tribute was written of Daniel and published in the *Millennial Star*:

> As the season for emigration advances, we are made deeply sensible of the departure of many noble spirits from our field of labour this side the Atlantic. . . . Few have laboured in these missions with that interest and effect for the salvation of souls which Elder Spencer has done; his absence, therefore, will be so much more keenly felt. Ever humble, and devoted to the interests of the Church . . . he was a tower of strength to them that abode in his counsels; and for childlike obedience and humility, he was an illustrious example for all who were blessed with his acquaintance. . . . Nearly all the Conferences in the British Isles have been blessed by his personal ministrations, nor have his valuable labours been limited to Britain. . . . We feel that a strong man has gone from us, and that in the strength of Israel's God he will be a source of great joy to the emigrating Saints. We have appointed Elder Spencer our Agent in the United States, to forward the European-Through-Emigration of Saints on to Utah this season.[8]

Upon learning Franklin D. Richards had appointed Daniel to superintend the whole of the emigration to the West, John Taylor sent out the following directive:

> The brethren, therefore, will receive him in that capacity, listen to his suggestions, and carry out his plans. I would further recommend that a constant intercourse be kept up with Bro. Spencer by the different parties employed in this business, that he may be thoroughly posted in relation to all matters, so that no delay may be occasioned; but that as the passengers arrive at the place of outfit, they may immediately proceed on their journey. He will confer with me from time to time. There is more loss, unpleasantness, and sickness occasioned by detention than perhaps by any other thing. I wish the passengers, on their arrival at the place of outfitting, to be prepared to start the next day, or in a day or two, at furthest.[9]

In Iowa, Daniel Spencer surrounded himself with trusted and proven men. John Taylor described them as "efficient a body of men to assist him as perhaps ever were assembled together for an object of the kind." These men were responsible for acquiring property to be used at the sight of outfitting, overseeing arrangements for the handcarts, wagons, and the oxen to pull the wagons. They also had responsibility to oversee arrangements for tents and food, including acquiring cattle to provide meat and milk, tons of flour, and other basic food staples and necessities to see the emigrants through to the next supply station, located in Florence, Nebraska, some 275 miles west. The reports of the scarcity of food and cattle in the Salt Lake Valley at the time directed John Taylor to give specific directions to the amount of food and cattle he felt should be sent with the Saints immigrating in 1856:

> From the reports we get from the valley, of the great loss of cattle, and the very great scarcity of provisions, as well as the helplessness of many now on their way to Utah, having carefully examined the subject, I am more than ever convinced of the necessity of being very careful in our moves about the emigration. They ought to have 60 lbs. of breadstuff for every person to start with, instead of 55 lbs. per person; and I wish to propose, that you send an extra team loaded with flour to each of the two first companies of 400 persons each.

Elder Taylor also recommended to forward cattle and flour to Fort Laramie: "By the time of the arrival of the later companies at Laramie, there will be some return from the new crop, which, with this advanced supply, will likely relieve them of much suffering."[10]

In relation to the handcarts specifically, Elder John Taylor recorded: "I have forwarded to Bros. Webb and Spencer President Young's instructions to me respecting this business. I hope they will be carried out as far as practicable, suggesting that great attention be paid to their strength, and that the best of seasoned timber be used. Not having been informed as to the exact numbers of the European emigration who would want hand-carts, I found it impossible to make any correct estimate as to the number that would be required."[11]

Initially, John Taylor arranged for the construction of one hundred handcarts to be built in St. Louis:

> These were made according to a schedule given by a committee of Elders who had just traversed the plains. They are a very neat article, well finished, ironed, and painted, well adapted for the purpose, and will cost about twenty dollars. Some time ago I appointed Elder George D. Grant to have another hundred made in Iowa City in a more primitive style, and without iron. These will cost about ten dollars each. Elder Grant is sanguine that they will answer the purpose. Elder Chauncey Webb is superintending the manufacture of a number more, and anticipates being able to make

> them for a still smaller sum. By having this variety we shall at least have a test of all.

Under the direction of Daniel Spencer, the remaining handcarts needed were constructed by the immigration officials in Iowa.[12]

In April 1856, twenty-one-year-old Joseph B. Elder was asked to assist with the season's immigration, specifically in the selection and purchase of the oxen, beef cattle, and cows. He was also asked to assist in driving and breaking the cattle. Joseph sacrificed much to do so, dropping out of college in Illinois and enduring much mocking and persecution from professors, fellow students, and other associates. Joseph worked with George D. Grant for almost four months and wrote the stock were some of the worst he ever undertook to drive and were the meanest cattle he ever had anything to do with. He originally planned on traveling to the Salt Lake Valley with the returning missionaries but was instead asked to travel with the Willie Handcart Company.[13]

While in Iowa City, the weather was unrelenting. Thunderstorms raged and the weather continued to be unfavorable with wind, rain, heat, and unbearable humidity. Although some tents were sewn on board the emigrant ships, there were not sufficient tents to protect most of the Saints from the inclement weather. Of his arrival in Iowa City, fifteen-year-old George Cunningham of the Willie Company described:

> Everything seemed beautiful and pleasant as far as the eye could reach. We had not been there long ere night set in. The sky began to gleam with lightning streaks, followed in rapid succession until some parts of the firmament seemed entirely in a blaze. The rain commenced to fall in torrents, the wind blew most terrible. We were there without the least particle of shelter, no tent, no cover whatever. Water was swimming everywhere, everyone in an uproar. Children were crying, mothers sighing. . . . I think that it is written somewhere that the devil is prince and power of the air. If so, he must have been in an awful rage; for such storms continued for several successive nights.[14]

The inclemency of the weather, in addition to the lack of sufficient shelter, attributed to much illness within the camp. While in Iowa, thirteen-year-old Elizabeth "Betsey" Smith, of the Willie

Company, became deathly ill with scarlet fever. Betsey was traveling with her widowed mother, Marjorie McEwan Bain Smith, sisters Jane and Mary, brother Alexander, half-sister Marjory "May" Bain, and May's friend Euphemia Mitchell, whose mother disowned her when she learned of her baptism. While Marjorie was away from the tent warming some broth, Betsey overheard two women mention she was dying. When her mother returned, she noticed tears in Betsey's eyes and asked if she was feeling worse. Betsey responded, "Mother, they think I am dying" and with great faith and conviction she proclaimed: "I want to live and go to the Valley." In Betsey's words: "My dear mother, at that time in her fifty-second year, then went and brought the elders, who administered to me and rebuked the disease, commanding it to leave both me and the camp. My recovery was rapid."[15]

By the time the Saints from the *Horizon*, captained by Edward Martin, arrived in Iowa, officials had run out of sufficient lumber for the handcarts and had began cutting the wood themselves with timber located six miles from their camp. The women of both companies, captained by James G. Willie and Edward Martin, made the tents and wagon covers. "Everybody that could handle a saw, plane and drawknife was put to work, and the making of the carts was rushed." John Chislett recorded the following regarding the handcarts: "They had to be made on the camp-ground. They were made in a hurry, some of them of very insufficiently seasoned timber, and strength was sacrificed to weight until the production was a fragile structure, with nothing to recommend it but lightness."[16]

In Iowa City, the weight limit for luggage was reduced from the previous seventy-five pounds per person over twelve years old allowed to a mere seventeen pounds per person. In Liverpool, emigrants were counseled about the unnecessary burden of additional luggage: "needless luggage burdens the Company with a worse than useless expenditure for transportation through the United States, takes up room in the often crowded condition of the passengers themselves, and burdens them with useless labour in taking care of and handling it, and finally has to be abandoned at the place of outfit. . . . It is far better for them to dispose of their extra articles, and use the means to add to their comfort on their way, than to finally have to abandon them as useless." The reduction of luggage to seventeen pounds necessitated emigrants to dispose of much of their already meager belongings. Josiah Rogerson of the Martin Company described: "A market was found for all this extra luggage with the residents at Iowa City, the buyer putting his own price on the article, the seller having to take that, give it away or burn it, and many a hundred dollars' worth were thus bartered for one-third to half its value." John Jaques of the Martin Company noted: "Many things were sold cheaply to residents of that vicinity, and many more things were left on the camping ground for anybody to take or leave at his pleasure." Even seasoned travelers to the valley, like Levi Savage of the Willie Company, noted just how little seventeen pounds was: "This makes us rather destitute for wearing apparel and bedding." John Chislett noted, "Each person was limited to seventeen pounds of clothing and bedding, making eighty-five pounds of luggage to each cart. To this were added such cooking utensils as the little mess of five required. But their cuisine being scanty, not many articles were needed, and I presume that average would not exceed fifteen to twenty pounds, making in all a little over a hundred pounds on each cart. The carts being so poorly made, could not be laden heavily, even had the people been able to haul them."[17]

James G. Willie, a returning missionary, was appointed to be the leader of the fourth handcart company, numbering 500 persons with 120 handcarts. Elders Millen Atwood, Levi Savage, William Woodward, John Chislett, and Johan Ahmanson were called to preside over groups of 100. "To each hundred there were five round tents, with twenty persons to a tent; twenty hand-carts, or one to every five persons; and one Chicago wagon, drawn by three yoke of oxen, to haul provisions and tents." Many of the groups of twenty were largely made up of women and children with few men. "The strength of the company was equalized as much as possible by distributing the young men among the different families to help them. Several carts were drawn by young girls exclusively."[18]

Edward Martin was appointed the leader of the fifth handcart company, along with Daniel Tyler. Edward was a returning missionary. At the request of Franklin D. Richards, he spent the last few months of his mission in Liverpool overseeing the emigration of

4,395 Saints. The Martin Company was originally divided into two groups, with Edward Martin as one leader and Jesse Haven as the other. Franklin D. Richards later consolidated this group under the leadership of Edward Martin in Florence, Nebraska. The combined total of the company numbered 575 persons with 146 handcarts.[19]

Dan Jones, who was returning from a mission to Wales, was appointed captain of a wagon company. William B. Hodgetts was appointed as subcaptain of 185 persons with 33 wagons, and John A. Hunt subcaptain of 200 persons with 50 wagons. However, Dan would not serve long in this capacity, and Captains Hodgetts and Hunt would be asked to take on full responsibilities as captains of their respective groups, enabling Dan to accompany Franklin D. Richards and the returning missionaries. At the Platte Bridge, Dan parted with the returning missionaries to remain with his brother to recover a cached thrashing machine.[20]

Once all of the preparations were finalized, the handcarts and wagons were loaded, and the companies were prepared to depart. Although companies were supposed to remain only a few days at Iowa City, members of the Willie and Martin Companies were delayed for weeks. After such a long delay, they were excited at the prospects of continuing on with their journey to the valley they so longed to reach. Sixty-two-year-old Peder Madsen, appointed to serve as clerk to the Danish Saints in the Willie Handcart Company, recorded: "We are happy that the time is near for the journey to continue. We will gather experiences that will follow us into eternity. The Lord will bless and preserve the faithful who will do his will." Of leaving Iowa, eleven-year-old Mary Ann James wrote: "After leaving Council Bluffs, Iowa, we started on what is known as the most remarkable journey recorded in the annals of history."[21]

9

SURELY THE BLESSINGS OF THE LORD WERE WITH US

IOWA CITY, IOWA, TO FLORENCE, NEBRASKA

WILLIE COMPANY
JULY 15–AUGUST 11, 1856

On Tuesday, July 15, the Willie Company left Iowa City and set out for Florence, Nebraska, some 277 miles west. The terrain on the trail was often difficult, and the emigrants expended all their strength and energy to get through each day. Levi Savage noted: "Some of the Saints, both old and young, were nearly overcome, yet they endured much better than could be expected. Surely the blessings of the Lord were with us." Adding to the difficulties were the extreme and often adverse weather conditions of wind, stifling heat, humidity, and torrential rainstorms. John Chislett pens:

> As we traveled along, we presented a singular, and sometimes an affecting appearance. The young and strong went along gaily with their carts, but the old people and little children were to be seen straggling a long distance in the rear. Sometimes, when the little folks had walked as far as they could, their fathers would take them on their carts, and thus increase the load that was already becoming too heavy as the day advanced. But what will parents not do to benefit their children in time of trouble? The most affecting scene, however, was to see a mother carrying her child at the breast, mile after mile, until nearly exhausted. The heat was intense, and

> the dust suffocating, which rendered our daily journeys toilsome in the extreme.[1]

Shortly after the handcart companies began their trek westward, weather conditions also took a toll on the handcarts that were hastily constructed with unseasoned wood. Every day seemed to bring a new set of challenges, as recorded by Levi Savage on July 23. He noted: "The weak are getting strong. The lame and aged get along exceedingly well." A day later on July 24 he noted: "Several in camp are severely ill. Our rations are very short. . . . It is not enough. There is some complaining." John Chislett described: "Our rations consisted of ten ounces of flour to each adult per day, and half that amount to children under eight years of age. Besides our flour we had occasionally a little rice, sugar, coffee, and bacon. But these items (especially the last) were so small and infrequent that they scarcely deserve mentioning. Any hearty man could eat his daily allowance for breakfast. In fact, some of our men did this, and then worked all day without dinner and went to bed supperless or begged food at the farmhouses as we traveled along."[2]

While the handcart companies passed through towns and settlements on their way to Florence, the local residents harassed and threatened them. Levi Savage noted the threats and disturbances occurred almost daily. On July 25, the local sheriff stopped the company, producing a warrant to search the wagons. It was thought the women were being detained against their wishes with ropes. The sheriff's search proved the report had no foundation, and he departed without further incident. Later on that same evening, a group of thirty men attempted to disturb the company but left after finding the company on guard.[3]

Fifteen-year-old George Cunningham recorded: "People would mock, sneer, and deride us on every occasion for being such fools as they termed us, and would often throw out inducements to get us to stop. . . . When we went through a town or settlement, pulling our handcarts as we always had to do, people would turn out in crowds to laugh at us, crying 'gee-haw' as if we were oxen. . . . This did not discourage us in the least, for we knew we were on the right track."[4]

Gratefully, the company was met with occasional kindness, as noted in the company journal on Thursday, July 31, at Fort Des

Moines: "Mr. Charles Good, a respectable gentleman from the City who seemed very favorable to the Gospel from no impure motive brought a present of 15 pairs of children's boots & being given with a free spirit we received them. John Chislett noted: "The people in Iowa were very good in giving to those who asked for food, expressing their sympathy for us whenever they visited our camp—which they did in large numbers if we stopped near a settlement."[5]

Along with these kindnesses, the Saints were also met with persuasions to leave the company. John Chislett recorded: "They tried to dissuade us from going to Salt Lake in that way, and offered us employment and homes among them. A few of our company left us from time to time; but the elders constantly warned us against 'the Gentiles' and by close watching succeeded in keeping the company tolerably complete." On August 2, the Willie Company journal noted: "A great many of the towns people came to see us & got trying to get the sisters away." Twenty-year-old Emily Hill and her sister, twenty-three-year old Julia, were handed anonymous letters. Emily described:

> Surely if we had been natural or unnatural curiosities we could not have been commented on or stared at any more by the people surrounding us. "Mormons, men, women and children, and worse, a lot of young girls, bound for Salt Lake and going to pull hand carts! Shocking!" . . . Anonymous letters, and warnings from sympathizing outsiders were mysteriously conveyed to us, setting forth the hardships and impossibilities of such a journey, and offering us inducements to stay. Many who started out with us backed out in a few days; my sister broke down and was unable to walk and I remember asking myself (footsore and weary with the first week of walking and working) if it was possible for me, faith or no faith, to walk twelve hundred miles further. The flesh certainly was weak but the spirit was willing, I set down my foot that I would try, and by the blessing of God I pulled a hand cart a thousand miles and never rode one step.[6]

On Monday, August 11, the Willie Company passed through Council Bluffs. Levi Savage recorded that some local residents came out to "make sport" of the handcart Saints. James McGaw—age thirty-two and Church agent and presiding authority in Florence, Nebraska—stood up to those verbally abusing the Saints and "consequently, got into a fist fight with them. He whipped one or two of them, but received no material injury to himself except getting his hair well pulled." The company then proceeded on to the Missouri River and was ferried across to the camp in Florence, Nebraska, making the 277-mile journey in 27 days.[7]

Haven & Martin Companies
July 22–August 22, 1856

Just prior to the departure of the Haven and Martin Companies from Iowa City, Brigham Young was apprised of the late departure of the Saints from Liverpool. In a letter dated July 19, President Young wrote: "The emigration are all late, owing, I suppose, to the difficulty in obtaining ships. It would be much better when it can be accomplished, to have the emigrants shipped earlier in the season. They should be landed early in May, and not much, if any, after the first of that month in Boston or New York." He also wrote of his intentions to send out wagons loaded with flour to meet the handcart trains and their plan of sending detachments of teams with flour every week as long as it was necessary.[8]

Jesse Haven's Company left Iowa on July 22, and Edward Martin's Company left on July 25. Both companies made little initial progress on account of many returning back to Iowa due to thunderstorms, sickness, loss of animals, handcart repairs, and unfinished preparations. The Hodgett and Hunt wagon companies began their journey on July 30 and August 1.[9]

On the trail, the Haven and Martin Companies experienced challenges similar to the Willie Company, with the difficult terrain, adverse weather conditions, physical exhaustion, harassment from the local townspeople, and the lack of food rations. Captain Jesse Haven also recorded the dissension experienced within his company and noted the dissatisfaction with the provisions: "Saints complain that the provision provided is not sufficient for them. Some dissatisfaction on the account of it." Five days later Captain Haven wrote he had concluded the provisions would not hold out.[10]

Of the extreme weather experienced, John William Southwell recalled:

> One of the most horrible electric storms I ever saw fell upon us accompanied with hail and rain. It proved a perfect deluge. In this flat clay soil in the space of ten minutes the roads became almost impassable and oh what a scene to behold. Four hundred men, women and children struggling to keep their feet. Here was no sign of a shelter. Our tents were rolled up in the wagons. After everyone was drenched and many were unable to move out of their tracks the captain gave orders to pitch camp and set up the tents the best they could in the mud and quick as possible this was done. It proved a temporary shelter for the old people and children. They were protected from the rain but they were still ankle [deep] in the mud. At this stage of the game the younger men displayed their heroism. Near our intended camp ground was a large patch of young willows and they attacked the willow patch with ax and pocket knives and in as short a time as possible they had enough ground covered on which we raised our tents, spread down the bedding, and then a good old farmer living in the distance gave us wood from a pile of dry willows which was soon piled up and a fire built. In the meantime the storm had spent its fury and men, women and children were soon standing and turning themselves around, drying their wet and bespattered clothing. Many a prayer went up asking the Lord to bless and prosper the old gentleman who had furnished us with the means to make us comfortable once more. With exception of a little hot tea, we ate a cold supper, had our night's service and laid our weary bodies down to rest. The storm having left the roads in such a bad condition the captain concluded to lay over one day, which dried up the road.[11]

John Jaques described the following incident of the harassment experienced from the locals: "When in camp, near Marengo, a crowd of rowdy young men on horseback visited one of the companies of handcart emigrants and seemed disposed to create a disturbance, but they subsequently rode off without, though during their stay they gave the emigrants a sample of western profanity oaths and 'by Gods' rolling from their tongues about as frequently as other words, and with much more gusto!"[12]

John William Southwell recorded:

> The usual mobocratic spirit we had witnessed all along the route filled the souls of the people and they felt to vie with each other in uttering oaths and curses upon us as we passed along thru their settlements. God forgive them. We passed along pleasantly for

> two days. The third day we came to a halt by a nice stream and in the foothills was grass for the oxen. The teams were out to feed and instantly two men started for them cursing the . . . Mormons, declaring they would kill every [one] of them. Captain Haven met them and in his gentlemanly way apologized and offered them pay in order to secure a night's feed for the poor, hungry brutes. This kind act on his part took them by surprise and they consented to leave them there without further trouble. The singing of the young ladies at evening service drew the attention of the kinder disposed people and in the morning they brought butter and milk into camp and expressed themselves as being pleased with the way we conducted ourselves traveling thru the country. At their request on breaking up camp we sang the hand cart song which pleased them. They bid us success on our journey. This circumstance is one that a kind word turneth away wrath and as Jesus said to his disciples, do good to them that hate you, is truly exemplified in this case.[13]

Although weary from the difficulties of pulling a handcart, twenty-two-year-old Samuel Openshaw continued to take notice of the beauties and blessings around him: "We started about seven o'clock this morning and traveled through a beautiful country where we could stand and gaze upon the prairies as far as the eye could carry, even until the prairies themselves seemed to meet the sky on all sides, without being able to see a house."[14]

Sixty-eight-year-old George P. Waugh, or "Father Waugh" as he was affectionately called, was a wise, kindhearted, and robust counselor to Edward Martin on the ship *Horizon*. Father Waugh was appointed to serve as captain over the aged and infirm in the Martin Company. Each morning, as noted by John William Southwell, Father Waugh would "muster them together, make an early start and travel them so far as they were able to walk. Those who tired out would fall back to be taken up by some young man and carried to camp on his hand cart, which was a light, frail article. Being built of very light material and tied with rawhide in place of whoop iron which could not be obtained at that time . . . they would be frequently breaking down and thus hindering the company's progress in their long march."[15]

The Haven Handcart Company reached Florence on August 19, two days following the departure of the Willie Company. Franklin D.

Richards and his group of returning missionaries arrived on August 21. The following day, on August 22, the Martin Company was ferried across the river to Florence. Samuel Openshaw described their arrival: "Some looked upon us as if we were deceived; others who were old apostates came with all the subtilty of the devil, and all the cunning they have gained by their own experience, trying to turn the saints to the right hand or to the left, but thank[s] be to God, but few or none adhered to their advice." The final arrival of the season was the Hunt and Hodgett Wagon Companies on August 28.[16]

10

THE DEBATE

FLORENCE, NEBRASKA

WILLIE COMPANY
AUGUST 11–16, 1856

In Florence, Nebraska, James McGaw was called to oversee the emigration. James was born in 1823 in Upper Canada. At age eighteen, he traveled to Illinois, where he was first introduced to the gospel and was baptized on October 11, 1841. Shortly after his baptism, James served a mission to Indiana and two missions to Texas. At age twenty-eight, James became captain of the Eleventh Pioneer Company, traveling to the Salt Lake Valley in 1852. The journey for this company was met with sickness and deaths attributed to cholera. In April 1854, James oversaw the immigration in New Orleans. Following subsequent council from President Young to adopt a more northern and healthy route through the States to avoid sickness, James traveled to Florence early in the spring of 1856 and began making arrangements for outfitting the emigrant companies at the site of old Winter Quarters. James was assisted by William H. Kimball, along with many others who worked tirelessly to fence off fields and corrals, put in grain, build a warehouse, and arrange for supplies of food, equipment, and tools. They contracted for the use of timber and fuel, and found ferriages to cross the Missouri, Elk Horn, and Loup Fork rivers. Florence became a critical supply station for the Saints, it being the last station operated by Church officials until reaching the Salt Lake Valley. The remainder of the more than one-thousand-mile journey to the valley was across a vast wilderness area with few opportunities to obtain supplies.[1]

In Florence, many apostate Mormons sought to convince the new arrivals to leave the handcart companies. J. H. Latey noted that along with the merry countenances and buoyant steps of those thrilled to be continuing on with their journey were those

> allured by the fine promises and high wages; others there are whose faith is not of that nature to stand the trials they are called upon to undergo, and back out from five to fifty in a company of 300. . . . Those weak in the faith soon find those who will make them weaker; those who have backed out before them come up with their long faces, smooth words, and melancholy tone, prating away their words of comfort . . . but it is all right, the sort that are led away from the line of their duty by such spurious promises and oily tongues—well never mind that—are not wanted in the Valley, and by staying here they save themselves two journeys—one to Utah and one back.[2]

After nearly a month's travel, the Fourth Handcart Company, captained by James G. Willie, arrived in Florence on Monday, August 11. The company spent the next few days repairing handcarts and tents, loading provisions, and determining who intended to continue on to the valley. "The companies stay here longer than they otherwise would in consequence of their carts being unfit for their journey across the plains; some requiring new axles, and the whole of them having to have a piece of iron screwed on to prevent the wheel from wearing away the wood." By this time, shoes and clothing were also wearing out. "Measurements of the feet of those who needed shoes were taken, and those who had shoes that were too small were given to the ones who could fit them. The others will instead get new shoes."[3]

While in Florence, a debate ensued whether the company should continue with the journey that season or stay the winter in Nebraska. Few were aware of the difficulties and dangers of traveling so late in the season. Not only was there a strong possibility of experiencing severe and extreme weather, but official calculations also indicated that their food supplies were insufficient to make it to South Pass, where resupply teams were expected. Also noted was the fact that teams were already weak and many were failing fast. Levi Savage wrote: "Many are going to stop. Others are faltering and I myself am not in favor of, but much opposed to, taking women and children through when they are destitute of clothing, when we all know that we are bound to be caught in the snow and severe cold weather long before we reach the valley." John Chislett noted: "The elders seemed to be divided in their judgment as to the practicability of our reaching Utah in safety at so late a season of the year, and the idea was entertained for a day or two of making our winter quarters on the Elkhorn, Wood river, or some eligible location in Nebraska; but it did not meet with general approval. A monster meeting was called to consult the people about it."[4]

On Wednesday, August 13, a meeting was held in which James G. Willie, Levi Savage, and Millen Atwood addressed the Saints. Captain Willie exhorted the company to press forward regardless of the sacrifice. Following his address, Levi Savage was invited to speak. Levi was among the few aware of the dangers of traveling this late in the season.

Levi Savage

Thirty-six-year-old Levi Savage was born in Ohio in 1820. At age twenty-three, he was introduced to the gospel and was baptized three years later in 1846. Shortly thereafter, Levi enlisted for service in the Mormon Battalion and through the trials and privations experienced, he was transformed into a true frontiersman. Upon returning from their service, some members of the Battalion came across and buried the remains of the Donner Party. The images of these horrific scenes presented a revolting and distressing spectacle and were indelibly burned into their hearts and minds. Upon his arrival in the Salt Lake Valley, Levi learned of the death of his mother near Council Bluffs, Iowa. Levi married in January 1848 and was blessed with a son in 1851. Eleven months later his wife, Jane, passed away, leaving Levi a widower with an infant son.

In October 1852, Levi was called to serve a mission to Siam (Thailand). He left his son in the care of his sister. Because of a civil war, he was never able to serve in Siam and instead served in the Far

East Mission in Burma. He experienced very little success while he labored under the most adverse and trying circumstances. In May 1855, he wrote President Richards informing him of his intentions to return home. Levi arrived in Iowa City just prior to the departure of the Fourth and Fifth Handcart Companies in 1856 and was asked to travel with the Willie Company. In Florence, when the debate ensued whether to continue on to the Salt Lake Valley, Levi's life experiences no doubt influenced his plea for the company to wait until spring. Levi boldly "declared positively that to his certain knowledge we could not cross the mountains with a mixed company of aged people, women, and little children, so late in the season without much suffering, sickness, and death. He therefore advised going into winter quarters without delay; but he was rebuked by the other elders for want of faith."[5]

Levi recalled his comments to the Saints, declaring that

> we were liable to have to wade in snow up to our knees and shovel at night, lay ourselves in a thin blanket and lie on the frozen ground without a bed. I said that it was not like having a wagon that we could go into and wrap ourselves in as much as we like and lay down. "No," said I, "we are without wagons, destitute of clothing and could not carry it if we had it. We must go as we are. The handcart system I do not condemn. I think it preferable to unbroken oxen and experienced teamsters. The lateness of the season was my only objection to leaving this point for the mountains at this time." I spoke warmly upon the subject, but spoke truth, and if Elder Willey did not want me to act in the place where I am, he is at full liberty to place another man in my stead.[6]

James G. Willie then stood and reprimanded Levi for his comments. Levi confidently replied to the reprimand that if Captain Willie did not want him to continue in the position as captain, he was at liberty to call another man to serve in his stead and declared with great conviction: "Brethren and sisters, what I have said I know to be true; but, seeing you are to go forward, I will go with you, will help you all I can, will work with you, will rest with you, will suffer with you, and if necessary, I will die with you. May God in his mercy bless and preserve us. Amen."[7]

Elder Atwood then spoke and exhorted all to pray to know for themselves whether they should go or stay, for it was their privilege to know for themselves. The meeting was then dismissed. John Chislett wrote: "The emigrants were entirely ignorant of the country and climate—simple, honest, eager to go to 'Zion' at once."[8]

James Family

William and Jane James were among those who attended the meeting that evening. They were emigrating with their seven children, having lost six-month old Jane on board the ship *Thornton*. Their sixteen-year-old daughter, Emma, recalled:

> I think that the thing which I will remember for the rest of my life and wish that we had heeded what was said by a brother [Levi] Savage, with tears streaming down his cheeks he pleaded with the people. "Brothers and sisters, wait until spring to make this journey. Some of the strong may get through in case of bad weather, but the bones of the weak and old will strew the way." I can remember that when he finished there was a long time of silence. I was frightened. Father looked pale and sick. I turned to mother to see what she was thinking, and all that I saw was her old determined look. She was ready to go on tomorrow. There were many others like her. We really didn't have much choice. There was no work here for us to keep ourselves through the winter, and our family had to live. "We must put our trust in the Lord," said mother, and that was that.[9]

Oakey Family

Thomas and Ann Collett Oakey were among the members of the United Brethren congregation to be converted to the gospel by Wilford Woodruff in 1840. They were traveling to the valley with their seven children. Following the discussion of continuing on to the Salt Lake Valley, fourteen-year-old Joseph decided to leave the company: "One day during the noon meal, Joseph turned to one of the younger children, handed his plate to him and left the camp. His parents were frantic when he did not return in the evening. They searched through the handcart train, along the trail, and visited the houses and farms in the area, but were unable to find Joseph and had no choice but to continue on." During that time of terrible grief for the Oakeys, Ann was given a priesthood blessing "in which she was promised she would one day see her son again."[10]

After spending five days in Florence, a majority of the Fourth Handcart Company, with Captains Millen Atwood, Levi Savage, William Woodward, John Chislett, and Johan A. Ahamason, left Florence on Saturday, August 16; the rest of the company followed a day later. The company now consisted of 404 persons, 87 handcarts, and 6 wagons. In addition, a wagon company consisting of 26 persons and 4 wagons, captained by Andrew L. Siler, was added to the Willie Company. For a short time, Colonel Almon W. Babbitt, Secretary of the Utah Territory, accompanied them.[11]

Before departing, the handcarts were each loaded with a ninety-eight-pound sack of flour in hopes this extra flour would see them through to South Pass, where the resupply teams were thought to be stationed. John Chislett described: "Some of the people grumbled at this, but the majority bore it without a murmur. Our flour ration was increased to a pound per day; fresh beef was issued occasionally, and each 'hundred' had three or four milk cows. The flour on the carts was used first, the weakest parties being the first relieved of their burdens."[12]

At this point in the journey, William James noted: "The Saints were put on a strict schedule. Each member had his chores for the company as well as for his own family. The strong were to pull the carts. Everyone over seven years of age was expected to walk. The very old and the very young could ride. The young men were expected to act as herders for the cattle. . . . The young women and girls were expected to look after the children who were walking and to gather in the fuel for the camp at night."[13]

Haven & Martin Companies
August 19–25, 1856

The Haven Company arrived on August 19 in Florence with nearly all of their handcarts in need of repair; they immediately began repair efforts and other preparations to continue their journey westward. The company was given notice to be ready to depart Florence by noon on the twenty-second. Just as Captain Haven was ready to give the company notice to pull their tents, Cyrus H. Wheelock instructed him that the company was to tarry until the following day, when Franklin D. Richards combined the Jesse Haven and Edward Martin Handcart Companies and placed Edward Martin in charge with Daniel Tyler and John Toone as counselors.[14]

On the evening of Sunday, August 24, the now-consolidated Martin Company gathered together to discuss undertaking the journey so late in the season. John Jaques noted: "Owing to the lateness of the season, the important question was debated, whether the emigrants should winter in that vicinity or continue the long and wearisome journey to Salt Lake."[15]

In reporting to President Brigham Young, Franklin D. Richards described the meeting as follows: "When we had a meeting at Florence, we called upon the Saints to express their faith to the people, and requested to know of them, even if they knew that they should be swallowed up in storms, whether they would stop or turn back. They voted, with loud acclamations, that they would go on. Such confidence and joyful performance of so arduous labors to accomplish their gathering will bring the choice blessings of God upon them."[16]

Josiah Rogerson recalled:

> I can hear, even now, the voice of President Richards, as he stood there and reasoned with us in his fatherly and gentlemanly manner, as to the lateness of the season, as to the possibility of the storms coming on earlier than usual, that no doubt many of the infants and aged might fall by the way, and some others through disease and from the impurities of the water in the streams, fatigue and exhaustion; and that it was left for us now to decide, whether we would go on and take the risks and chances of these possible and probably fatalities; or remain there in and around Florence, Council Bluffs and other villages in the vicinity till an earlier date for starting the next year; that if we chose and decided to stay, we could have what provisions and supplies were in the store or warehouse there and ready for loading into our wagons for the journey; that he would purchase for us what more he could with means still in his hands, and assist us in every other way for our remaining there till next spring, and about the only encouraging words we remember as to our not staying and going ahead were when he said that as it had been one of the largest season's emigrations that had ever been shipped from the British Isles,

> since he had presided at Liverpool, that it contained hundreds of the first converts to Mormonism from 1837 to 1850, and that the majority of the latter had never been able to emigrate themselves, after their eighteen years in the faith, and doubtless never would have been able, that they were thus far on their way to Zion, he would be gratified by the help and favor of God to see all reach there in safety that season.[17]

Benjamin Platt added further detail:

> Apostle Franklin D. Richards called a meeting and advised us to stop at Florence until the next season; but . . . we declared we would go through or die trying and we prevailed, and he seeing we were determined he consented but he said he did not want anyone to try [who] could not walk every foot of the way. . . . He told us that President Young had promised to send out teams to meet us and that we might have ten weeks of Indian summer and we might get within reach of the teams before the cold weather set in.[18]

Josiah Rogerson also recalled that during the meeting, John D. T. McAllister, Cyrus H. Wheelock, George D. Grant, and others urged the company to move forward. He also noted one lone voice, Chancey W. Webb, urged them to winter in Florence or surrounding areas. A few others spoke, and a vote was called. The Martin Company chose to continue forward. John Jaques penned: "Unfortunately, warm enthusiasm prevailed over sound judgment and cool command. And it was determined to finish the journey the same season." John's account continues: "Before starting from Florence a general lightening of baggage took place. Some of the emigrants sold their extra baggage, some was deposited in store, to be forwarded afterwards another season."[19]

The company was provided with six wagons loaded to the bows with provisions. In addition, each handcart was loaded with a sack of flour, except where children were numerous in the family. Josiah Rogerson noted: "It was a load for the carts, and a load, indeed, for the drawers."[20]

The Martin Company departed Florence on August 25, nine days after the Willie Company departed. The company now consisted of 576 persons, 146 handcarts, and 7 wagons. William Wignall, Peter Mayo, Thomas Ord, John Toone, Robert Holt, and a man named Robinson, were called to serve as captains over 100.[21]

Cyrus H. Wheelock noted: "All were in good spirits, and generally in good health, and full of confidence that they should reach the mountains in season to escape the severe storms. . . . I have never seen more union among the Saints anywhere than is manifested in the handcart companies. And hundreds bear record of the truth of the words of President Young, wherein he promised them increasing strength by the way."[22]

A representative of the Council Bluff Bugle wrote the following in regards to the Handcart Companies:

> First, they have toiled wearily o'er the hundreds of miles which separated their native hills from the Eurpoean sea-port from which they were to embark—then see them on crowded ships, braving the dangers of the broad Atlantic—afterwards, they travel patiently one thousand inland miles to Iowa City, thence to start on foot for a journey over hill, plain, desert, and mountain, fourteen hundred miles, to reach the "Happy Valley." This is enthusiasm—this is heroism indeed. Though we cannot coincide with them in their belief, it is impossible to restrain our admiration of their self-sacrificing devotion to the principles of their faith.[23]

At the close of the immigration season in Florence, Franklin D. Richards reported to Brigham Young in a letter dated September 3:

> The operations of the season are likely to turn out quite as favorably with regard to cost of outfit as we have at any time expected or hoped. But for the lateness of the rear companies, everything seems equally propitious for a safe and profitable wind-up at the far end. From the beginning we have done all in our power to hasten matters pertaining to emigration, therefore we confidently look for the blessing of God to crown our humble efforts with success, and for the safe arrival of our brethren the poor Saints in Utah, though they may experience some cold.[24]

11

MOVING FORWARD FULL OF HOPE AND FAITH

FLORENCE, NEBRASKA, TO FORT LARAMIE, WYOMING

WILLIE COMPANY
AUGUST 16–SEPTEMBER 29, 1856

John Chislett recorded:

> Everything seemed to be propitious, and we moved gaily forward full of hope and faith. At our camp each evening could be heard songs of joy, merry peals of laughter, and bon mots on our condition and prospects. Brother Savage's warning was forgotten in the mirthful ease of the hour. The only drawbacks to this part of our journey were the constant breaking down of carts and the delays caused by repairing them. The axles and boxes being of wood, and being ground out by the dust that found its way there in spite of our efforts to keep it out, together with the extra weight put on the carts, had the effect of breaking the axles at the shoulder. All kinds of expedients were resorted to as remedies for the growing evil, but with variable success. Some wrapped their axles with leather obtained from bootlegs; others with tin, obtained by sacrificing tin-plates, kettles, or buckets from their mess outfit. Besides these inconveniences, there was felt a great lack of a proper lubricator. Of anything suitable for this purpose we had none at all. The poor folks had to use their bacon (already totally insufficient for their wants) to grease their axles, and some even used their soap, of which they had very little, to make their carts trundle somewhat easier. In about twenty days, however, the flour being consumed, breakdowns became less frequent, and we

> jogged along finely. We traveled from ten to twenty miles per day, averaging about fifteen miles. The people felt well, so did our cattle, and our immediate prospects of a prosperous journey were good. But the fates seemed to be against us.[1]

JOSEPH & EMILY WALL

Shortly after leaving Florence, seventeen-year-old Joseph Wall, of England, became gravely ill. Joseph and his sixteen-year-old sister, Emily, were traveling to the valley without their parents and siblings because the expense of sending the entire family together was too great. Before leaving England, Joseph and Emily were promised by Orson Hyde "if they were true and faithful and obeyed the counsel of those in authority over them, they would arrive in Zion in safety." As Joseph's health worsened, it was decided to leave him to be picked up or buried by the Martin Company. With the remembrance of the blessing given at the hands of an Apostle of the Lord, Emily did not want to leave her brother behind and insisted on pulling Joseph in a handcart. With the aid of a young girl, Emily pulled Joseph until he was well again.[2]

Travel became even more physically demanding for the Willie Company as they ascended the sandy hills with the handcarts. The company often avoided traveling during the midday hours because of the extreme heat and humidity. To add to the difficulty, traveling on the open prairie, at times, meant long distances between drinkable water sources and a lack of wood for fuel.

On Monday, August 25, as the Martin Company was departing Florence, the Willie Company was nearly 120 miles west. Thirteen-year-old Elizabeth "Betsey" Smith, who had been healed by the power of the priesthood in Iowa City, recorded:

> One day, especially, stands out from among the remainder. The wind blew fresh, as if its breezes came from the sea. It kept blowing harder until it became fierce. Clouds arose; the thunder and lightening were appalling. Even the ox teams ahead refused to face the storm. . . . The captain said, "Let us pray." And there was offered such a prayer. He told the Lord our circumstances. He talked to God, as one man talks to another, and as if the Lord was very near. I felt that He was and many others felt the same. Then the storm

> parted on the right and to the left. We hurried on to camp, got our tents pitched, and some fires built, when the storm burst in all its fury. We had camped on a sidehill and the water ran through the tents in little creeks.[3]

CALDWELL FAMILY

On Saturday, August 30, while fourteen-year-old Thomas Caldwell, of Scotland, was holding a cow for a young girl to milk, the cow broke from his hold and ran away. His mother Margaret recorded: "The cow broke and ran catching Thomas' foot in the rope, throwing him to the ground and dragging him quite a distance. When he released the rope, the cow turned and stepped on him, which broke his collar bone. This left me with a great deal of pulling to do. . . . Thomas' collar bone did not heal like it should, gangrene set in and I had quite a time clearing it up." Thomas's mother relied heavily upon her son. His father was thought to have abandoned the family, and the oldest brother, William, had stayed behind to serve out the remainder of his commitment in the Scottish Army. Seventeen-year-old brother Robert was unable to assist the family because of his company responsibilities. Following the accident, Thomas was administered to by President Willie, and his shoulder and arm were bandaged."[4]

JAMES FAMILY

Early in September, the Willie Company neared the Platte River and entered buffalo country. Buffalo could be seen in all directions, and the Saints enjoyed a plentiful amount of fresh meat. However, on the evening of September 3, the buffalo caused devastating loss for the Willie Company. Sixteen-year-old Emma James recorded,

> One evening as we prepared to stop for the night a large herd of buffalo came thundering toward us. It sounded like thunder at first then the big black animals came straight for our carts. We were so scared that we were rooted to the ground. One of the captains seeing what was going on, ran for the carts which were still coming in, jerked out some of the carts to make a path for the steady stream of animals and let them go through. They went past us like a train roaring along. I'm sure that but for the quick thinking of these men

> that many of us would have been trampled to death. The animals acted as if they were craz[y] the way they ran. We hoped that we wouldn't meet such a large herd soon again[.] After they had gone somebody called out that the cattle had gone with them. This was our only supply of meat so the men started right out after them. The men on foot soon lost the sight of the herd. Those of us who were left made preparation for the night hoping the men would be back with our cattle by dark. As the sun went down a terrible storm came up. A strong wind tore the tents out of our hands and sent everything flying in all direction. The thunder and lightening was like nothing we had ever seen before. We had all we could do to keep track of each other. The noise terrified the children so that they ran for any shelter that they could find. Soon we all did [the same] thing for the rain came down in torrents and in a matter of minutes. We were soaked to the skin. The men came in from the hunt empty-handed. But in time to help gather up our belongings and get ready for our meal. We all went to bed wet and cold. The cattle were never found. Even the tracks had [been] washed away by the rain. This was to prove a serious thing for the company. With no oxen or mules to pull the wagons it was necessary to hitch the milk cows to the wagon. It was a sorry group which started out on the trail next morning.

Emma James was traveling with her parents, William and Jane James, and her siblings: nineteen-year-old Sarah, fourteen-year-old Reuben, eleven-year-old Mary Ann, nine-year-old Martha, six-year-old George, and five-year-old John Parley. Her infant sister died on board the ship *Thornton*.[5]

On the morning of September 4, the Willie Company was now 265 miles west of Florence and without thirty of their oxen. Colonel Almon Babbitt overtook the company and "reported that the Cheyennes had attacked a small California train and killed a woman and that the U.S. Troops had killed 13 Cheyennes and taken a number of horses." Throughout the day, President James G. Willie sent out search parties to look for the oxen. The final group of searchers returned at dark reporting no sign of the animals.[6]

The following morning, James G. Willie, Levi Savage, and others set out in search of the oxen. The Abraham O. Smoot and Orin Porter Rockwell Wagon Companies overtook the Willie Company in the evening. Captains Smoot and Rockwell visited the Saints and offered words of comfort in their then present emergency. In the evening, the search parties returned without the missing oxen. Leaders met in council that evening and initially it was decided the company would be split into two divisions. The first group would use their animals to move forward and then send back the animals to help bring the second group forward.[7]

On September 6, the remaining cattle were yoked and the company moved forward. As they did so, twenty-one-year-old Joseph B. Elder and nineteen-year-old Andrew Smith were given the responsibility to search for the missing cattle with instructions not to return until after they had met up with President Franklin D. Richards. After an attempt was made with the plan formulated the previous evening, it quickly became obvious the company could not move forward in this manner. The gravity of the situation began to sink in. In reflecting upon their situation, Captain Andrew Siler shared that he felt this experience was preparing their minds for a coming trial of their faith.[8]

The following morning, the company gathered together. John Chislett, William Woodward, Levi Savage, Andrew Siler, Millen Atwood, and James G. Willie addressed the Saints, speaking clearly of the difficulties of their present situation. They were counseled of the "absolute necessity for doing away with the spirit of grumbling, strife, pilfering and disregard of counsel" and they were asked to replace it with the "spirit of contentment, peace, union, and strict obedience." The owners of wagons were asked to consecrate their wagons and teams and everything they owned to be used in the present emergency. All were urged to obey the counsel of the leaders placed over them "without rebelling or grumbling openly or secretly." The whole strength of the company was to be focused upon the "resumption and speedy and final completion of the journey." They were asked to carry out all that might be required of them "even though it should be to leave their luggage on the plains" or if they should be "required by their Captain to draw 4 or 5 hundred pounds of flour they must do it cheerfully and the Waggon Company must act on the same principle by carrying anything and everything which might be required of them by like authority." A vote was taken asking the Saints to sustain the various officers in their respective positions and in carrying out such measures as would be required of them. The vote was unanimous in support. Following the vote, all "immediately went to work to execute the will of President Willie which was cheerfully responded to."[9]

Following a three-day search for the missing cattle, the company reluctantly gave it up, and they prepared to move forward the best they could. John Chislett noted:

> We had only about enough oxen left to put one yoke to each wagon; but, as they were each loaded with about three thousand pounds of flour, the teams could not of course move them. We then yoked up our beef cattle, milk cows, and, in fact, everything that could bear a yoke even two-year old heifers. The stock was wild and could pull but little, and we were unable, with all our stock, to move our loads. As a last resort we again loaded a sack of flour on each cart. It was really hard for the folks to lose the use of their milk cows, have beef rations stopped, and haul one hundred pounds more on their carts. Every man and woman, however, worked to their utmost to put forward towards the goal of their hopes.[10]

Ann Jewel Rowley recalled: "This was the beginning of our great hardships and probably was the cause of most of them, for we had spent valuable time looking for the oxen. This loss in turn, reduced our meat supply, and because there wasn't enough cattle to pull the supply wagons, a hundred pounds of flour was placed in each handcart. Our handcarts were not designed for such heavy loads and were constantly breaking down."[11]

George Cunningham penned:

> We had between six and seven hundred miles to travel to accomplish our journey, which we would be compelled to do or perish in the mountain snows. We therefore came to the conclusion to take the provisions out of the wagons and put them on the handcarts. . . . Here we plodded along through the mud with all the courage that we could muster. Our bright young sisters helped us by doing all they could to encourage us in every shape, and whenever an opportunity afforded, they would try to cheer us along with their beautiful strains of vocal music. They seemed to have songs very appropriate for every occasion. This was much help to us under such stiff circumstances.[12]

Reeder & Hurren Families

The Reeder and Hurren families were among those to shoulder the extra burden by adding additional sacks of flour to their handcart. Nineteen-year-old Robert Reeder wrote: "Some had one, others two or three, and, if my memory serves me right, Brother Hurren, being considered the strongest man the company had, had five sacks put on his cart besides two small girls that were not able to walk and all his baggage and cooking utensils. His wife helped in pulling the cart and walked the entire trail." Members of the Reeder family were introduced to the gospel and were baptized in England in the early 1850s. In 1856, widower fifty-four-year-old David Reeder, his seventeen-year-old daughter, Caroline, nineteen-year-old son, Robert, twenty-six-year-old daughter, Eliza, and her husband, twenty-nine-year-old James Hurren, and their three children immigrated to the Salt Lake Valley on board the *Thornton*. On July 15, while in Iowa, Eliza gave birth to their fourth child. The child lived only a few short weeks, passing away on July 28. The journey thus far for the Reeder and Hurren families had been extremely physically exhausting. Their family consisted of three strong men who were often called upon to assist with the cattle, not only during the day but at night as well. Robert wrote of the difficulty those in charge had in finding men who were willing to help:

> We had to herd those cattle night and day. There were lots of us to change off if all would have taken a part, but it was a very rainy country, and some would not take their turn, especially in the nighttime. I can well remember those who had charge used to come to us and say, "Will you go and herd again tonight as we cannot get anyone else to go." Me and my father and my brother-in-law, James Hurren, have gone three and four nights out of a week in the pouring rain, wet through from head to foot and in the water part of the time up to our knees—anything to help get fitted out and started on the road.[13]

On September 12, John Chislett described: "One evening, as we were camped on the west bank of the North Bluff Fork of the Platte, a grand outfit of carriages and light wagons was driven into our camp from the East. Each vehicle was drawn by four horses or mules, and all the appointments seemed to be first rate. The occupants we soon found to be the apostle F. D. Richards, elders W. H. Kimball, G. D. Grant, Joseph A. Young, C. G. Webb, N. H. Felt, W. C. Dunbar and others who were returning to Utah from missions abroad. They camped with us for the night, and in the morning a general meeting was called." During the meeting President Richards addressed the Saints "impressing on their minds the absolute necessity of literal and prompt obedience and reminding them that Prest. Willie was invested with absolute authority to direct the affairs of this camp." President Richards then severely reprimanded Levi Savage for his actions in Florence as well as comments made to James G. Willie regarding Captain Siler's wagons. John Chislett's account continues: "He had been advised of the opposition brother Savage had made, and he rebuked him very severely in open meeting for his lack of faith in God." This incident was noted by many others including William Woodward: "A severe reprimand was given to Levi Savage for speaking before the camp in an improper manner to Brother Willie and also speaking as he did at Florence."[14]

George Cunningham mentioned that not only was Levi Savage reprimanded in the meeting, but Millen Atwood and the entire company were also reproved "for the dissensions that had been allowed to creep into camp. He said that the hand of God had been heavy upon us for this cause. Brother Savage was called up and was told that he would have to take back what he said at Florence of which I have already mentioned or be tried for his fellowship. He was forced to do so."

Levi was completely caught off guard at this rebuke and noted, "A meeting of the Saints was called, not on the campground as usual, but a short distance one side. I supposed it was for prayers. After singing and prayers Brother Richards commenced to speak, and I soon perceived that the meeting was called in consequence of the wrong impression made by my expressing myself so freely at Florence concerning our crossing the plains so late in the season. The impression left was that I condemned the handcart scheme, which is very wrong. I never conveyed such an idea, nor felt to do so, but, quite to the contrary, I am in favor of it."

Levi went on to mention:

> Also, the meeting was called, more particular in consequence of someone, unknown to me, informing Brother Richards of the disagreeable words that took place between Brother Willie and myself concerning Brother Siler's teams traveling between the handcarts and fund wagons, which I supposed was settled. When I asked Brother Willie's and the Saints' forgiveness for all that I had said and done wrong, Brother Richards reprimanded me sharply. Brother Willie said that I had manifested a bad spirit from Iowa City. This is something unknown to me and something he never before expressed. I had always the best of feelings toward him and supposed he had toward me until now.

The Willie Company then hastily prepared to depart, crossing the mile-wide North Platte River, which took all day.[15]

By mid-September, the Saints experienced typical fall weather: cold, strong winds, rain, and sharp frost one day and warm and pleasant the next. Travel continued to be difficult as they ascended the sandy bluffs. The handcarts were in constant need of repairs. On many occasions, teams did not have the strength to pull the wagons and had to be doubled. Feed for the animals was also becoming scarce. Levi Savage penned: "The Saints slow in rising and getting breakfast early, notwithstanding Brother Willey's repeated order to arise at the sound of the bugle (daylight). Apparently not realizing the necessity of our making as much distance as possible in order to reach the Valley before too severe cold weather, some complain of hard treatment, because we urge them along. . . . The old appear to be failing considerably."[16]

Margaret Ann Caldwell noted: "The handcarts were frail, the material too green. . . . They kept breaking so that only a few miles could be made a day. After becoming accustomed to walking it wasn't too bad. [The first] frost came on the 17th day of September."[17]

Just prior to the arrival of the Willie Company at Fort Laramie, they learned of the death of Colonel Babbitt and the two men who accompanied him.[18]

Martin and Richards Companies
August 25–September 28, 1856

On Monday, August 25, the Martin Company left Florence for Fort Laramie, which was more than 520 miles west. That same day, the

Willie Company, who left nine days earlier, recorded being 120 miles west of Florence. The Hodgett Wagon Company left Florence on August 28, with the Hunt Company following on August 31. President Franklin D. Richards and his company of returning missionaries left on September 3.[19]

Griffith Family

Sixteen-year-old Margaret Ann Griffith recorded that the company left Florence "as happy a lot of people as ever crossed the plains. Little did we realize on that bright September morning the hardships through which we were destined to pass or the suffering, sickness and death awaiting us ere we reached that long hoped for haven of rest among the saints in the valley of the mountains. It never occurred to my young mind, being but sixteen years of age, that we should experience anything but joy and happiness on our long pilgrimage to that promised land." John Taylor baptized Margaret's parents in 1840, and a year later her father was called to serve as a branch president, laboring diligently for fifteen years. Margaret's mother passed away while giving birth in 1853, leaving her father a widower with five children. Margaret immigrated to the Salt Lake Valley with her father; step-mother, Elizabeth Webb; and her siblings, twelve-year-old John, eight-year-old Jane, and six-year-old Herbert.[20]

During this time, the physical strain placed upon some weary members of the company was more than their bodies could endure. Suffering and sickness brought many nigh unto death. Along with these trials came great blessings as faith and determination increased, the priesthood was exercised in powerful and magnificent ways, and countless members of the company, true to the gospel that they loved, were willing to serve, sacrifice, and shoulder additional responsibilities.

Bailey Family

John and Jane Bailey of England, who joined the Church in 1844, were traveling to the valley with their children: eighteen-year-old Langley, fifteen-year-old John, twelve-year-old Thomas, and five-year-old David. Between Iowa and Florence, Langley became deathly ill:

> I was taken down with hemorrhage of the bowels. I was unable to walk, had to be hauled on Bro. Isaac Wardle and my brother John's cart. After reaching Florence a doctor was consulted [and] said I must not go another step or I would die and be buried on the roadside. A captain named Tune [John Toone] would not administer to me, said he did not have faith enough to raise the dead. Mother on hearing that Apostle F. D. Richards and C. H. Wheelock had arrived in camp got them to administer to me. They promised me I would live to reach the valleys. All this time I was unconscious of what was going on. The doctor called again to see me, told father he would take care of the family and fit us out next year to pursue our journey. Father thanked him kindly, he pled with father to stop, said it was too late to make the trip.

With great faith, the Baileys decided to continue the journey. Upon regaining consciousness, Langley, feeling as if he was causing too much of a burden to others, noted he had plans

> to get away, lay down under a sagebrush and die. I saw my father and mother and my cart pass by, I stretched out to die; just then a voice said, "Your mother is hunting you, jump up." I saw mother in haste coming towards me, wanted to know what had gone wrong with me. I told her I had planned to lay down and die. I felt it was too much to pull me on the cart, at the same time have as much luggage as they could manage, [she] scolded me a little. She reminded [me] what I was promised by Apostle F. D. Richards. I rode on the cart until the teams from the Valley met us.[21]

Loader & Jaques Families

Of the trials experienced by the Loader and Jaques families, Patience Loader recalled:

> We seemed to endure the days travel pretty well for the first hundred miles then my poor dear fathers health began to fail him and before we got to Florence he became very weak and sick his legs and feet began to swell. Some days he was not able to pull the cart and when we arrived at Florence we put up the tent made the bed and he went to bed we did not think he could live. Franklin Richards came into the tent to see him. My father said he wished to be administered to and Brother Richards and three other brethren administered to him and blessed him and told him that he should get better and

> continue his journey and get to Salt Lake City. This seemed to give him new strength and courage.

Franklin D. Richards and John Taylor also administered to Tamar Loader, who was sick with mountain fever. In the blessing, she was promised she would be able to walk before she arrived in Utah.[22]

After a few hours of rest, the Loader family resumed their journey. Patience recorded: "That afternoon we had not traveled far when my poor sick father fell down and we had to stop to get him up on his feet. . . . we started on again we had not traveled far before he fell down again he was so weak and worn down we got him up again but we told [him] he could not pull the cart again that day so my sister Maria came and worked with me inside the shafts and Jane and Sarah pulled on the rope until we got into camp."[23]

On the evening of Wednesday, August 27, when the Martin Company was just west of Florence, Patience described:

> That night, my sister, Zilpha Jaques, was confined at twelve-o'clock and my sister, Tamar, was very sick with mountain fever. . . . The next morning the company got ready to start. The captain came to our tent and told us to be ready to start as soon as we could get ready. There lay my sister, Zilpha, on the ground just gave birth to a child. She was lying on some quilts in one corner of the tent and my sister, Tamar, [was] lying on quilts in the other corner of the tent, neither of the poor things able to move. The Captain Edward Martin said, "Put them up on the wagon," as there was a wagon for the sick [who were] unable to walk. I asked, "Can one of us ride with them to take care of them." He said, "No, they will have to take care of themselves," Then I said, "They will not go. We will stay here for a day or two and take care of our two sick sisters." So we was left there all alone as the company started about seven o'clock that morning. We was there all day alone with our sick and when night came my poor father and my brother-in-law, John Jacques, had to be up all night to make [a] big fire to keep the wolves away from us. I never heard such a terrible howling of wolves in my life as we experienced that lonesome night. We was all very glad to see daylight.[24]

In the morning, Joseph A. Young, a returning missionary helping the group driving Church stock to the valley, rode into the Loader camp. He was sent to investigate the large fire witnessed the previous evening. Patience recorded:

> When he came into the tent and saw my sister with her new born babe lying on the ground on some quilts he was overcome with sympathy. The tears ran down his cheeks. Then he blessed my sister and tried to comfort and cheer her. . . . Then he turned to see my sister lying in the opposite corner of the tent sick with mountain fever, he ask[ed] us what we was going to do and no one to help us or accompany us to overtake the company. We told him we expected to start that morning as we could not stay there any longer as we would not catch up with the company and we could not travel all the way alone.

Joseph returned to his camp with a report of the fire and the plight of the Loader family. The Loaders proceeded to pack up camp and attempted to catch the Martin Company. Patience described:

> We packed our handcart, struck our tent, packed it on my handcart, then lay my sister Tamar on that, then Brother Jacques packed his cart and put his wife, my sister, and her two children on the cart. We tied the tent poles alongside of the cart, our cooking utensils we tied under the cart with our days provisions. [W]e again started on our journey. This was very [difficult] on my poor dear sick father after having to be up all night, no rest or sleep . . . stand[ing] guard to keep the wolves away from us. It surely did prove that God was with us for my poor father seemed better that day than he had been for a week past. Surely God gave him new strength that day for we traveled 22 miles before we came up with the company.

As they were thus employed in their attempts to overtake the Martin Company, Moses Cluff, who was in the company with Joseph A. Young, rode into their camp to offer assistance. Patience noted: "He fetched a rope with him and tied it to our handcart then to the pummel of his saddle and gave us a rest first he helped Brother Jaques away then he help[ed] my dear father and us girls for which I was very thankful."[25]

Moses Cluff

Moses Cluff was among the missionaries called to serve in 1852 during the special conference held in Salt Lake City. He was originally called to serve in Prussia, but because missionaries were banished from that location, he ended up serving in England. Moses was appointed president of several conferences and served in that capacity until the time of his release in 1856. While on his mission, Moses met Rebecca Culey Langman, whom he later married upon his arrival in the Salt Lake Valley. Rebecca traveled to the valley with the Martin Company, while Moses took charge of the "Church herd which consisted of loose cattle and young stock to be sent with the last company of emigrants."[26]

Patience Loader's account continued:

> Brother Cluff had not left us very long we hardly was out of sight of him when five great Indians came out of a cave in the mountains got on their horses and came to meet us. They was all painted bare naked except their brich cloth had their tomahawks and hatchet bows and arrows. They stopped us in the road [and] talked but we could not understand them when they saw our sick, and my sister with her new born babe they moved out of the road and motioned for us to go on. I think this was as near to being killed by Indians as I wish to be. . . . They was quite impodent in their manners to us and made fun of us pulling the handcart. We was somewhat afraid of them and I daresay they could see we was afraid of them. At the same time we put our faith and trust in God our Father that he would take care of us and not let those Indians hurt us or do us harm. I know it was nothing but the power of God that saved us from those Indians that day we was all alone traveling in the mountains and hills all that day.[27]

Several members of the Martin Company recorded encounters with the Indians, which caused much anxiety. Upon meeting a large group of Sioux Indians on their way to fight the Pawnee tribe, Peter McBride recorded: "Fear held the whole camp in its grip as they all expected to be annihilated." Through interpreters, the Saints learned the Indians would not attack them because of the large number of women and children in their company. Samuel Openshaw recorded the Indians were "committing depredations behind and before. In fact, they made an open attack in day light upon Fort Kearney. On the twenty second of August the soldiers killed a great number of them, which has stirred them up against the white man, but they keep out of our way."[28]

Guarding of the Cattle

For a time, the Martin Company had the responsibility of guarding the Church herd. Immigration officials were driving a large amount of cattle to the valley because of the Church had lost half of its stock due to a severe and harsh winter season and American Indians driving a considerable number away. James Bleak often guarded the cattle. He noted in his journal nine consecutive days of guard duty, three of which he was on guard from six o'clock in the evening to the following morning.[29]

Josiah Rogerson described the rigors of guard duty:

> Our night guarding began as soon as the oxen were unyoked and the mules unharnessed, not later than 6 to 7 p.m. The moment we dropped our cart we had to spring into this arduous duty every other night for six hours. One week, every night as soon as we reached camp until midnight . . . and the next week every other night roused from our quilts by midnight and on guard until 6 a.m., when the oxen and mules were ordered to be brought for yoking and harnessing. . . . The only "winks" the writer got in this service was from 6 to 7 a.m. while his mother was cooking him a little breakfast.[30]

During this time Josiah Rogerson recalled:

> Our rations during these ten weeks was one pound of flour per day for adults, six ounces for the children under 9 years, a few ounces of bacon in proportion to the flour and the adults and children, and once or twice a week a few ounces of tea and sugar to the family. . . . Even with the above rations, limited in variety and quantity, the able bodied adults and middle-aged had stood the journey fairly well and were all right and good for another 500 miles, but every other night guarding for six hours was beginning to tell on the fathers of families and the less hardy young men, who were now showing the effects of such hardship in their lean and haggard faces and frames.[31]

Among those traveling in the Martin Company this season were "the 'cleanings up' of that year's emigration, and comprising the halt, lame, feeble, and from the babe in the arms to the East Indian veteran." A large portion of the old and feeble members of the company set out early in the morning with their captain, Father Waugh. Among these was a man of whom John William Southwell wrote: "In his company was one of the worst cripples I ever saw to be a traveler.

His lower limbs were paralyzed and his body badly deformed but he was strong in the faith. He was able to propel himself with surprising speed with the use of crutches." One afternoon, John and a few other men were asked to search for this man, who had gotten lost. Around sunset, they brought him back into camp having found him in time to save his life "to our horror we saw around an old tree two large gray wolves prowling around, and half a dozen eagles hovering over the tree waiting for him to quit his screams and gestulations with his crutches so they would pounce upon him and devour him in his cramped position under the roots of the tree screaming out his death knell." This man was put in the handcart. But all the while he begged his rescuers to let him walk. He had made a promise to Brother Tyler that he would not be a hindrance to the company, and he would walk every foot of the way. He was buried on the banks of the Elkhorn River a few days later.[32]

FRANKLIN D. RICHARDS COMPANY

On Sunday, September 7, Franklin D. Richards and his company of returning missionaries met the Martin Company. They stopped long enough to spend an evening with the company, offering encouragement and counsel.

> Brother Franklin then made a speech which was applauded to the echo. He told us that we would soon be relieved of the responsibilities of the bank of cattle that were now forming so much extra labor, such as reducing our forces at the hand carts as well as double the number of men to guard through the night instead of giving them their much needed rest. . . . A meeting was held by the authorities with the following results. The herd was taken possession of by two horsemen who were with the party and were driven by them the remainder of the journey to Salt Lake City. Before starting, however, two small animals were killed and distributed among the people, being the first beef we had been the recipient of on the journey.[33]

Similar to the Willie Company, the Martin Company found travel more difficult during this part of the journey. Finding sources of drinkable water at times became challenging; at one point, the company traveled two days without water. One afternoon, the company was coming upon a pond of water, when, "parched with thirst, the cattle rushed pell mell into the pond and stirred up the mud until the water was thick and black, before the people had supplied themselves for their own use. But it was all the water available, and so it was used for cooking purposes, making coffee, tea, bread and porridge or hasty pudding, which when made, was quite black, but was eaten and drunk nevertheless." The company also had great difficulty finding sufficient wood for fuel. "There is no wood upon the prairies, only at rivers and creeks, and having nothing cooked, we were obliged to lie down without supper." The company often used buffalo chips when sources of wood were scarce.[34]

John William Southwell described further difficulties:

> The next days march lay across the river to the south side. We crossed on a small ferry boat. The boat was a flimsy affair and the first load of flour that we placed upon it sank the thing to the bottom. The whole load was badly soaked and we had a hard time taking it from its bath and unloading it to prevent it from being a total loss. With this accident occurring we were detained all day in crossing this small stream. However, it gave us a rest. We buried our dead, drained our flour, pitched camp, and spent the remainder of the day washing, mending and taking a little sport which was enjoyed by all hands.[35]

John's account continued: "Before leaving the now scattering towns of Iowa it was made known to us that we must reduce the amount of our spare luggage. There was an inspector sent among us to judge of what we actually needed. The remainder was to be sold. I was well clothed for the present as the days were warm and filled with good sunshine and we still enjoying our full ration of flour and with what small change we had we could buy little luxuries of the settlers but the time will come when the wisdom of this order will be questioned."[36]

Though trials became more intense and travel more difficult, members of the Martin Company were blessed with deeply personal and spiritual experiences that witnessed of the power of God. Many saw their trials and challenges in a different light, and with a perspective that further strengthened their faith and testimony. Their love, compassion, and devotion for one another also increased as members of the company served others who could not do so for themselves. Patience Loader testified:

> It seemed the Lord fitted the back for the burden every day. We realized that the hand of God was over us and that he made good his promises unto us day by day as we know God our Father has promised us these blessings if we will call on him in faith. We know that his promises never fail and this we proved day by day we knew that we had not strength of our own to perform such hardships if our Heavenly Father had not help[ed] us and we prayed unto God continually for his help and we always acknowledged his goodness unto us day by day. Sometimes in the morning I would feel so tired and feel that I could not pull the cart the day through then the still small voice would whisper in my ear "as thy day thy strength shall be." This would give me new strength and energy and thus we traveled on day after day week after week.[37]

The Martin Company camped near Fort Kearney on September 12. Until this point the weather had remained extremely hot with severe thunderstorms that often halted the progress of the company. On September 16, Samuel Openshaw described the weather as follows: "The weather is extremely hot which makes it hard traveling. . . . It would truly be an amusing and interesting scene if the people of the old country could have a bird's eye view of us when in camp; to see everyone busy—some fetching water, others gathering Buffalo chips, some cooking and so forth upon these wild prairies where the air is not tainted with the smoke of cities or factories, but is quiet here. One may see a creek at a distance and start and travel one hour towards it, yet you seem no nigher than you did when you started." The following day was a much different report on the weather from Samuel: "When we started out it was a very hard, sandy road and the wind was extremely cold, as if we had come into a different climate all at once." Three days later, Samuel recorded: "We started at and left the sandy bluffs on our right, went about three miles and then crossed a creek about knee deep; the weather being cold, it felt disagreeable to go into the water." He also reported rain that night, which continued on into the next day, delaying their travel and making it impossible for them to cook because the buffalo chips were wet.[38]

Jaques & Loader Families

Toward the end of September, James Loader's health became critical. Patience recorded: "My sister Zilpha called to [me] saying 'Patience come quick our father is dieing.' . . . Poor dear father realizing he had to leave us he was too weak to talk to us he looked on us all with tears in his eyes then he said to mother with great difficulty he said you know I love my children then he closed his eyes. [This] was the last words he ever said. He seem[ed]to fall asleep he breathed quiet and peaceful." The Loaders were instructed to prepare to leave camp shortly. They asked if someone could ride with their dying father in the wagons and were told no. Patience continued:

> [T]hat day we had a very hard journey as we had to travel through the sandy bluffs it was very hard pulling so much up hill and deep sand we got to the top of the hill about one o'clock. This was the 23 of September [1856]. The sun was scorching hot so bad for my dear dieing father on the top a hill not the least shade for him. We had to stay there all day but very little to eat until all the companies got up the hill. So many gave out and the wagons was loaded with the tents and what provisions there was some of the oxen gave out. That was a terrible day never to be forgotten. . . . The last of them did not get up until it was dark.[39]

Following that grueling and brutal pull into camp on September 24, James Loader was administered to. At the conclusion of the blessing, with a smile on his face, he spoke the word *amen*, and shortly thereafter peacefully slipped from this life to the next. The next morning James was wrapped in a quilt and placed in a grave next to seventy-three-year-old William Mason Jones, thirteen miles east of Ash Hollow.

> This was a severe trial here we had to [w]rap my dear father in a quilt. . . . I will never forget the sound of that dirt being shoveled into my poor fathers body. It seemed to me that it would break every bone in his body. It did indeed seem a great trial to have to leave our dear father behind that morning knowing we had looked upon that sweet smiling face for the last time on earth but not without a hope of meeting him again in the morning of the resurrection for he had been a faithful servant of God and bore testimony to the truth of the gospel of Jesus Christ. . . . It was a very sorrowful day and we all grieved greatly.[40]

McBride Family

After leaving Florence, both Robert and Margaret McBride's health began to fail rapidly. The responsibility of pulling the handcart and caring for the younger children (eight-year-old Ether, six-year-old Peter, and two-year-old Margaret) fell upon the shoulders of sixteen-year-old Janetta and thirteen-year-old Heber. Heber wrote:

> I being the oldest boy just past 13 years and my sister [Margaret Alice McBride] 3 years older than me we had to pull the handcart all the way but Mother being sick and nothing for her comfort she failed very fast. She would start out in the morning and walk as far as she could. Then she would give out and lie down and wait till we came along, and we would take her on our cart and haul her along till we came to camp. But it was not long before our provisions began to get short and we was reduced to one-half pound of flour and children to ¼ lb per day, and nothing else with it only water and sometimes a very little tea. The food we had was not enough. . . . No tongue or pen could tell what my sister and I passed through, our parents both sick and us young. It seemed as though death would be a blessing. For we used to pray that we might die to get out of our misery for by this time it was getting very cold weather and our clothing almost worn out and not enough of bedclothes to keep us warm. We would lay and suffer from night till morning with the cold. By this time the team was give out entirely and we had to take more load on our carts and had to haul Father and Mother. Sometimes we would find mother laying by the side of the road first then we would get her on the cart and haul her along until we would find Father lying as if he was dead. Then Mother would be rested a little and she would try and walk and Father would get on and ride and then we used to cry and feel so bad. We did not know what to do but we would never get into camp till away after dark and then we would have to hunt something to make a fire.[41]

Mellor Family

Prior to their departure on the ship *Horizon*, James Mellor and his wife, Mary Ann, were confronted with the death of their twin daughters in Liverpool. During this portion of the journey, sixteen-year-old Louisa recorded:

> My mother, still being weak, finally gave up and said she could go no further. The company could not wait for her, so she bade my father goodbye and kissed each one of the children Godspeed. Then my mother sat down on a boulder and wept. I told my sister, Elizabeth, to take good care of the twins and the rest of the family, and that I would stay with mother. I went a few yards away and prayed with faith that God would help us, that He would protect us from devouring wolves, and asked that he would let us reach camp. As I was going back to where my Mother was sitting I found a pie in the road. I picked it up and gave it to mother to eat. After resting awhile we started on our journey, thanking God for the blessings. A few miles before we reached camp we met my father coming out to meet us. We arrived in camp at 10:00 pm. Many times after that Mother felt like giving up and quitting; but then she would remember how wonderful the Lord had been to spare her so many times, and offered a prayer of gratitude instead.[42]

Franklin D. Richards Company
September 24–28, 1856

From Fort Laramie to the Salt Lake Valley, Franklin D. Richards and his company of returning missionaries met up with three separate groups of re-supply teams. On September 24, they met John Smith and two other men near Independence Rock. They were reportedly hauling six hundred pounds of flour. President Richards instructed John to cache the flour at the Little Sandy River located sixty miles west of the Sixth Crossing of the Sweetwater River and to return to the valley with the missionaries. On September 27, they met up with William Smith and two other men, fifteen miles east of Pacific Springs with two wagons of flour. These men were counseled to cache their flour and go on to meet the Willie Company. The following day they met up with Brother Talcott three miles east of the Big Sandy. These men were also instructed to go with their teams to assist the Willie Company. It is unclear what happened to these re-supply teams other than a mention in the Smoot Wagon Company history on October 2, of meeting up with a relief wagon at the last crossing of the Platte River.[43]

Arrival of the First Three Handcart Companies Salt Lake City, Utah September 26–October 2, 1856

On September 26, just over two months after they left Florence, the first two handcart companies arrived in the Salt Lake Valley ahead of the wagon trains with a less than average amount of mortality. Their arrival was anxiously anticipated, and they were met by hundreds thronging to see and welcome them into the valley. "And thus has been successfully accomplished a plan, devised by the wisdom and forethought of our President, for rapidly gathering the poor, almost entirely independent of the wealth so closely hoarded beyond their reach."[44]

Of the arrival of Edmund Ellsworth in the Valley, Wilford Woodruff stated: "When I saw brother Ellsworth come into this city covered with dust and drawing a handcart, I felt that he had gained greater honor than the riches of this world could bestow, and he looked better to me than he would have done had he been clothed with the most costly apparel that human ingenuity can produce; he looked better, I say, to me than a man adorned with jewels and finery of every description. The honor any man can obtain by his faithfulness in this cause and kingdom is worth far more than all the honors and riches of the world."[45]

The third handcart company, made up almost entirely of Welsh Saints, captained by Edward Bunker, arrived in the Salt Lake Valley on Thursday, October 2.[46]

12

STARK REALIZATIONS

FORT LARAMIE, SALT LAKE VALLEY, SCOTT'S BLUFF

WILLIE COMPANY
OCTOBER 1, 1856

REEDER & HURREN FAMILIES

Early in the morning on October 1, twenty-six-year-old Eliza Reeder Hurren, nineteen-year-old Robert Reeder, and seventeen-year-old Caroline Reeder awoke to find their father, fifty-four-year-old David, dead. David, his son Robert, and his son-in-law, James Hurren, were among the stalwart members of the company willing to take on additional burdens and responsibilities on the trail. These additional responsibilities proved to be extremely physically exhausting and soon took their toll. "My father, David Reeder, would start out in the morning and pull his cart until he would drop on the road. He did this day after day until he did not arise early on 7 October, 1856. He was found dead in his bed. . . . Sister Eliza wrapped a cherished sheet around him and we placed him in a shallow grave, hoping the wolves would not disturb. We must go on our way in silent mourning and in a weakened condition." David was preceded in death by his wife, Lydia, who died shortly after giving birth to Caroline and his granddaughter, Selena Hurren, who was born in Iowa and lived only a few short weeks.[1]

The Willie Company arrived in Fort Laramie on Wednesday, October 1, having made the 522-mile journey from Florence to Fort Laramie in 46 days. Upon their arrival, Captain Willie received a letter left by President Richards notifying him of the unsuccessful attempts to secure cattle and other much needed supplies for the companies to follow. President Richards also noted they might expect supplies from the valley by the time they reached South Pass, located nearly 280 miles to the west.[2]

The Willie Company was now 509 miles from the Salt Lake Valley and faced with the stark realities of their present situation. John Chislett recorded the following: "Captain Willie called a meeting to take into consideration our circumstances, condition, and prospects, and to see what could be done. It was ascertained that at our present rate of travel and consumption of flour, the latter would be exhausted when we were about three hundred and fifty miles from our destination! It was resolved to reduce our allowance from one pound to three-quarters of a pound per day, and at the same time to make every effort in our power to travel faster. We continued this rate of rations from Laramie to Independence Rock."[3]

At Laramie, several members of the Willie Company took their watches and rings and other keepsakes to the Fort to buy provisions. At this time, several women were persuaded by military officers and apostates to leave the company.[4]

Caldwell Family & Christina McNeil

Nine-year-old Agnes Caldwell recalled the experience of her mother, Margaret, while at the fort:

> Mother, in Company with her fifteen-year-old boy and a young lady, Christina McNeil, who was making the trip under Mother's care, visited one of the generals in command at the fort to obtain permission to trade some trinkets and silver spoons for flour and meat. The officer said he himself could not use any of the things but to leave the young lady in his office while mother went to another station, where he assured her she would be able to obtain the things she desired. He seemed very kind, and not wishing to arouse any feeling of ill will, she left Christina and Thomas. During her absence the officer used the time in trying to persuade Christena to stay there,

> proposing to her and showing her the gold he had, telling her what a fine lady he would make of her. Then he tried discouraging her, pointing out to her how the handcart company would never reach Utah, because of the severe cold, and that they would die of cold and hunger and exposure. Like all noble girls, and true to the cause for which she had left her native Scotland, her family, home, and friends just to be in Utah, she told him in plain language she would take her chances with the others even though it might mean death. She was greatly relieved to have Mother return. The officer, however, seemed to admire her very much for her loyalty to her faith and gave her a large cured ham and wished her well in her chosen adventure.[5]

The Willie Company remained only a short time at Fort Laramie and continued on with their journey the same day they arrived. The independent wagon teams traveling with the Willie Company under the direction of Andrew Siler remained behind. "When we arrived at Fort Laramie there was a letter from Bro. Richards directing the families traveling with us in private wagons to remain at Laramie till the wagon companies east of us arrived, & then travel with them."[6]

Franklin D. Richards Company Salt Lake Valley October 4, 1856

On October 4, Franklin D. Richards and his company of returning missionaries arrived in the valley, having left Florence a month earlier on September 4. Brigham Young called upon Franklin D. Richards and others to attend an evening meeting with the First Presidency. Brigham Young stated: "The object of my meeting the brethren here is to find out what we need to do tomorrow. It is the day for calling up on the Bishops." It was at this time that Brigham Young was apprised of the Willie, Martin, Hunt, and Hodgett Companies' decision to continue on to the valley that season.[7]

During the meeting, President Young suggested: "Suppose we take the first company we come to as we go back and we will see what you think they will need." Those present discussed each company remaining on the trail, beginning with the company nearest to the valley and noted their possible needs.[8]

WILLIE COMPANY
WEST OF FORT LARAMIE
OCTOBER 4, 1856

As Franklin D. Richards met with the First Presidency, the Willie Company was a few days west of Fort Laramie. October 4 was the first day of their reduced rations of twelve ounces of flour. Levi Savage recorded some in the company had been stealing provisions; consequently a guard was posted outside the supply wagons. Also of note, three deaths were recorded: sixty-one-year-old Benjamin Culley, sixty-eight-year-old George Ingra, and two-year-old Daniel Gadd.[9]

GADD FAMILY

Two-year-old Daniel Gadd was a twin son of Samuel and Eliza Chapman Gadd. Samuel was among the faithful and dedicated early converts who joined the Church in 1841. His wife, Eliza, did not join the Church, yet she not only supported her husband in his new faith and leadership positions, but also agreed to emigrate to America with their eight children in order to keep the family together. Burying one of the twins on this October day must have been devastating for Eliza, but it would prove only the beginning of what she would be called upon to endure.[10]

MARTIN COMPANY
SCOTTS BLUFF
OCTOBER 4, 1856

OPENSHAW FAMILY

On October 4, the Martin Company passed through Scotts Bluff, 559 miles from the Salt Lake Valley. Up until this point in the journey, twenty-two-year-old Samuel Openshaw had been keeping a daily record of his experiences. October 3 was his last daily entry. Samuel was traveling to the valley with his parents, William and Ann Openshaw, who were among the first to accept the gospel in England in 1840. The family made great sacrifices to save enough to emigrate by working seemingly endless hours in the linen mills. Samuel's brothers, Roger and Eli, were blessed to emigrate in March 1854 to prepare the way for the family. Roger left behind his wife, Eliza Booth Openshaw, in the care of his family. Little did Roger know when he left in 1854, he would never see his wife again. Eliza and her sister-in-law Eleanor became sick in early September and had to be hauled in the handcarts. Samuel recorded the difficulties in pulling the women in the handcart and continued to record the decline in Eliza's health. He did not include the events of Eliza's death, nor of the physical and emotional difficulties experienced by his family during this time, but he later finished his account with his recollections.[11]

13

GO AND BRING IN THOSE PEOPLE NOW ON THE PLAINS

URGENT CALL TO ACTION

SALT LAKE VALLEY
OCTOBER 5–7, 1856

At general conference held in the Salt Lake Valley on Sunday, October 5, Brigham Young must have felt the sheer magnitude and gravity of the plight of all who remained on the trail at the time. It was that feeling, now resting heavily upon his shoulders, which prompted his urgent call to action:

> I will now give this people the subject and the text for the Elders who may speak to-day and during the conference, it is this, on the 5th day of October, 1856, many of our brethren and sisters are on the plains with hand-carts, and probably many are now 700 miles from this place, and they must be brought here, we must send assistance to them. The text will be, "to get them here." . . . That is my religion; that is the dictation of the Holy Ghost that I possess, it is to save the people. . . . I shall call upon the Bishops this day, I shall not wait until to-morrow, nor until next day, for 60 good mule teams and 12 or 15 wagons. I do not want to send oxen, I want good horses and mules. They are in this Territory, and we must have them; also 12 tons of flour and 40 good teamsters, besides those that drive the teams . . . to take charge of the teams that are now managed by men, women and children, who know nothing about driving them; second 60 or 65 good spans of mules,

> or horses. . . . I will tell you all that your faith, religion, and profession of religion, will never save one soul of you in the celestial kingdom of our God, unless you carry out just such principles as I am now teaching you. Go and bring in those people now on the plains, and attend strictly to those things which we call temporal, or temporal duties, otherwise your faith will be in vain; the preaching you have heard will be in vain to you, and you will sink to hell, unless you attend to the things we tell you. Any man or woman can reason this out in their own minds, without trouble. The gospel has been already preached to those brethren and sisters now on the plains; they have believed and obeyed it, and are willing to do anything for salvation; they are doing all they can do, and the Lord has done all that is required of him to do, and has given us power to bring them in from the plains.[1]

During the conference, Daniel Spencer, who oversaw the immigration in Iowa City, was invited to speak, and he shared the following:

> Many of the people that started with plenty of means to come through with teams divided their means to help those that had none, and enrolled themselves as pullers of carts, and such circumstances are common this season; they devoted all to assist the poor, and they have felt cheerful. . . . Well, now, we feel for those brethren and sisters that are still upon the plains, for we have been with them in the old countries and seen their faith and diligence, and now we feel to plead with you to assist them. . . . The emigration is late, quite late, but it is useless for me to undertake to explain why it is so. They are late, but the faith of those that have been associated with them is that the God of heaven will control the elements, providing that you, my brethren and sisters, render them that assistance which he has given you ability to do.[2]

When Franklin D. Richards spoke, he specifically petitioned the sisters as follows:

> I would like to say a word to the sisters here, for they have a tremendous influence sometimes. Let me say to some of those that came out in the earlier years of our settlement in these valleys, you thought the journey quite long enough, and that if it had been a week, a fortnight or a month longer, you did not know how you could have endured it. Many of you came in wagons, bringing the

> comforts of life with you in abundance. Sisters think of those fatiguing times, and stir up your good men in behalf of those who are footing it, and pulling hand-carts 1,300 miles, instead of riding 1,000 as you did. The aged, the infirm and bowed down, and those who have been lame from their birth, are coming along upon their crutches; and they think it is a good job if they can walk the most of the way through the day, and avoid riding all they can. Indeed persons of nearly all ages and conditions are coming . . . arise up and bring those Saints in, for it is late in the season, and ten to one they will have snow storms to encounter; though the Lord will not let them suffer any more than they have grace to bear. It is our highest privilege to do all we can to ameliorate the sufferings of those brethren that are thus trying to work out their emigration. . . . Concerning the hand-cart companies this year, it is an experiment. We cannot yet tell you exactly what it costs to come through in that way; what we know that it is going to cost those on the other side of the mountains cold feet and a great deal of affliction and sorrow, unless we help them.[3]

Harvey H. Cluff wrote: "I attended the October conference of that year which opened on the 6th as usual, having walked from Provo to Salt Lake City. . . . The response to the call of president Young was most remarkable. . . . Being in Salt Lake City and of an ambitious turn of mind, I volunteered to go. One thing which attracted me, in addition of the interest in the handcart people, was my brother Moses. He was on the plains returning from a mission to England."[4]

This call for action could not have come at a more difficult time for the Saints in the valley. Heber C. Kimball recorded:

> The times are said to be more close this season than they have ever been in the valleys; and this is universal through all the settlements. There are not more than one half the people that have bread, and they have not more than one half or one quarter of a pound a day to a person. A great portion of the people are digging roots, and hundreds and thousands, their teams being dead, are under the necessity of spading their ground to put in their grain. There is not any settlement or people, in any part of the Territory, but what feel the scarcity of food, money, cattle, horses, &c.; and there is a pretty universal break with our merchants, as there is no one to buy their goods, and their stock are mostly dead. . . . Brother Brigham,

> myself, and others have been crying unto this people for more than three years, to lay up their grain for a time when they would have much need of it.[5]

In spite of the difficulties experienced by the Saints, the call for action was answered immediately with all they could spare and more. "Such a spirit of brotherly love as was shown forth by the Latter-day Saints on that occasion was perhaps never before witnessed in a religious community. It seemed that every man, woman and child within the limits of Salt Lake was alive to the situation. While the men were going in every direction gathering up supplies, the women were making quilts, mending underwear, knitting mittens, darning socks, patching trousers, and even taking clothes from their own backs to send to the shivering pilgrims hundreds of miles out on the plains."[6]

It was written in the *Deseret News*:

> For never have we witnessed a greater general alacrity in answering to the calls of the First Presidency, and in turning out at such a time of the year with animals, provisions and clothing abundance, to rescue brethren and sisters that the most who went forth had never seen. . . . No person abroad can realize the immense self-denial and drawback upon plans for comfort, comprised in sending out so many fine teams and active men to encounter the inclemency of mountain cold and storms at this season of the year. Well may sinners be astonished and dismayed at the love of the Saints, seeing that they are ready, at the word, to cheerfully endure privation and hardship for the truth's sake and the salvation of man.[7]

Addressing the Saints in the morning session of conference, Brigham Young called for teams to be ready to start the following morning and requested volunteers to come forward and give their names. Among the first to volunteer were six men who had just returned to the valley a few days earlier with Franklin D. Richards: James Ferguson, George D. Grant, William H. Kimball, Chauncey G. Webb, Cyrus H. Wheelock, and Joseph A. Young.[8]

Daniel W. Jones was among those present in the morning session of conference. He wrote: "Brother Young was in earnest; he seemed moved by a spirit that would admit of no delay. . . . Brother Young called upon every one present to lend a hand in fitting up these teams. As I was going out with the crowd, Brother Wells spoke to me saying: 'You are a good hand for the trip; get ready.' Soon after Bishop Hunter said the same thing to me. Also Brother Grant met me and said: 'I want you on this trip.' I began to think it time to decide, so I answered, 'all right.'"[9]

DANIEL W. JONES

Daniel W. Jones, as described by historian Wallace Stegner, was "an ex-Missouri Puke, an orphan, a harder Huckleberry Finn who from the age of eleven had made his tough way on a tough frontier." Daniel described himself as "probably as willful a boy as ever lived" never controlled except through kindness, which he did not often meet with. Stegner's description continued: "Like Huckleberry, rather than submit to being civilized, he had lit out for the territories: the Mexican War led him into the Southwest as a member of the Missouri Volunteers, and for some years afterward he lived among hair-trigger borderers in Texas and New Mexico." For a time, Daniel continued living a wild and reckless life "indulging in many of the wild and reckless ways of the people." While he was driving sheep from Santa Fe, he accidentally shot himself and almost lost his life. It was then he began to turn his life around. In order to save his life, Daniel was encouraged to get to a Mormon settlement. He was told of their kindness and was assured they would take care of him. Daniel agreed and was carried for fifteen days to Spanish Fork, Utah, and taken care of in the home of Bishop Isaac Higbee. Wallace Stegner described how the experience with this family changed his life: "The kindness with which he was treated smote his orphan heart; he found himself hankering after the security of the Mormon confidence in the Lord. Before long he joined the Church, married a Mormon girl, and settled down."[10]

Daniel W. Jones recorded the following individuals who initially volunteered to assist in the rescue efforts: George D. Grant, Robert T. Burton, William Kimball, Cyrus H. Wheelock, Charles F. Decker, Joseph A. Young, Chauncey Webb, Harvey H. Cluff, David P. Kimball, George W. Grant, Edwin M. Peck, Joel Parrish, Henry Goldsbrough, Thomas Alexander, Benjamin Hampton, Thomas Ricks, Abel Garr, Charles Grey, Al Huntington, "Handsome Cupid,"

Stephen Taylor, William K. Broomhead, Ira Nebeker, Redick Allred, Amos Fairbanks, and Tom Bankhead.[11]

Many of these men were among the young, rugged, and strong "Minute Men," born under great tribulation. Their parents were

> driven from county to county and from state to state, until they were utterly stripped of all earthly possessions. Even then, they were not allowed to rest until they had been driven into the wilderness, some twelve hundred miles from civilization, and there left in the midst of cruel savages and wild beasts, with starvation staring them in the face. Most of our pioneer boys were born while their grief-stricken parents were passing through these terrible hardships. These little fellows naturally partook of the spirit with which they were surrounded, and this undoubtedly went far towards qualifying them for the hard and trying mission they were destined to fulfill later on. The majority of them were descendants of our Pilgrim Fathers, and their grandsires stood shoulder to shoulder with the brave patriots who made this the most glorious nation on earth. . . . When emigration from the old countries began to pour into Utah, the burden of pioneer life commenced to weigh heavily upon their young shoulders. New settlements had to be built, roads and bridges made, hostile Indians subdued, and the wild beasts looked after. These responsibilities, with many others just as important, kept them moving almost continuously.[12]

As members of the Minute Men, they often rode

> thirty-five or forty miles a day, over a rough country, through the hot sun of summer, or the cold weather of winter. . . . They scarcely ever built fires, on such occasions, since the smoke by day or the light by night might reveal . . . their whereabouts. Their covering at night generally consisted of their damp saddle blankets, with their saddles for pillows. . . . They were compelled to swim rivers, during cold weather . . . fording treacherous mountain streams during high water. . . . When they ran short of provisions they killed wild game and jerked the meat. Once in a while, they entered barren regions where game was not found. Then they were compelled to live on the meat of their faithful saddle animals.[13]

It would take volumes to place properly before the people all the heroic acts performed by our early day pioneer boys. They were instruments in the hands of the Lord in making it possible for the

> thousands of emigrants, who came to Utah in early days, to dwell in peace in these valleys of the mountains. These boys were naturally intelligent, honest, truthful, virtuous, God-fearing and as tender-hearted as children. Of course, they were somewhat rough, as they had but little time to attend school, and to enjoy the comforts of home life. . . . They were a cheerful lot of fellows, under the most trying circumstances, and not a word of complaint was ever heard to come from their lips. It is remarkable, in view of conditions, how few of them lost their lives, either in Indian fights or by accident. It seemed like the powers of heaven were watching over them.[14]

"This generation of Latter-day Saints will never fully appreciate what our pioneer boys have done towards the establishment of the Church in these valleys and the founding of homes, until the books spoken of in John the Revelator shall have been opened. When the dead, small and great, shall stand before God, to be judged according to their works, these brave 'Mormon' boys, a few of whom are still with us, will undoubtedly be found in the front ranks among the noble and great ones 'which came out of great tribulation.'"[15]

On the evening of October 6, the first Rescue Company to be dispatched met with Brigham Young, who offered counsel and priesthood blessings "that fairly made them quake. After an affectionate parting, the boys returned to their homes for a good night's rest."[16]

On the morning of October 7, with wagons laden with supplies, the first Rescue Company left the Salt Lake Valley, under the direction of George D. Grant, with William H. Kimball and Robert T. Burton as assistants. Cyrus H. Wheelock was called to serve as chaplain, Charles F. Decker as guide, and Daniel W. Jones as chief cook. "A better outfit and one more adapted to the work before us I do not think could have possibly been selected if a week had been spent in fitting up. Besides the wagons and teams, several men went horseback. We had good teams and provisions in abundance. But best of all, those going were alive to the work and were of the best material possible for the occasion."[17]

This Rescue Company set out in hopes of meeting the Willie Handcart Company near the Green River, 130 miles east of the Salt Lake Valley. Little did they realize the dangers and privations they soon would be faced with, or the sacrifices and the heroic efforts it would require in bringing the remaining handcart and wagon companies to the Salt Lake Valley. Before nightfall, this initial rescue company experienced a light snowstorm. Dan Jones recorded: "The weather soon became cold and stormy. We traveled hard, never taking time to stop for dinner."[18]

14

STOUT HEARTS AND GREAT FAITH

FORT LARAMIE TO THE PLATTE RIVER BRIDGE

WILLIE COMPANY
OCTOBER 5–13, 1856

For the Willie Company, the journey from Fort Laramie to the Platte River Bridge was extremely difficult. It must have brought to their minds the stark realization of the reservations expressed by Levi Savage in Florence: "I myself am not in favor of, but much opposed to, taking women and children through when they are destitute of clothing, when we all know that we are bound to be caught in the snow and severe cold weather long before we reach the valley."[1]

John Chislett recorded:

> We had not traveled far up the Sweetwater before the nights, which had gradually been getting colder since we left Laramie, became very severe. The mountains before us, as we approached nearer to them, revealed themselves to view mantled nearly to their base in snow, and tokens of a coming storm were discernible in the clouds which each day seemed to lower around us. In our frequent crossings of the Sweetwater, we had really 'a hard road to travel.' The water was beautiful to the eye, as it rolled over its rocky bed as clear as crystal; but when we waded it time after time at each ford to get the carts, the women, and the children over, the beautiful stream, with its romantic surroundings . . . lost to us its beauty, and the chill which it sent through our systems drove out from our minds all holy

and devout aspirations, and left a void, a sadness, and—in some cases—doubts as to the justice of an overruling Providence.

John's account continued:

Our seventeen pounds of clothing and bedding was now altogether insufficient for our comfort. Nearly all suffered more or less at night from cold. Instead of getting up in the morning strong, refreshed, vigorous, and prepared for the hardships of another day of toil, the poor "Saints" were to be seen crawling out from their tents looking haggard, benumbed, and showing an utter lack of that vitality so necessary to our success. Cold weather, scarcity of food, lassitude and fatigue from over-exertion, soon produced their effects. Our old and infirm people began to droop, and they no sooner lost spirit and courage than death's stamp could be traced upon their features. Life went out as smoothly as a lamp ceases to burn when the oil is gone. At first the deaths occurred slowly and irregularly, but in a few days at more frequent intervals, until we soon thought it unusual to leave a camp-ground without burying one or more persons. Death was not long confined in its ravages to the old and infirm, but the young and naturally strong were among its victim. Men who were, so to speak, as strong as lions when we started on our journey, and who had been our best supports, were compelled to succumb to the grim monster. These men were worn down by hunger, scarcity of clothing and bedding, and too much labour in helping their families. Weakness and debility were accompanied by dysentery. This we could not stop or even alleviate, no proper medicines being in the camp; and in almost every instance it carried off the parties attacked. It was surprising to an unmarried man to witness the devotion of men to their families and to their faith, under these trying circumstances. Many a father pulled his cart, with his little children on it, until the day preceding his death. I have seen some pull their carts in the morning, give out during the day, and die before next morning. These people died with the calm faith and fortitude of martyrs. Their greatest regret seemed to be leaving their families behind them, and their bodies on the plains or mountains instead of being laid in the consecrated ground of Zion. The sorrow and mourning of the bereaved, as they saw their husbands and fathers rudely interred, were affecting in the extreme, and none but a heart of stone could repress a tear of sympathy at the sad spectacle.[2]

GADD FAMILY

On Thursday, October 9, just five days after the death of one of Eliza Chapman Gadd's two-year-old twins, Eliza's husband, Samuel, was overcome with the effects of pneumonia. Eliza's eighteen-year-old son, Alfred, recorded: "We went eighteen miles. My father was dying before we left this morning, but they put him in a wagon, and when we saw him at noon, he was dead." Eliza was now a widow with seven children.[3]

Not only were members of the company reaching their physical limits, but the oxen teams, pulling their life-sustaining supplies, were reaching theirs as well. Levi Savage recorded: "When we arose we found the best ox in our train, dead; In the weak state of our teams, the loss impaired it much . . . our old people are nearly all failing fast . . . three of our working cows gave out and one died, and the remainder of our oxen were nearly overcome."[4]

John Chislett recorded:

> Each death weakened our forces. In my hundred I could not raise enough men to pitch a tent when we encamped, and now it was that I had to exert myself to the utmost. I wonder why I did not die, as many did who were stronger than I was. When we pitched our camp in the evening of each day, I had to lift the sick from the wagon and carry them to the fire, and in the morning carry them again on my back to the wagon. When any in my hundred died I had to inter them; often helping to dig the grave myself. In performing these sad offices I always offered up a heartfelt prayer to that God who beheld our sufferings, and begged him to avert destruction from us and send us help.[5]

The countless heartfelt prayers being offered up at this time were not only heard, but were also being answered, as rescue efforts were already underway.

SUSANNAH STONE

Twenty-five-year-old Susannah Stone was traveling alone to the valley in the Willie Company. At age seventeen, she was baptized and soon desired more than anything to gather with the Saints in Zion. Her family and friends greatly opposed Susannah's emigration and did all within their power to dissuade her. Despite this, she worked and saved for eight years and was able to emigrate with the Saints. Although Susannah's journey to the Salt Lake Valley was filled with difficulties, her faith sustained her in her greatest time of need, and she was blessed to receive help and encouragement from beyond the veil. Susannah wrote:

> I am thankful that I was counted worthy to be a pioneer and a hand cart girl. . . . It was hard to endure, but the Lord gave us strength and courage. . . . We waded through the cold streams many times, but we murmured not, for our faith in God and our testimony of His work were supreme. . . . Only once did my courage fail. One cold, dreary afternoon, my feet having been frosted, I felt that I could go no further, and withdrew a little from the company, and sat down to await the end, being somewhat in a stupor. After a time, I was aroused by a voice, which seemed as audible as anything could be, and which spoke to my very soul of the promises and blessings I had received, and which should surely be fulfilled, and that I had a mission to perform in Zion. I received strength, and was filled with the Spirit of the Lord, and arose, and traveled on with a light heart.[6]

Mortensen Family

It was during this time of great difficulty that Helena "Lena" Mortensen of Denmark recorded:

> We had to have stout hearts and great faith in meeting these great trials, misfortunes and sickness pain and death, burying beloved dead ones, who gave their lives for the sake of the gospel. We wept as we went on our journey. We went before the Lord and pleaded for Him to make good the promises which were given us by His servant when we were in old Denmark. How we implored Him to raise the sick and give us strength to carry our burdens without complaints. For we had the lame to haul on our handcarts, the maimed to care for and our beloved dead ones to bury by the wayside, never to see again the place where they were laid to rest.

And they were often reminded of Jeremiah's vision and prophecy recorded in the 31st chapter: "For there shall be a day that the watchman upon Ephraim shall cry, 'arise ye, and let us go up to Zion unto the Lord our God . . . Behold, I will bring them from the north country and gather them from the coasts of the earth, and with them the blind and the lame, the woman with child and they that travaileth with child together, a great company shall return hither. They shall come with weeping, and supplication will I lead them.'"[7]

On October 10, the Willie Company stopped near the Platte River Bridge at the trading post and obtained thirty-seven buffalo robes left by Franklin D. Richards and continued on six miles near the old "Mormon Ferry" site. The Mormon Ferry was established in 1847 when Brigham Young and those traveling in the first Mormon Pioneer Emigrant Company arrived at the upper crossing of the North Platte. During the spring runoff in June and July, this river swelled to 450 feet wide with strong currents and depths from 10 to 15 feet, this posing many dangers to the Saints. With the great number of Saints, Brigham Young knew were soon to follow, he commissioned the construction of a ferry.[8]

The Mormon Ferry operated until 1852, when a toll bridge was constructed across the river. This first bridge operated only a short time before washing away in a spring flood. By 1853, construction on the second toll bridge was completed. The bridge was 835 feet long and 15 feet wide built of wood, stone, and iron. It was built 10 feet above the high water mark. The toll to cross was five dollars per wagon during high water months, the fee decreasing during low water months. This toll bridge eventually put the ferries out of business. Without the means available to cross the river on the bridge, the Willie Company forded the Platte River without incident. The Martin Company would not reach this river crossing until nine days later; their experience would be much different.[9]

Martin Company
Fort Laramie
October 8–9, 1856

The Martin Company reached Fort Laramie on October 8, a week behind the Willie Company. They traveled the 522-mile distance from Florence to Fort Laramie in 45 days. The following morning, members of the company went to the fort to sell watches, jewelry, and other heirlooms and keepsakes in hopes of obtaining some provisions. Stationed at the fort were three companies of

United States infantry and cavalry who persisted in their efforts to persuade men from the Martin Company to enlist. These officers implored the men not to risk their lives on this journey to the Salt Lake Valley so late in the season.[10]

WILLIAM ASHTON

William Ashton, of England, was among the number of men persuaded to leave the company and enlist at this time. William's journey to the valley thus far was filled with heartache: his two-year-old daughter, Elizabeth, died on the *Horizon* on July 2; his wife, Sarah Ann Barlow, died on August 26, shortly after giving birth; his newborn daughter, Sarah Ann, died on September 11. These deaths proved to be too much for William, and he placed his remaining children—eleven-year-old Betsy, seven-year-old Sarah, and four-year-old Mary—in the care of the Martin Company. Before reaching the valley, eleven-year-old Betsy would also die.[11]

The Martin Company departed from Fort Laramie on October 10. They were now 509 miles from the Salt Lake Valley. At their present rate of travel, the company leaders calculated they would run out of provisions long before they reached their destination. Later in the evening, fifteen-year-old Josiah Rogerson and his older brother William were among twenty men detailed to return to Fort Laramie with ten handcarts to obtain seventy-five to one hundred buffalo robes purchased by Franklin D. Richards. The robes were distributed among the company the following day.[12]

15

SUCH TENDER DEVOTION

Independence Rock to Sweetwater River, Fort Laramie to Deer Creek

Willie Company
Independence Rock to Sweetwater River
October 14–17, 1856

On October 14, the Willie Company camped about a mile west of Independence Rock. With over 330 miles remaining in their journey, Captain Willie received a letter from Franklin D. Richards informing him they might expect supplies at South Pass. John Chislett recorded: "An examination of our stock of flour showed us that it would be gone before we reached that point. Our only alternative was to still further reduce our bill of fare. The issue of flour was then to average ten ounces per day to each person over ten years of age, and to be divided thus: working men to receive twelve ounces, women and old men nine ounces, and children from four to eight ounces, according to age and size." On reduced rations the general health of the company declined rapidly. Levi Savage recorded: "The people are getting weak, and failing very fast, a great many sick. Our teams are also failing fast, and it requires great exertion to make any progress."[1]

Reeder and Hurren Families

Between October 15 and 17, five deaths occurred in the Willie Company. Among the dead was seventeen-year-old Caroline Reeder, who passed away on October 15, just two weeks following the death of her father, David Reeder. Her brother Robert penned the following of Caroline's death:

> Our rations were growing shorter, and we reduced them by common consent from day to day. Nights were getting colder, and some would sit down by the roadside and die. My younger sister, Caroline, seventeen years old, after traveling all day and seeing the camp being made for the night, took off her apron to tie some sagebrush in to bring into the camp. She sat down to rest, leaning on her bundle, exhausted. They found her chilled and dying and carried her to camp. She died without gaining consciousness. She, too, was placed in an unmarked grave near Three Crossings—Sweetwater [River]. She died the evening of October 15, 1856. Her death was another real loss to us, but we must hurry on in threatening weather and colder nights on the Windriver Pass.[2]

The Martin Handcart Company, along with the Hunt and Hodgett Wagon Companies, would not reach the area near Independence Rock until seventeen days later on November 1.[3]

Martin Company
Fort Laramie to Deer Creek
October 10–17, 1856

During this time between Fort Laramie and Deer Creek, members of the Martin Company began to feel the physical effects of the reduced rations. John Jaques describes:

> Well, at the time when this great appetite was fairly roused up and had put on its strength and was still further strengthened and sharpened by the increasing coldness of the weather, the extra pinching time commenced. Soon after Fort Laramie was passed, it was deemed advisable to curtail the rations in order to make them hold out as long as possible. The pound of flour fell to three fourths of a pound, then to half a pound, and subsequently yet lower. Still the company toiled on through the Black Hills, where the feed grew scarcer for the cattle also. As the necessities of man and beast

> increased their daily food diminished, at the time when it was as the emigrants might have said, with Sir Walter Scott, "like a summer—dried fountain, when our wants were the sorest."[4]

John continued:

> Up to this time the daily pound of flour ration had been regularly served out, but it was never enough to stay the stomachs of the emigrants, and the longer they were on the plains and in the mountains, the hungrier they grew. . . . It is an appetite that could not be satisfied. At least that was the experience of the handcart people. You felt as if you could almost eat a rusty nail or gnaw a file. You are ten times as hungry as a hunter, yes, as ten hunters, all the day long and every time you woke up in the night, and so you continue to your journey's end, and for some time after. Eating is the grand passion of a pedestrian on the plains, an insatiable passion, for he never gets enough to eat.[5]

To add to the difficulties experienced during this time, John described the continual breakdown of the handcarts: "In the Black Hills the roads were harder, more rocky and more hilly, and this told upon the handcarts, causing them to fail more rapidly, become more rickety, and need more frequent repairing."[6]

As members of both the Willie and Martin Handcart Companies were being tried and tested well beyond their physical limits, these moments allowed their God-given capabilities of compassion and brotherly love to be refined. These were the moments that these pioneers will forever be remembered for, moments that bring the reader to a new level of understanding of what an honor it must have been to be numbered among their companies. John Bond, a member of the Hodgett Wagon Company, witnessed such acts and documented this event:

> The saints begin to show weariness of the journey by the sunken eyes and emaciated forms from constant travel leaving the dear ones on the plains in an exhausted condition on arriving in camp missing the loved ones, though fatigued themselves they return back on the plains to find them on the road powerless to go on farther, put them on their carts, pull and tug with them until they arrive in camp near midnight their shoes were worn out, their toes protruding from the shoes in a bleeding condition. In the same way some were compelled

> to stay on the way and pull sand burrs from their feet shedding many tears. Alas! It was painful and sorrowful to see the mothers carry their babes on the way giving them the bosom in languid and tired steps with sorrowful hearts. While the husbands were pulling two and three children on the carts who had sore and bleeding feet for want of shoes and were powerless to walk on farther. A sad, sad sight to see indeed. . . . The usual way the hand-cart Saints lay down on the way, getting more exhausted as their allowance of food did not seem adequate for them to pull their carts and live on, and it was fast telling on them. But friends go back on the plains and help them into camp. Though it fatigued in doing so yet they have faith in God to protect the famished and that they will receive the desired relief and camp shortly.[7]

John Bond continued:

> The wind is blowing hard and snow is seen on the Laramie Peak in the distance, giving every indication that a storm is near at hand. The wolves are following the trains making their monotonous howlings in all directions a hideous sound to the ears. The snow-capped peaks bring much alarm for fear of the suffering ones in tent life as their bed clothing is badly worn from lying on the campground getting damp and cold to lay on, their wearing apparel is in a very bad condition with worn out shoes, their toes are protruding and bleeding from them. It is a shocking and heart-aching sight to see, and their care worn and emaciated forms with tears rolling down their sunburned cheeks, God pity them. He knows of their wounded and aching hearts.[8]

Jaques & Loader Families

By Tuesday, October 14, John Jaques had nearly reached his limits of physical exhaustion, and he turned to his wife for help in pulling the handcart. She had delivered a baby just west of Florence. In his journal, John noted he was not feeling well and wrote that his legs and hands were swollen and he was short of breath. Since leaving Florence, John was overwhelmed with his company leadership responsibilities along with the weighty responsibilities of caring for his young family and in-laws. Since leaving Iowa, John hauled his wife, his sister-in-law, or his sick two-year-old daughter and newborn son in the handcart. He also assumed additional responsibilities for the Loader family after his father-in-law passed away. "Thenceforth, until the close of the journey, although noteworthy events were on the increase, and some of them were indelibly impressed on the minds of the emigrants, yet they were so fully occupied in taking care of themselves that they had little time to spare to note details with exactness."[9]

The Martin Company reached Deer Creek on Friday, October 17. Westward progress was slowing down considerably as the company, on reduced rations of twelve ounces of flour for adults and six ounces for children, was quickly wearing down. With the meager amount of flour rationed, many stirred in enough water to make a thin gruel, bring it to a near boil so it would thicken, and drank it. Others would take the thin gruel and fry it on a griddle, making thin cakes, or bake them to make biscuits.[10]

At their present rate of travel, calculations indicated the Martin Company would not reach supply wagons, thought to be stationed at South Pass, until a week after their supplies had run out. Feeling as if there was no other alternative, desperate measures were taken in order to lighten the loads of the weary Saints and allow them to travel faster. The luggage allowance was further reduced. John Jaques described: "At Deer creek, on the 17th of October, owing to the growing weakness of emigrants and teams, the baggage including bedding and cooking utensils, was reduced to ten pounds per head, children under 8 years, five pounds. Good blankets and other bedding and clothing were burned as they could not be carried further, though needed more badly than ever, for there was yet 400 miles of winter to go through."[11]

Josiah Rogerson wrote:

> During the afternoon Captain Edward Martin advised the whole camp to lighten up their extra luggage bags and canvas sacks as much as possible, by discarding and burning every article of wearing apparel that could be dispensed with, save and except our best and warm coats, cloaks, etc., for the coming cold weather, and the wisdom of this timely counsel was soon afterward realized. When many of the canvas bags were opened it was readily seen that the heads of many families were hauling and pulling luggage in the shape of books, trinkets, and half worn-out clothing that could

> be dispensed with beneficially, and many piles of this unnecessary loading were burned here . . . several members of our company were permitted and selected to take such articles of apparel (in lightening up our loads) to the fort and sell and barter the same for flour, dried buffalo meat, tea, sugar and medicines. In several instances this advice, carried out, was the means of saving lives during the subsequent weeks of snow and hardships intervening between this time and our arrival in Utah.

Josiah Rogerson described filling an empty flour sack with light summer dresses, night gowns, knitted decanter stands, linen bureau, and mirror bric-a-brac. He then traveled a few miles to the Platte Bridge, where he bartered with the American Indians for a substantially large quantity of jerked buffalo meat, black and cayenne pepper, tea, sugar, soda, and bread. "The results and success of my bartering trip that day saved the lives of several in our family, and the liberality of my mother, with many a cup of buffalo beef soup, seasoned well with pepper, alleviated the sufferings and saved the lives of several more."[12]

Mortensen Family

Prior to leaving Denmark, the Mortensen family received a blessing promising they would have strength, health, and wisdom, and that they would reach the Salt Lake Valley in safety. The family was truly blessed with strength, health, and wisdom on this journey. Along the way, forty-seven-year-old Helena, or "Lena," gathered berries and herbs and used them in teas, soups, and stews. When food rations became dangerously low, Lena was able to make a little bread from the bran she remembered was in a pin cushion she brought along with her. She was resourceful with her flour rations, using the flour to make small biscuits and keeping them in her apron to give little pieces to the family throughout the day. On one occasion, after a difficult day of pulling the family handcart in heavy sands, eighteen-year-old Hans was so weak and faint that he felt as if he could go no further. Lena gave him a small amount of fruit juice and a crust of one of the biscuits and offered words of encouragement: "Be brave, my boy—We must go on." This was enough to give Hans the strength to continue with his weighty responsibilities. Along with pulling the handcart, Hans and his thirteen-year-old brother, Lars, also had the responsibility of carrying five-year-old Caroline on their shoulders. The boys also shared the responsibility of burial duty, with Lena donating her hand-woven sheets to cover the bodies of those who died. When times became even more difficult, Lena took the rawhide from the handcart, scraped and boiled it, and made soup. Her ten-year-old daughter Mettie became so hungry at one point that she took a crust of bread from the pocket of a woman who had passed away, and throughout her life she expressed her regrets for doing so. Although fifty-year-old Peder faced many physical limitations on the journey, he also was blessed with great resourcefulness. When the shoes of his children wore out, he took pieces of smooth shingles and oiled them. He then attached the old, worn-out shoe and boot tops to the shingles in order to save his children's feet. In spite of the difficulties, the Mortensen family would all be blessed to reach the Salt Lake Valley.[13]

16

OUR HEARTS BEGAN TO ACHE

FORT BRIDGER TO SOUTH PASS

RESCUE COMPANY
FORT BRIDGER TO SOUTH PASS
OCTOBER 12–18, 1856

After traveling 113 miles in six days, on October 12, Captain George D. Grant's Rescue Company reached Fort Bridger. They had high hopes of reaching the Willie Company near the Green River within a few days. At the fort, they purchased supplies and cached flour for the return trip. Daniel W. Jones recorded: "We began to feel great anxiety about the emigrants as the weather was now cold and stormy, and we, strong men with good outfits, found the nights severe. What must be the condition of those we were to meet? Many old men and women, little children, mothers with nursing babes, crossing the plains pulling hand-carts. Our hearts began to ache when we reached Green River and yet no word of them. Here an express was sent on ahead with a light wagon to meet and cheer the people up." On October 14, with no sign of either the Willie or Martin Handcart Companies, Captain Grant sent a four-man express team ahead to search for them. The Express Company consisted of Cyrus H. Wheelock, Joseph A. Young, Stephen Taylor, and Abel Garr with light wagons and fast horses. These men were instructed to go no further than Independence Rock.[1]

On October 17, the Rescue Company camped on Little Sandy located 204 miles from the Salt Lake Valley. Robert T. Burton noted:

> From that time on they encountered increasingly cold days and bitter nights. When an animal was killed to take to the immigrants, there was no need to salt the beef—it froze during quartering and stayed frozen. It now seemed necessary to leave more teams behind so that they might be able to assist when the immigrant parties came through. Therefore, Reddick Allred was stationed on the Sweetwater River with flour, cattle, eleven guards, and four wagons. He would soon be joined from the west by three additional wagons and six men. Had any one in the relief party forseen the condition of either of the handcart companies, they would have gathered all the stores and teams at Fort Bridger, Green River, and South Pass and traveled day and night until their animals broke. It was just as well they did not know, for the relief effort would already require more strength and supplies than they carried. Their pace would already stretch every man to the breaking point.[2]

REDICK NEWTON ALLRED

Redick Newton Allred was born February 21, 1822, in Tennessee. In 1831, while living in Missouri, he heard the gospel preached by Hyrum Smith. Redick and his twin brother, Reddin, were baptized in the spring of 1833, and thereafter endured terrible persecution. While in Nauvoo, Redick worked on the Nauvoo Temple as a mason. In 1841, he was called to serve a mission, but on his way to Pennsylvania, he stopped in Cincinnati for health reasons. In 1843, at age twenty-one, Redick married Lucy Hoyt. Prior to the Prophet Joseph Smith's imprisonment in Carthage, Redick was warned about the death of the prophet and his brother Hyrum in a dream.

Following their deaths, Redick attended a meeting where he witnessed the mantle of Joseph Smith placed upon the shoulders of Brigham Young as Brigham took the stand and spoke. The experience was a spiritual witness to Redick, and the Spirit testified to him with such power and authority that no doubt existed in his mind that Brigham Young was the prophet of the Church. Redick endured the persecutions and subsequent expulsion from Nauvoo by the mobs. In Council Bluffs, he joined the Mormon Battalion, leaving behind his wife, a daughter, and a son who was born shortly after his departure. After faithfully enduring countless hardships, Redick completed his service in the Battalion and set off to be reunited with his family. While passing the Sierra-Nevada Mountains, he and his fellow Battalion members came across the winter camp of the ill-fated Donner Party. Before reaching Council Bluffs, these men experienced terrible difficulties, having nearly starved to death while traversing through deep snow and ice-filled rivers. Redick's brother-in-law died in his arms.

In 1852, Redick was called to serve a mission in the Hawaiian Islands, where he presided over the Island of Maui until 1854, when his health began to fail, and he was advised to return home. Redick sailed to America and remained in San Francisco for a time to regain his health. He arrived in the Salt Lake Valley in July 1856 to find his family in desperate circumstances because of the loss of two successive seasons of crops. Provisions were difficult to come by, and Redick had no money. He rode through nearby settlements offering anything he had for food. He finally contacted a man who let him have corn and potatoes on credit.

A few months later, at the October general conference, Redick heard Brigham Young's call to action and willingly responded. While crossing Big Mountain, Redick's health rapidly declined as he was affected with pleurisy, an infection of the membrane surrounding the lungs. This condition made breathing severely painful. At South Pass, Redick accepted the assignment to establish a relief station and remained steadfast at his post when others faltered.[3]

17

GOD ONLY CAN UNDERSTAND WHAT WE WENT THROUGH

DEER CREEK TO ROCKY RIDGE, PLATTE RIVER BRIDGE TO RED BUTTES

WILLIE COMPANY DEER CREEK TO BASE OF ROCKY RIDGE OCTOBER 18–22, 1856

On October 18, Levi Savage noted the air was cool but fair. The company nooned at the Sweetwater and forded the river after dinner. Twelve-year-old John Oborn, traveling with his parents, Joseph and Maria, recalled: "Our scant rations had reached the point where the amount ordinarily consumed for one meal now had to suffice a full day. From here on it is beyond my power of description to write. God only can understand and realize the torture and privation, exposure and starvation that we went through. . . . During these terrible times it seemed only a matter of days before all would perish. We had resorted to the eating of anything that could be chewed, bark and leaves from trees, etc. We youngsters ate the rawhide from our boots."[1]

Fifteen-year-old George Cunningham recalled:

> The nights now began to be very cold and the feed was very poor. Our provisions were running out fast. Starvation looked us in the face. We were put on rations of six ounces of flour per day and nothing else. The old and weak began to die off, and a great many of the young and strong soon followed suit. We were several weeks on this

> small ration. They were reduced to half that amount. At last we were caught in a heavy snow storm on the Sweetwater, and the last of our flour was gone. The captain called us together, and said that all the provisions were gone, except some few crackers which he had saved for the sick and the small children. There were only one or two hundred pounds of them. He said that all hands would be treated alike; that he would kill every critter in the train before any of us should die of starvation. The weather turned to be extremely cold. Many died from the effect of want and cold, I myself have helped to bury (or partly bury, as they were only put a small distance underground—might just as well have been left open for the wolves) ten to fifteen in a single day. Our Captain intended to keep his word, and commenced to kill off the cattle, but they were nearly as poor as we were. We used to boil the bones and drink the soup and eat what little meat there was. We greedily devoured the hides also. I myself have took a piece of hide when I could get it, scorched off the hair on the fire, roasted it a little on the coals, cut it in little pieces so that I could swallow it and bolted it down my throat for supper and thought it was most delicious. Many were frozen to death. I think that there were only five or six men in camp towards the last but what were frozen. Our captain drove all he could and did his duty. He was badly frozen and came very close to dying. Some would sacrifice themselves by giving their food or perhaps some old blanket that covered them. In common cares, we cannot tell what our friends and neighbors are, but there are circumstances which undoubtedly proved them. While laboring under those trials and afflictions, I lay down one night and fell asleep. I dreamed a dream. That morning had come, the storm had subsided some and that we had started out on the road. I thought that I saw two men coming toward us on horseback. They were riding very swiftly and soon came up to us. They said that they had volunteered to come to our rescue and that they would go on further east to meet a company which was still behind us and that on the morrow, we could meet a number of wagons loaded with provisions for us. They were dressed in blue soldier overcoats and had Spanish saddles on their horses. I examined them, particularly the saddles as they were new to me. I also could discern every expression of their countenance. They seemed to rejoice and be exceedingly glad that they had come to our relief and saved us.

The following day, George Cunningham's dream was fulfilled in every detail.[2]

On October 19, the last of the flour was rationed out and all that remained was "six small beefs and 400 pounds of biscuits to provision over 400 people." The weather changed drastically, the company "encountered a very severely cold and blustering snowstorm." This storm especially affected the women and little children, and they began to suffer much. Worn-out clothing and shoes were insufficient to protect the Saints from the cold. Many began to tie rags, burlap, or canvas around their feet in the attempt to keep their shoes together and to protect their feet from the elements.[3]

ROWLEY FAMILY

Among the five deaths recorded on October 19 was twenty-eight-year-old Eliza "Ann" Rowley. Eliza's stepmother, Ann Jewell Rowley, wrote: "I watched with alarm, my stepdaughter Eliza, grow weaker each day. She was never very strong. I had always devoted a lot of love and care to her, but she passed away one day and was buried off to the side of the trail. Her long journey was at an end, but ours had a long way yet to go." It was during these most desperate of times that the sweet and tender mercies of God manifested themselves. Ann continued:

> Our handcarts were not designed for such heavy loads and we were constantly breaking down. They had been made of green lumber and were affected by the weather. Rawhide strips was used to wrap the iron rims to the wheels and the wood would shrink and the rawhide would come loose. It hurt me to see my children go hungry. I watched as they cut the loose rawhide from the cart wheels, roast off the hair, and chew the hide. There came a time, when there seemed to be no food at all. Some of the men left to hunt buffalo. Night was coming and there was no food for the evening meal. I asked God's help as I always did. I got on my knees, remembering two hard sea biscuits that were still in my trunk. They had been left over from the sea voyage. They were not large, and were so hard, they couldn't be broken. Surely, that was not enough to feed 8 people, but 5 loaves and 2 fishes were not enough to feed 5,000 people either, but through a miracle, Jesus had done it. So, with God's help, nothing is impossible. I found the biscuits and put them in a dutch oven and covered them with water and asked for God's blessing, then I put the lid on the pan and set it on the coals. When I took off the lid a little

later, I found the pan filled with food. I kneeled with my family and thanked God for his goodness. That night my family had sufficient food.[4]

John Chislett recalled: "We traveled on in misery and sorrow day after day. Sometimes we made a pretty good distance, but at other times we were only able to make a few miles' progress. Finally we were overtaken by a snowstorm which the shrill wind blew furiously about us. The snow fell several inches deep as we traveled along, but we dared not stop, for we had a sixteen-mile journey to make, and short of it we could not get wood and water." They were still more than fifty miles from South Pass, where they hoped to receive the supplies they so desperately prayed were waiting for them.[5]

Express Rescue Company Finds Willie Company

While the Willie Company stopped around noon, thirteen-year-old Elizabeth "Betsey" Smith and her sister, seventeen-year-old Jane, walked over a hill to the west in search of fuel for their fire. They were met by members of the Express Rescue Company sent ahead of the Main Rescue Company five days earlier, on October 14, by George D. Grant. Joseph A. Young and Cyrus H. Wheelock were moved to tears at the sight of their condition and offered words of encouragement. Their emotions grew deeper and more heartsick as they neared the main body of the company.[6]

Near midday, John Chislett recorded: "As we were resting for a short time at noon, a light wagon was driven into our camp from the west. Its occupants were Joseph A. Young and Stephen Taylor. They informed us that a train of supplies was on the way, and we might expect to meet it in a day or two. More welcome messengers never came from the courts of glory than these two young men were to us."[7]

John Oborn wrote: "Those of you who have never had this experience cannot realize how thankful we were or how we thanked God for our rescue. Mother and I were cared for by a dear brother, who was very kind to us. He seemed like an angel form heaven."[8]

At the sight of sisters Emily and Julia Hill, Joseph A. Young was again overcome with emotion. Joseph had become acquainted with the girls in England. In conversation with Joseph, Emily questioned why he was crying. Joseph replied, "'Oh, because you look so starved and the provision wagons are a mile away.' Then, feeling in his pocket, he produced a small onion. 'Eat this,' he said. But emotion checked the feeling of hunger for the moment, and she carried the onion in her hand. Near the fire lay a man, apparently dying. To him she handed it, and he declared afterward that it had saved his life."[9]

The Express Rescue Company was traveling light and did not have anything to offer the Willie Company other than encouragement and the hope that help was nigh at hand. William Woodward noted: "An express from the relief train met us about Ice Springs on the Sweetwater valley. C.H. Wheelock, Jos. A. Young, Steve Taylor and a Bro Garr. Some of these brethren advised us to give out all the flour we had at night to our famished people. We did so. A snow fell on us that night about a foot deep. It was a sorry sight, over 400 people with hand carts, short of bedding, & to sleep on the cold ground. One thought is enough for a lifetime." Members of the Express Rescue Company continued with all haste to find the Martin Company. Little did they realize how far they would have to travel to reach them.[10]

After a short rest, the Willie Company pressed forward, reaching the Sixth Crossing of the Sweetwater after dark. John Chislett recorded: "We pursued our journey with renewed hope and after untold toil and fatigue, doubling teams frequently, going back to fetch up the straggling carts, and encouraging those who had dropped by the way to a little more exertion in view of our soon-to-be improved condition, we finally, late at night, got all to camp—the wind howling frightfully and the snow eddying around us in fitful gusts. But we had found a good camp among the willows, and after warming and partially drying ourselves before good fires, we ate our scant fare, paid our usual devotions to the Deity, and retired to rest with hopes of coming aid."[11]

Elizabeth "Betsey" Smith, who almost died of scarlet fever in Iowa City, noted the struggles experienced by her widowed mother, Marjorie McEwan Bain Smith, at this time:

> My mother was taken very sick with cramp and cholera, a very fatal trouble in our weakened condition. We all felt bad about mother. I remember thinking, "Many are dying; mother may die, and what a dark world it would be without our dear mother!" As I gathered the sage to burn on our camp-fire, I couldn't keep from crying. When I met mother, she asked me what was the matter. I told her how badly I felt. She said, 'Do not feel like that; pray for me. I have been out yonder in the snow praying to the Lord to spare our lives, that we might get through to the Valley. I will never murmur nor complain, whatever we pass through, when we get there.' God heard our prayers, and she kept her word. Even when, in years following, she went blind with age, she never murmured.[12]

On Monday, October 20, the Willie Company awoke to four inches of snow on the ground, and it continued to snow throughout the day. Levi Savage noted: "The cattle and people are so much reduced with short food and hard work that except we get assistance, we surely cannot move far in this now. Brothers Willie and [Joseph] Elder started on horseback about ten o'clock to search for the wagons that Wheelock reported a short distance in our advance. This morning we issued the last bread, or breadstuffs, in our possession."[13]

John Chislett wrote:

> Being surrounded by snow a foot deep, out of provisions, many of our people sick, and our cattle dying, it was decided that we should remain in our present camp until the supply-train reached us. It was also resolved in council that Captain Willie with one man [Joseph Elder] should go in search of the supply-train and apprise its leader of our condition, and hasten him to our help. When this was done we settled down and made our camp as comfortable as we could. As Captain Willie and his companion left for the west, many a heart was lifted in prayer for their success and speedy return. They were absent three days—three days which I shall never forget. The scanty allowance of hard bread and poor beef, distributed as described, was mostly consumed the first day by the hungry, ravenous, famished souls.[14]

James Simon Willie, grandson to James G. Willie, related the following regarding the account of his grandfather leaving camp that day in search of the Rescue Company: "When Grandfather left to get help, he said that he wouldn't be gone very long, and when he came back he would have help; the Lord wouldn't let them die where they were."[15]

John Chislett described how desperate their food situation had become:

> The morning before the storm, or, rather, the morning of the day on which it came, we issued the last ration of flour. On this fatal morning, therefore, we had none to issue. We had, however, a barrel or two of hard bread which Captain Willie had procured at Fort Laramie in view of our destitution. This was equally and fairly divided among all the company. Two of our poor broken-down cattle were killed and their carcasses issued for beef. With this we were informed that we would have to subsist until the coming supplies reached us. All that now remained in our commissary were a few pounds each of sugar and dried apples, about a quarter of a sack of rice and a small quantity possibly 20 or 25 lbs. of hard bread.[16]

John continued:

> We killed more cattle and issued the meat; but, eating it without bread, did not satisfy hunger, and to those who were suffering from dysentery it did more harm than good. This terrible disease increased rapidly amongst us during these three days, and several died from exhaustion. Before we renewed our journey the camp became so offensive and filthy that words would fail to describe its condition, and even common decency forbids the attempt. Suffice it to say that all the disgusting scenes which the reader might imagine would certainly not equal the terrible reality. It was enough to make the heavens weep. The recollection of it unmans me even now—those three days! During that time I visited the sick, the widows whose husbands died in serving them, and the aged who could not help themselves, to know for myself where to dispense the few articles that had been placed in my charge for distribution. Such craving hunger I never saw before, and may God in his mercy spare me the sight again.[17]

James Family

Nineteen-year-old Sarah James related the following:

> We were cold all the time. It was either rain, or snow, or wind. Even when you wrapped up in a blanket your teeth chattered. Father told us one night that the flour was gone and that the word was that

> we might not get help for some time. Father was white and drawn. I know that mother was worr[i]ed about him for he was getting weaker all the time and seemed to feel that there was no use in all the struggle. Mother had taken as much of the load off his shoulders as she could in pulling the cart. We girls and Ruebin [Reuben] did most of the work so that father could rest a lot. Mother didn't have much to say and I wondered if she remembered that council meeting in camp Iowa and wished that we had taken the advice of more experienced people. I'm sure that many of us had those thoughts. We were grateful one morning when we heard that the captain had ordered all the animals in the company killed so that we could have fresh meat. We were so hungry that we didn't stop to think what it would do for our wagons. How good the soup tasted made from the bones of those cows although there wasn't any fat on them. The hides we used to roast after taking all the hair off of them. I even decided to cook the tatters of my shoes and make soup of them. It brought a smile to my father's sad face when I made the suggestion but mother was a bit impatient with me and told me that I'd have to eat the muddy things myself.[18]

Linford Family

On October 21, there were four deaths in the company. Among the dead was forty-nine-year-old John Linford. In England, John and his wife, Maria, were converted to the gospel by Joseph Fielding. They were baptized in December 1842. John was a successful owner of a shoemaking business, and when his membership in the Church was discovered, customers and family members, unable to persuade John to give up his newfound religion, vowed to starve him by withholding their business. Before the way was made open for the Linford family to emigrate in 1856, they endured years of persecution. Once in America, John became ill with fever and ague in Iowa, gradually growing worse until he could no longer walk. Levi Savage, true to the promise he made to go with the company, to work with them, to suffer with them, and to help them with all he had, offered the last of his flour to John. Eleven-year-old Amasa Linford wrote: "While father was sick and just before he died of starvation, Levi Savage emptied his flour sack to make him some skilly as it was called; after eating this he died." Maria and her boys, seventeen-year-old George, fourteen-year-old Joseph and eleven-year-old Amasa continued on and were blessed with strength and courage. "Mother told me that my brother George was at times the only able bodied man in their company. The snow was lying deep on the ground, the streams of water were very cold, and the elderly women could hardly be persuaded to cross them; they said that they would rather die. George would often carry them through the water on his back."[19]

These were desperate hours for members of the Willie Company, hours that required members to reach well beyond their physical capacity to endure. It was during these hours they came to understand in great measure true Christlike love for one another as they reached out with selfless and simple acts of kindness and compassion for one another.

Margaret Caldwell wrote:

> Provisions had all been given out and used; children began crying for bread. For three days we were snowed in with these meager rations. I boiled a small piece of buffalo meat, seasoned it with salt crackers, and thickened it with a little flour, then divided it with others desperately in need of food. Two young boys on guard, remembered it for years after as being the best thing they ever ate. I was greatly blessed as my endurance and strength seemed to increase. Elizabeth, my 12 year old, had her toes frozen and because of the continuous walking had to have her toes amputated upon our arrival in Salt Lake.[20]

Nine-year-old Agnes Caldwell recalled:

> Winter came in October with eighteen inches of snow, but in spite of this we did not suffer from hunger, due to Mother's careful and frugal planning. In Iowa City Mother sold a quilt and a bedspread for the sum of twenty-four cents. With this she bought food. She had a way with Indians: she traded trinkets for dried meat, which proved to be of great help to us on the journey. Frequently it would be stormy so that a fire could not be built; then mother would allow each of us to have a piece of dried meat on a piece of bread. As food became more and more scarce and the weather colder, she would stew a little of this meat and make a delicious gravy over it. I guess the reason it tasted so good is that we were allowed only a small portion at each meal.[21]

Main Rescue Company

For days, storms passed to the right and left of the main rescue company, but on Sunday, October 19, as the company camped near the mouth of Willow Creek, it began to storm. Rescuer Harvey H. Cluff wrote: "This relief party proceeded on their journey as rapidly as possible, and in due time crossed over the South Pass without encountering any obstructions by storms or otherwise. . . . Passing over the summit, a distance of nine miles, they camped on the first crossing of Sweetwater River. Here, during the night, a heavy snow storm set in which continued during the following two days. This raging blizzard from the north compelled the relief party to seek shelter some miles down the river where the growth of willows was dense enough to break the force of the wind and afford shelter to animals and some protection to the camp." Had this rescue company known Captain James G. Willie and Joseph B. Elder were making an ascent up and over Rocky Ridge during this storm, they would have pressed forward with all haste.[22]

Of this experience, Harvey H. Cluff wrote:

> Quietly resting in the seclusion of the willow copse, three miles from the road, I volunteered to take a sign board and place it at a conspicuous place at the main road. This was designed to direct the express party who was expected to return about this time. So they would not miss us. In facing the northern blast up hill I found it quite difficult to keep from freezing. I had only been back to camp a short time when two men rode up from Willie's handcart company. The signboard had done the work of salvation. Had Captain Willie and his fellow traveler [Joseph Elder], from his company, continued on the road they certainly would have perished as they would have reached the Sweetwater where the storm first struck us. The handcart company was then 25 miles from our camp, and as they had traveled that distance without food for themselves or horses and no bedding, they must have perished. I have always regarded this act of mine as the means of their salvation. And why not? An act of that importance is worthy of record and hence I give a place here.[23]

Harvey continued:

> Preparations were made and early in the morning of the following day we were on the road pushing our way for Captain Willie's

> camp. The depth of snow made traveling extremely difficult and the whole day was spent before we reached camp. It was about sunset when we came in sight of the camp; which greatly resembled an Eskimo Village fully one mile away. The snow being a foot deep and paths having been made from tent to tent gave the camp that appearance. As we reached an eminence overlooking the camp, which was located on a sagebrush plain near the river a mile away. When the people of the camp sighted us approaching, they set up such a shout as to echo through the hills.[24]

Main Rescue Company Reaches Willie Company

Of the arrival of the Main Rescue Company, John Chislett recorded:

> On the evening of the third day after Captain Willie's departure, just as the sun was sinking beautifully behind the distant hills, on an eminence immediately west of our camp several covered wagons, each drawn by four horses, were seen coming towards us. The news ran through the camp like wildfire, and all who were able to leave their beds turned out en masse to see them. A few minutes brought them sufficiently near to reveal our faithful captain slightly in advance of the train. Shouts of joy rent the air; strong men wept till tears ran freely down their furrowed and sun-burnt cheeks, and little children partook of the joy which some of them hardly understood, and fairly danced around with gladness. Restraint was set aside in the general rejoicing, and as the brethren entered our camp the sisters fell upon them and deluged them with kisses. The brethren were so overcome that they could not for some time utter a word, but in choking silenced repressed all demonstration of those emotions that evidently mastered them. Soon, however feeling was somewhat abated, and such a shaking of hands, such words of welcome, and such invocation of God's blessing have seldom been witnessed.[25]

John continued: "Among the brethren who came to our succour were elders W. H. Kimball and G. D. Grant. They had remained but a few days in the Valley before starting back to meet us. May God ever bless them for their generous, unselfish kindness and their manly fortitude! They felt that they had, in a great measure, contributed to our sad position; but how nobly, how faithfully, how bravely they worked to bring us safely to the Valley—to the Zion of our hopes!"[26]

Harvey H. Cluff described:

> Arriving within the confines of this emigrant camp a most thrilling and touching scene was enacted, melting to tears the stoutest hearts. . . . This was certainly the most timely arrival of a relief party recorded in history for the salvation of a people. Five hundred people with handcarts a scanty supply of clothing, bedding and less supply of provision, upon the plains in snow ten inches deep. The limited supply of food ordinarily would be very small, and of this limited supply scarcely a bite of substantial of food was left in camp. Think of it ye mountaineers. Four hundred miles from any possible supply of provisions. You no longer wonder at the joy manifested by that perishing people when they saw salvation pull into their camp. Twenty odd wagons drawn by four animals to each and each wagon loaded into the bows with vegetables, meat, flour, groceries, clothing for both sexes, and bedding and footwear. To give an idea of the critical conditions of those people I will say that our camp was pitched about fifty yards from the tents of the emigrants and each meal was over in our camp and the bones and crumbs from our meals were thrown out on the snow, young men would gather them up knaw and suck them as long as they gathered any substance.[27]

Words completely fail to describe the appalling conditions in which the rescuers found the Willie Company. The extent of the suffering they had experienced, and for that matter, the extent to which they would continue to experience, it was more than they could have ever possibly imagined. It is sufficient to say that it was enough to make the heavens weep. Immediately the rescuers rendered all the help they possibly could. They gathered wood, built large fires, and distributed flour, potatoes, onions, warm clothing, quilts, blankets, buffalo robes, and woolen socks.

That evening, John Chislett recorded: "For the first time in quite a period, the songs of Zion were to be heard in the camp, and peals of laughter issued from the little knots of people as they chatted around the fires. The change seemed almost miraculous, so sudden was it from grave to gay, from sorrow to gladness, form mourning to rejoicing. With the cravings of hunger satisfied, and with hearts filled with gratitude to God and our good brethren, we all united in prayer, and then retired to rest."[28]

John continued: "The next morning the small company which came to our relief divided; one half, under G. D. Grant, going east to meet Martin's company, and the other half, under W. H. Kimball, remaining with us. From this point until we reached the Valley, W. H. Kimball took full charge of us." Of the wagons in this Rescue Company, six remained with the Willie Company and eight continued east, bound for the Martin Company. James Simon Willie, grandson to James G. Willie, related the following regarding the account of his grandfather's concern for the Martin Company: "Grandfather told them [the rescuers] to give them just as little as they could and go on, taking what was needed to the Martin Handcart Company who were worse off than they were." Harvey H. Cluff recorded: "Six four-mule teams, well loaded with clothing and provisions, were left with Captain Willie's company, and the rest of the relief party pushed on as rapidly as possible, deeply impressed with what had already been witnessed that the other hand-cart companies were in a much worse condition than the one already passed."[29]

The Willie Company, under the direction of William H. Kimball, resumed their westward journey, traveling eleven miles and then camping on the Sweetwater at the base of Rocky Ridge, where many slept directly on the ground with only a blanket to protect them from the elements. John Chislett recorded: "The weather grew colder each day, and many got their feet so badly frozen that they could not walk, and had to be lifted from place to place. Some got their fingers frozen; others their ears; and one woman lost her sight by the frost. These severities of the weather also increased our number of deaths, so that we buried several each day."[30]

Martin Company
Platte River Bridge to Red Buttes
October 19–22, 1856

The Martin Company reached the last crossing of the Platte River on Sunday, October 19, nine days behind the Willie Company. John Jaques noted the company "crossed the Platte for the last time at Red Buttes, about 5 miles above the bridge. . . . That was a bitter cold day. Winter came on all at once, and that was the first day of it. The river was wide, the current strong, the water exceedingly cold and up to the wagon beds in the deepest parts, and the bed of the river was covered with cobble stones. Some of the men carried some of the women on their backs or in their arms, but others of the women tied up their skirts and waded through, like heroines as they were, and as they had done through many other rivers and creeks."[31]

On this bitterly cold day in October, John Bond of the Hodgett Wagon Company recorded:

> Arriving at the river at noon Oct. 19th and camp on the west side of the river near to the same. Here I was detailed to herd the cattle while my sisters made dinner ready. While herding it commenced to rain and then the rain turned to sleet while the air commenced to get colder just as the courageous Hand-cart Saints arrived at the opposite side of the river. . . . Here the weaker ones pleaded to the captain to unload one of the wagons and haul them over the river as they could not stand the cold water in their condition, the water running so rapid in their weak condition. The weak ones still begging and [w]ringing their hands in tears and shivering with cold.

True to the strength of their character, John Bond recalled, twenty-one-year-old John Laty, nineteen-year-old George H. Haines, fourteen-year-old George Dove of the Hodgett Wagon Company, and thirty-three-year-old Thomas J. Franklin and forty-three-year-old John Toone of the Martin Company, and others, exhausted themselves as they carried the weaker members of the company across the icy river on their backs. "Those noble heroes went backward and forward several times carrying them on their backs, the weaker ones, which is worthy of commendation for their kindheartedness and worthy to be handed down to future generations."[32]

McBride Family

Although he had been struggling with his health since Florence, Robert McBride was among the stalwart men blessed with the strength, fortitude, and courage to make several trips across the river, saving the lives of many members of the company. His son Peter wrote: "He had worked all day pulling, pushing, wading through the icy river, and he made about twenty-five trips across the river helping to get all the people and carts across."[33]

Loader Family

Just prior to the river crossing, Amy Britnell Loader, who had lost her husband three weeks prior, spent some time visiting acquaintances in the Hodgett Wagon Company. She visited with Ann Ballan, who selflessly gave her some bread and molasses. She also visited with Nathan Porter, a returning missionary from England, whom her daughters Patience and Maria cared for while he was recovering from an illness in New York. When Nathan learned of James Loader's death, he volunteered to carry the family members across the river on his mule and then pull the handcart across for them. Patience Loader recorded:

> This we did not know that he intended doing so we started to cross the river and pull our own cart. The water was deep and very cold and we was drifted out of the regular crossing and we came near being drowned. The water came up to our arm pits. Poor mother was standing on the bank screaming, as we got near the bank I heard Mother say, "For God's sake some of you men help my poor girls." Mother said she had been watching us and could see we was drifting down the stream. Several of the brethren came down the bank of the river and pulled our cart up for us and we got up the best we could. Mother was there to meet us, her clothing was dry but ours was wet and cold and very soon frozen. Mother took one of her under skirts and put on one of us and her apron for another to keep the wet cloth from us for we had to travel several miles before we could camp. Here Mother took out from her apron the bread and molasses Sister Ballen gave her for us. She broke in pieces and gave each some. This was a great treat to us and we [were] all hungry. It seemed to give us new strength to travel on.[34]

Late in the afternoon on October 19, Josiah Rogerson crossed the river twice, and

> had to dodge in his wadings large cakes of mush-snow and ice—not a presage, but proof of the fact that the snowstorms had been ahead of us for several days in its headwaters and tributaries. The water was cold, indeed, and to numbers of our young women and middle-aged

> mothers and matrons, it proved a fatal crossing in the death of many and the ruining of the health of as many more, from which they never afterward recovered. . . . There were wet feet and soaked shoes and socks with the men, but many times worse the soaked skirts, dresses and underclothing of our sisters and mothers. We gave little care for the crossing of the main Platte river several times previous, and other streams during the warm weather, but this crossing has been remembered vividly by all from that day to the present.[35]

Sixteen-year-old Margaret Ann Griffith recorded: "I shall never forget the last time we crossed the Platte River. . . . Captain Jesse Haven's Company of wagons that traveled with us most of the way, brought their teams and took most of the women and children across and also the feeble men, my father among them; for he was so affected with rheumatism that he could not walk."[36]

John Jaques wrote: "The company was barely over when snow, hail and sleet began to fall, accompanied by piercing north wind, and camp was made on this side of the river. . . . That was a stinging night, and it told its tale on the oxen as well as on the people." The same storm that hit the Willie Company after passing Ice Springs also hit members of the Martin Company as they were still soaking wet and chilled to the bone from crossing the Platte River. The cold wind instantly froze their wet clothing. Because of the decision to lighten their load just two days before, they didn't have much left to alleviate their suffering.[37]

Patience Loader recalled:

> We had to travel in our wet clothes until we got to camp and our clothing was frozen on us and when we got to camp we had but very little dry clothing to put on. We had to make the best of our poor circumstances and put our trust in God our father that we may take no harm from our wet clothes. It was too late to go for wood and water, the wood was too far away. That night the ground was frozen to hard, we was unable to drive any tent pins in as the tent was wet when we took it down in the morning it was somewhat frozen so we stretched it open the best we could and got in under it until morning. Then the bugle sounded early in the morning for us to travel seven miles as we could not get any wood to make a fire. There was snow on the ground.[38]

Patience continued:

> [W]e had a good many sick people, more than could ride in the sick wagon, so Captain Martin appointed Brother [Waugh] to take charge of the invalids. . . . It was a terrible day. It snowed and drifted and the wind blew all day. We traveled seven miles and when we camped there was no sign of Brother [Waugh] and his sick brethren. Then captain Martin called for some of the brethren to go back and find the company of invalids and when it was getting dark they returned bringing nineteen, all frozen. I never knew if that was all that started out in the morning or not.[39]

Upon their arrival in camp, Patience and her sister Maria found they had to go a long way to find wood:

> We had to travel in the snow knee deep for nearly a mile to the cedars. We found nothing but green cedar, as all the dry wood on the ground was covered with snow. I asked one of the brethren to cut me down a shoulder stick, so he kindly gave us quite a large, heavy log. My sister took one end on her shoulder and I raised the other end to my shoulder and we started back to camp. We had not gone far when we both fell down with our load. The snow being so deep made it very hard work for us to get back to camp with our load, but after much hard work we got there. . . . As soon as I could get some wood chopped, I tried to make a fire and cook a little broth, as I had an old beef's head. I was always on the lookout for anything I could get to eat, not only for myself but for the rest of my family. We got off the skin from the beef head and chopped it in pieces the best I could, put it into the pot with some snow and boiled it for a long time. About four o'clock in the afternoon we were able to have some fine made broth. I cannot say that it tasted very good but it was flavored both with sage brush and from the smoky fire from the green cedar fire. So after it was cooked we all enjoyed it and felt very thankful to have that much. . . . We young folks had drank our broth my mother was still drinking hers the captain of the company came with two other brethren and fetched poor brother John Laurey to our tent since my poor father died this brother had staid in our tent as he had no friends with him, he was alone he was one of the poor invalids that was lost. Brother Toone said to Mother give him something warm. . . . We tried to give him a little [soup] with a teaspoon but we could not get the spoon between his teeth, poor dear man. He looked at us but could not speak a word. He was nearly

> dead frozen. [I]t got dark we rapped him up the best we could to try to get warm but he was too far gone. . . . He commenced to talk to himself, he called for his wife and children he had previously told me that he had a wife and nine children in London and that they would come out as soon as he could make money enough to send for them he said he was counseled to come to this country first and leave his family in England for a time. He was told that he could earn more money in this country than in England. He was a Tailor by trade and had never been accustomed to working outdoors. . . . In the night we could not hear him talking any more. I said to mother I think poor brother is dead. I have not heard him for the last hour. Mother asked me to get up and go to him. I got up but everything in the tent seemed so silent and then was such a sad feeling came over me it was so dark and dreary that I said to mother I cannot go to him. She said well get back in bed and try to get warm and wait until day light. Of course we did not sleep early as it was a little light I got up and went to the poor man found him dead frozen to the tent as I turned him over to look in his face never can I forget that sight. . . . We wrapped him in his own little blanket and the brethren came and took him away to bury him with eighteen more that had died during the night.[40]

Read Family

Prior to their emigration, Samuel and Elizabeth Georgina Quilley Read resided in London. They were well off, and their children were fortunate to attend the best boarding schools. Life changed drastically following their baptisms; they were ostracized for their acceptance of the restored gospel of Jesus Christ. It was at this time that Samuel and Elizabeth decided to sell their bookstore and join with the Saints in the Salt Lake Valley. Their oldest daughter, Clara, remained behind. With their children, fifteen-year-old Alicia, fourteen-year-old Samuel, eleven-year-old Thisbe, and seven-year-old Walter, they traveled to the valley in the Martin Company. Just outside of Newton, Iowa, on August 8, Elizabeth gave permission for seven-year-old Walter to go ahead of the company with those who were driving the herd; it was his birthday. He was last seen that day sitting on the side of the road waiting for the handcart company. After a frantic search, Walter was not found, and the family decided that Elizabeth and the girls would continue forward with the company while Samuel and his son Samuel would remain behind to search. Shortly thereafter, a man by the name of Ephraim Hanks rode into the Martin Company camp; he was on his way east carrying mail. Ephraim and Captain Martin served together in the Mormon Battalion. Upon finding out about the Reads' missing son, Ephraim agreed to take a letter to Samuel. On his return, Ephraim once again stopped with the Martin Company and delivered a letter to Elizabeth from Samuel. Unfortunately, Samuel had no information on the whereabouts of Walter.[41]

As the journey became more physically demanding for the Read family, Elizabeth was blessed with the assurance that she was not on this journey alone, that God knew of her and her situation, and that He was with her. With great conviction, Elizabeth testified to her daughters: "We'll live. We'll reach the Valley. Sometimes when I can't go on at all, sometimes when it seems that I can't pull another step, I feel someone beside me taking the load from me. I look around, wondering if I have been dreaming and if Pa is by my side. But he isn't. Nobody that we can see with our earthly eyes is there. It is the spirit of God between the shafts."[42]

At the last crossing of the Platte, Elizabeth instructed her daughters to get in the handcart and she would pull them across the river. At this time, Captain Martin volunteered to take the girls across for her. Captain Martin took Alicia first, while Thisbe waited for his return.

> There were cakes of mush ice floating in the stream, and one poor man had sunk down on a sandbar in the middle of the river. Too weak to rise he sat there with the water milling around his shoulders while a woman waded out, helped him to his feet and half carried him forward. Thisbe recognized the woman—Sister Leavitt—so the man, half curtained from her by the flying snow, must be poor Brother Horrocks, Sister Leavitt's brother-in-law. Sister Horrocks would be pulling the handcart with the three children on top of it. . . . Thisbe's eyes were attracted back to the river by a shout of alarm. There was a cart half overturned in the river. It was Ma's cart. She was doing her best to right it. Without hesitation Thisbe waded into the river, shoes, and all. She put her shoulder under the load, though the cold water lapped her face, cutting her breath off in a way

> that terrified her. Ma gave a great pull, someone else came quickly to help, and the cart was right side up again and climbing the far bank.

Elizabeth and Thisbe exited the river chilled to the bone. Elizabeth did her best to warm Thisbe, but she remained chilled and was hauled in the handcart until she regained strength. Elizabeth later recorded: "My dear children, we have suffered beyond anything you can imagine. We have seen our comrades weaken and die and be buried in trenches of snow. But in all this suffering we have come face to face with God. It was God who upheld us when our weary bodies would have given up the ghost. It was God who preserved Thisbe to us when it seemed that she would never live. Yes, my children, for the first time in my life I know God. I know that He hears our prayers, and that in his wisdom all is for the best."[43]

JACKSON FAMILY

Shortly after leaving Fort Laramie, Aaron Jackson became sick. Aaron was traveling with his wife, Elizabeth Horrocks, and their three children (seven-year-old Martha Ann, four-year-old Mary Elizabeth, two-year-old Aaron), and his nineteen-year-old sister-in-law, Mary Horrocks. Elizabeth described:

> During the time of leaving Laramie and reaching the Platte, my husband had been taken sick. He was afflicted with mountain fever. His appetite was good and he could eat more than his rations. But his ambition was gone. All attempts to arouse him to energy or much active exertion were futile. On the 19th of Oct. the last crossing of the Platte River was reached; but when we went into camp that noon day my husband was not there. Two of the company went back to look for him. They found him sitting by the roadside, resting. He was very weak. They assisted him into camp. When we resumed our journey he was put into a wagon, and rode a few miles to the bank of the river, when it was discovered that the teams had become so weak they were unable to haul the freight across the stream, so my husband was compelled to alight. . . . Some of the men carried some of the women on their backs or in their arms, but others of the women tied up their skirts and waded through, like the heroines that they were, and as they had gone thru many other rivers and creeks. My husband attempted to ford the stream. He had only gone a short distance when he reached a sand bar in the river on which he sank

down through weakness and exhaustion. My sister, Mary Horrocks Leavitt, waded through the water to his assistance. She raised him up to his feet. Shortly afterward, a man came along on horseback and conveyed him to the other side of the river, placed him on the bank and left him there. My sister then helped me to pull my cart with my three children and other matters on it. We had scarcely crossed the river when we were visited with a tremendous storm of snow, hail, sand and fierce winds. It was a terrible storm from which both the people and teams suffered. After crossing the river, my husband was put on a hand cart and hauled into camp; and indeed after that time he was unable to walk, and consequently provision had to be made for him to ride in a wagon. . . . As soon as possible after reaching camp I prepared a little of such scant articles of food as we then had. He tried to eat but failed. He had not the strength to swallow. I put him to bed as quickly as I could. He seemed to rest easy and fell asleep. About nine o'clock I retired. Bedding had become very scarce, so I did not disrobe. I slept until, as it appeared to me, about midnight. I was extremely cold. The weather was bitter. I listened to hear if my husband breathed—he lay so still. I could not hear him. I became alarmed. I put my hand on his body, when to my horror I discovered that my worst fears were confirmed. My husband was dead. He was cold and stiff—rigid in the arms of death. It was a bitter freezing night and the elements had sealed up his mortal frame. I called for help to the other inmates of the tent. They could render me no aid; and there was no alternative but to remain alone by the side of the corpse till morning. The night was enveloped in almost Egyptian darkness. There was nothing with which to produce a light or kindle a fire. Of course I could not sleep. I could only watch, wait, and pray for the dawn. But oh, how those dreary hours drew their tedious length along. When daylight came, some of the male part of the company prepared the body for burial. And oh, such a burial and funeral service. They did not remove his clothing—but he had but little. They wrapped him in a blanket and placed him in a pile with thirteen others who had died, and then covered him up in the snow. The ground was frozen so hard that they could not dig a grave. He was left there to sleep in peace until the trump of the Lord shall sound, and the dead in Christ shall awake and come forth in the morning of the first resurrection. We shall then again unite our hearts and lives, and eternity will furnish us with life forever more. I will not attempt to describe my feelings at finding myself thus left a widow with three children, under such excruciating circumstances. I

> cannot do it. But I believe the Recording Angel has inscribed in the archives above, and that my sufferings for the Gospel's sake will be sanctified unto me for my good. My sister Mary was the only relative I had to whom I could look for assistance in this trying ordeal, and she was sick. So severe was her affliction that she became deranged in her mind, and for several days she ate nothing but hard frozen snow. I could therefore appeal to the Lord alone; He who had promised to be a husband to the widow, and a father to the fatherless. I appealed to him and he came to my aid.[44]

On the evening of October 19, Josiah Rogerson woke at midnight to go on guard. He recalled: "It was one of the bitter cold, black frost nights, near the Black hills and, notwithstanding the hard journey the day before, I was awakened at midnight to go on guard again till 6 or 7 in the morning." On his way out of the tent, he accidentally stumbled on the feet of a fellow member of the tent. Josiah reached down and felt the stiff, cold face of Aaron Jackson. He did not wake Elizabeth but rather whispered the news to his mother. Earlier that day, Josiah was assigned to wheel Aaron in a handcart to camp after crossing the river. After putting up the tent, Josiah assisted Elizabeth in laying him in his blankets in the tent. Josiah describes returning to the tent after guard duty:

> Returning to my tent from the night's guarding, I found there in one of the most touching pictures of grief and bereavement in the annals of our journey. Mrs. Jackson, apparently but just awakened from her slumber, was sitting by the side of her dead husband; her face was suffused in tears, and between her bursts of grief and wails of sorrow, would wring her hands and tear her beautiful head of hair; her children blending their cries of "Father" with that of the mother. This was love, this was affection; grief of the heart and bereavement, the like of which I have never seen since. . . . Aaron's demise was not the only one by a half dozen that night.[45]

McBride Family

On October 20, the Martin Company awoke to four or five inches of wet, heavy snow. Robert McBride's strength had given out, and he could hardly sit up in the tent. He had spent the previous day assisting others across the Platte River. Because of his condition,

Robert's son Heber had no choice but to get him into one of the sick wagons. After arriving in camp that evening, Janetta and Heber went to look for their father, but the deep snow and the fierce winds made it impossible for them to find him. On the morning of October 21, while Janetta was preparing a meager breakfast, Heber went again to look for his father. By now the snow was about eighteen inches deep, and it was terribly cold. Heber found his father lying dead under a wagon. Of this experience, Heber wrote:

> I felt as though my heart would burst as I sat down beside him on the snow and took his hand in mine and cried Oh, Father, Father. There we was away out on the plains with hardly anything to eat and father dead and mother sick and a widow with five small children and not hardly able to live from day to another. After I had my cry out, I went back to the tent and told my mother and the children. Now to try to write to tell the feelings of Mother and the other children is out of the question. Now we were not all the family that was called upon to mourn the loss of a father this morning, for there was 13 men dead in camp. The men that was able to anything cleaned of[f] the snow and made a fire and thawed out the ground and dug a big hole and buried them all in one grave, some side by side and on top of one another any way to get them covered for I can as[s]ure you that the men had no heart to do any more than they had to. We never knew how Father died, weather he died in the wagon and was lifted out or he got out himself and fell down exhausted and froze to death.[46]

Josiah Rogerson recalled:

> The wind blew and the snow fell and beat in our faces all the time while making only four or five miles. As we tugged and pulled our carts the snow stuck and rolled up on the tires two and three inches deep, the ground having been quite dry before the snow fell. While it thawed some today as the snow fell, it must have been six or eight inches deep this afternoon when we camped. The next day, Tuesday, October 21, we made another four or five miles with the wind and snow falling and beating in our faces, and on Wednesday, October 22, I do not remember traveling, as the last two days' pulling in the snow had wilted and downed the best and strongest of our company.[47]

Samuel Openshaw noted:

> We now seeing the storms increasing upon us in the midst of an inclement and howling desert far away from an[y] human succor and having only a few days rations in the camp, summoned all our strength and efforts to make another move, but our oxen having died off and our strength being very much reduced—the snow, cold, and the blasting winds, it seemed impossible for us to travel, in fact, we were traveling all day, cold, hungry, and fatigued, and only traveled about 5 miles. We put up our tents and then shoveled out the snow and put it around the bottom of the tent in order to keep out the winds and to make ourselves somewhat comfortable. We continued here for several days.[48]

18

SEEMINGLY INSURMOUNTABLE ODDS

Rocky Ridge to Green River, Red Buttes to Avenue Hill, South Pass, Devil's Gate, Salt Lake Valley

Willie Company
Rocky Ridge to Green River
October 23–29, 1856

On the morning of October 23, the Willie Company was camped at the base of Rocky Ridge. Even under the best of conditions, the climb up the steep and rugged terrain was treacherous. On this October morning, the weather was extreme in its severity with the snow eighteen inches deep and the cold winds blew fiercely and pierced through their clothes. The Willie Company would make this climb under seemingly insurmountable odds in their already weakened condition. Once the emigrants reached the summit of Rocky Ridge, the difficulties were not over. They still had to cross three small creeks and Strawberry Creek before descending into their next campsite at Rock Creek Hollow. For many, this part of the journey was more than their bodies could endure.[1]

James Family

About nine o'clock in the morning, as the Willie Company made their climb up Rocky Ridge, forty-six-year-old William James and his fourteen-year-old son, Reuben, remained behind to finish their duty of burying the dead. William suffered from rheumatism and struggled with his health. His wife, Jane, and several of his children had been pulling the handcart for some time. Sixteen-year-old Emma James recalled:

> The day we reached the last crossing of the Sweetwater River I will never forget as long as I live. It was a bitter cold morning in October as we broke camp. As usual there were dead to be buried before we could go on. Father and R[e]uben were with the burial detail. Mother who was helping to pull the heaviest cart had stayed behind until they could finish their sad work. After a short service we with light cart went ahead to catch the rest of the company and mother and Reuben started to follow. Father collapsed and fell in the snow. He tried two or three times to get up with mother's help then finally he asked her to go on and when he felt rested he would come on with R[e]uben. Mother knew in her heart that he had given out but perhaps she said in a few minutes with some rest he could come on. She took the cart and hurried to follow us.

Eleven-year-old Mary Ann recalled: "Mother was placed in an awful position, her husband unable to go farther, and her little children far ahead hungry and freezing; what can she do? Father said, 'Go to the children; we will get in if we can.'"[2]

Jane James took the handcart and rushed to catch up to her children. Nineteen-year-old Sarah recalled: "She found us on the river bank. We were too frightened and tired to cross alone. We had forded this river before many times, but it had never seemed so far across. It was about 40 feet, I guess, to the other bank. Mother soon had us on our way. The water was icy, and soon our clothing was frozen to our bodies. Our feet were frozen numb. Cold and miserable, we reached the other bank, put on dry clothing, and joined the rest of the company."[3]

John Chislett recorded:

> A few days of bright freezing weather were succeeded by another snow-storm. The day we crossed the Rocky Ridge it was snowing a little—the wind hard from the north-west-and blowing so keenly that it almost pierced us through. We had to wrap ourselves closely in blankets, quilts, or whatever else we could get, to keep from freezing. Captain Willie still attended to the details of the company's

traveling, and this day he appointed me to bring up the rear. My duty was to stay behind everything and that nobody was left along the road. I had to bury a man who had died in my hundred, and I finished doing so after the company had started. In about half an hour, I set out on foot alone to do my duty as rear-guard to the camp. The ascent of the ridge commences soon after leaving camp, and I had not gone far up it before I overtook a cart that the folks could not pull through the snow, here about knee-deep. I helped them along, and we soon overtook another. By all hands getting to one cart we could travel; so we moved one of the carts a few rods, and then went back and brought up the other. After moving in this way for a while, we overtook other carts at different points of the hill, until we had six carts, not one of which could be moved by the parties owning it. I put our collective strength to three carts at a time, took them a short distance, and then brought up the other three. Thus by traveling over the hill three times—twice forward and once back—I succeeded after hours of toil in bringing my little company to the summit. The six carts were then trotted on gaily downhill, the intense cold stirring us to action. One or two parties who were with these carts gave up entirely, and but for the fact that we overtook one of our ox-teams that had been detained on the road, they must have perished on that Rocky Ridge. One old man named James (a farm-laborer from Glouchestershire), who had a large family, and who had worked very hard all the way, I found sitting by the roadside unable to pull his cart any farther. I could not get him into the wagon, as it was already overcrowded. He had a shotgun which he had brought from England, and which had been a great blessing to him and his family, for he was a good shot, and often had a mess of sage hens or rabbits for his family. I took the gun from the cart, put a small bundle on the end of it, placed it on his shoulder, and started him out with his little boy, twelve years old. His wife and two daughters older than the boy took the cart alone finely after reaching the summit. . . . We traveled along with the ox-team and overtook others, all so laden with the sick and helpless that they moved very slowly. The oxen had almost given out. Some of our folks with carts went ahead of the teams, for where the roads were good they could out-travel oxen; but we constantly overtook some stragglers, some with carts, some without, who had been unable to keep pace with the body of the company. We struggled along in this weary way until after dark, and by this time our "rear" numbered three wagons, eight handcarts, and nearly 40 persons. With the wagons were Millen Atwood, Levi Savage, and

William Woodward, captains of hundreds, faithful men who had worked hard all the way.[4]

John's account continued:

We finally came to a stream of water which was frozen over [Strawberry Creek]. We could not see where the company had crossed. If at the point where we struck the creek, then it had frozen over since we passed it. We started one team to cross, but the oxen broke through the ice and would not go over. No amount of shouting and whipping could induce them to stir an inch. We were afraid to try the other teams, for even should they cross we could not leave one in the creek and go on. There was no wood in the vicinity, so we could make no fire, and were uncertain what to do. We did not know the distance to the camp, but supposed it to be three or four miles. After consulting about it, we resolved that someone should go on foot to the camp to inform the captain of our situation. I was selected to perform the duty, and I set out with all speed. In crossing the creek I slipped through the ice and got my feet wet, my boots being nearly worn out. I had not gone far when I saw someone sitting by the roadside. I stopped to see who it was, and discovered the old man James and his little boy. The poor man was quite worn out. I got him to his feet and had him lean on me, and he walked a little distance, but not very far. I partly dragged, partly carried him a short distance farther, but he was quite helpless, and my strength failed me. Being obliged to leave him to go forward on my own errand, I put down a quilt I had wrapped around me, rolled him in it, and told the little boy to walk up and down by his father, and on no account to sit down, or he would be frozen to death. I told him to watch for teams that would come back, and to hail them when they came. This done I again set out for the camp, running nearly all the way and frequently falling down, for there were many obstructions and holes in the road. My boots were frozen stiff, so that I had not the free use of my feet, and it was only by rapid motion that I kept them from being badly frozen. As it was, both were nipped. After some time I came in sight of the campfires, which encouraged me. As I neared the camp I frequently overtook stragglers on foot, all pressing forward slowly. I stopped to speak to each one, cautioning them all against resting, as they would surely freeze to death. Finally, about 11 p.m., I reached the camp almost exhausted. I had exerted myself very much during the day in bringing the rear carts up the ridge, and had not eaten anything since breakfast. I reported to Captains Willie and Kimball the

> situation of the folks behind. They immediately got up some horses, and the boys from the Valley started back about midnight to help the ox-teams in. The night was very severe and many of the emigrants were frozen. It was 5 a.m. before the last team reached the camp. I told my companions about [William] James and his little boy. They found the little fellow keeping faithful watch over his father, who lay sleeping in my quilt just as I left him. They lifted [his father] into a wagon, still alive, but in sort of stupor. He died before morning. His last words were an enquiry as to the safety of his shot-gun.[5]

Throughout the night, Jane James and her children were up waiting for word of William and Reuben. Toward morning, as the last of the company reached camp, Jane received word of the condition of William, who was dead, and Reuben, who was badly frozen. Emma James recorded: "I can see my mother's face as she sat looking at the partly conscious Ruebin [Reuben]. Her eyes looked so dead that I was afraid. She didn't sit long however for my mother was never one to cry. When it was time to move out Mother had her family ready to go. She put her invalid son in the cart with her baby and we joined the train. Our mother was a strong woman and she would see us through anything." In tribute to her mother, Mary Ann James writes: "Imagine, if you can, my mother only a young woman of forty-one, her husband lying dead in a frozen wilderness, with seven little children, starved and freezing, crying for comfort. Her physical and mental endurance was surely nothing short of miraculous." This was the second terrible loss for Jane, as she had already buried her infant daughter in a watery grave while on board the *Thornton*.[6]

John Chislett, Millen Atwood, Levi Savage, William Woodward, and nameless others were up all night in attempts to ensure the safe arrival of all members of the Willie Company into the Rock Creek Hollow camp. They worked themselves near complete exhaustion, remaining determined to do all in their power to alleviate the members' suffering. These men should be noted among the stalwart unsung heroes of the company who were blessed with strength and courage beyond their natural abilities. They were also blessed with love and compassion for their fellow men, which saved the lives of countless Saints that fateful night.[7]

Andrew Smith

Nineteen-year-old Andrew Smith was also an unsung hero that night. He was traveling with his future father-in-law, fifty-seven-year-old Joseph McKay. From a young age, Andrew learned the value of hard work by herding cows, mining coal, and working in both a cotton mill and shawl factory near his home in Scotland. As a member of the Willie Company, Andrew carried additional responsibilities because of his willingness to work hard. While ascending Rocky Ridge, Joseph McKay collapsed and would have likely died were it not for Andrew, who found him and carried him over his shoulder up and over the summit. Andrew continued with this life-saving mission for others who were unable to make it up the summit on their own strength. Millen Atwood noticed his efforts and reportedly commented: "Hold on there, Andrew boy, hold on there. You've done enough, my boy. The Lord knows you've done enough!"[8]

The thought of grown men and women struggling and suffering in such a manner, some for over twenty hours, to make it up and over the summit of Rocky Ridge and into the Rock Creek Hollow campground stirs within the heart and mind emotions that words cannot adequately describe. Even more emotionally stirring are the thoughts of the young children suffering in even greater measure and degree.

Rowley Family

Three days following the death of her stepdaughter, Ann Jewell Rowley and her children struggled up Rocky Ridge.

> John being the oldest boy, had born the brunt of the hard work. I was grateful for my faith in God, for it was only through this faith, that I was able to carry on at all. I confess, it seemed at times, the Lord had deserted us. I watched John, so cold, drowsy and sick, want to lie down in his tracks, never to rise again. I had to stand helplessly while Captain Willie whipped him, to make him go on. Gladly, would I have taken the whipping myself. In traveling at night, in the frost of that altitude, Thomas' right hand froze while he was pushing on the back of the cart and when we stopped at night and his hand got warm, it swelled up, as Samuel said: "like a toad." John could finally go no farther and I felt my heart would break as I saw him laying beside the trail, waiting for the sick wagon. By the time he was picked up, his body was frozen in two places. . . . However, the Lord

> had not deserted us and I was ashamed for thinking for a moment, he had.[9]

Kirkwood Family

Eleven-year-old James Kirkwood was traveling to the Salt Lake Valley with his forty-six-year-old widowed mother, Margaret Campbell Kirkwood, and brothers: twenty-two-year-old Robert, nineteen-year-old Thomas, and four-year-old Joseph. The Kirkwood family joined the Church in Scotland in 1848. When emigrating in 1856, Margaret left behind the graves of her daughters Margaret, Ellen, and Catherine and of her husband, who died in December 1852. In Iowa, Margaret and her son Robert pulled the handcart containing Thomas, who was crippled, and their meager belongings. James had responsibility for his younger brother Joseph. While pulling the handcart up Rocky Ridge, one of Margaret's eyes froze, causing her to lose her sight. Sometime during the night, James and his four-year-old brother, Joseph, fell behind the main group. While no one knows the exact details of what took place between these two young boys as they struggled to make it into the Rock Creek Hollow campground, one can only imagine what they were called upon to endure. Rock Creek Hollow became James's final resting place. Carrying Joseph into camp, James placed Joseph down by the fire and died shortly thereafter from overexertion and exposure to the elements.[10]

Bodil Mortensen & Nielson Family

Nine-year-old Bodil Mortensen of Denmark was traveling to the Salt Lake Valley with family friends Jens and Elsie Rasmussen Nielson and their five-year-old son, Niels "Jens", whom Bodil was given responsibility. Although Jens and Elsie had money from the sale of their property and possessions to travel comfortably by wagon, they chose to selflessly part with their means and travel by handcart. While ascending Rocky Ridge, Jens Sr.'s feet became so frozen that they became useless. He was unable to pull the handcart any further. He pled with Elsie to leave him on the trail in the snow to die, begging her to go forward and save her life. With all the tender emotions of a loving and devoted wife, Elsie replied: "Get in the cart and ride, I can't leave you, I can pull the cart." With her petite frame of less than five feet, Elsie pulled Jens in the handcart while Bodil and Niels "Jens" trudged behind through the blinding snow. As they arrived at Rock Creek Hollow, Bodil must have been asked to collect some fuel for the fire. She obediently set out to fulfill her responsibility but never returned. Bodil was found the next morning, frozen to death, leaning against a handcart wheel. The sagebrush she had collected was still clutched in her hands. Five-year-old Jens also died. Jens Sr. later described his ordeal as follows: "No person can describe it, nor could it be comprehended or understood by any human living in this life, but those who were called to pass through it."[11]

Gadd Family

Eliza Chapman Gadd, who was not yet a member of the Church, had agreed to make the journey to the Salt Lake Valley with her husband to keep the family together. She had previously buried one of her two-year-old twin boys on October 4, and her husband five days later, on October 9. Eliza's ten-year-old son, Samuel, did not survive the difficulties of the night, joining his brother and father on the other side of the veil. It was during this time that Eliza also became snow blind. Her eight-year-old daughter, Mary Ann, led her by the hand while Eliza struggled to pull the handcart. In spite of the devastating losses and difficulties, Eliza continued on in great faith and courage. Seven days after her arrival in the Valley, on November 16, 1856, she was baptized.[12]

Redick N. Allred's Station
South Pass

After being stationed at South Pass for a week, Redick N. Allred received an express from William H. Kimball with news that the Willie Company had been found in deplorable condition. Redick took six teams and met the Willie Company fifteen miles below at the Rock Creek Hollow campsite. He noted: "In such a hard west wind that they could not travel facing the drifting snow even if they had been ready for duty. I found some dead and dying laying over the camp in the drifting snow that was being piled in heaps by the gale thus burying the dead."[13]

In the Rock Creek Hollow camp on the morning of October 24, John Chislett wrote: "There were so many dead and dying that it was decided to lie by for the day. In the forenoon I was appointed to go round the camp and collect the dead. I took with me two young men to assist me in the sad task, and we collected together, of all ages and both sexes, thirteen corpses, all stiffly frozen. We had a large square hole dug in which we buried these thirteen people, three or four abreast and three deep. When they did not fit in, we put one or two crosswise at the head or feet of the others. We covered them with willows and then with the earth." Among the dead, noted in the Willie Company journal on October 23, were sixty-seven-year-old James Gibb and sixty-six-year-old Chesterton Gilman. Among the dead noted the following day, on October 24, were forty-six-year-old William James, fifty-two-year-old Elizabeth Bailey, eleven-year-old James Kirkwood, ten-year-old Samuel Gadd, sixty-year-old Lars Wendin, forty-six-year-old Anne Olsen, twenty-two-year-old Ella Nilson, six-year-old Jens Nielson, nine-year-old Bodil Mortensen, forty-one-year-old Nils Anderson, and forty-one-year-old Ole Madsen. [14]

Among the dead noted in the company journal on the morning of October 25 were sixty-two-year-old Thomas Gurdlestone and twenty-two-year-old William Groves. These men were buried near the common grave at Rock Creek Hollow. The Company left Rock Creek Hollow later that morning, leaving behind sacred ground, hallowed by the suffering and sacrifices of the Willie Company. It was also recorded that sixty-four-year-old John Walters and forty-eight-year-old William Smith died that day.[15]

On October 26, the Willie Company made their way over South Pass. John Chislett described: "During the day we crowed the Sweetwater on the ice, which did not break, although our wagons were laden with sick people. The effects of our lack of food, and the terrible ordeal of the Rocky Ridge, still remained among us. Two or three died every day. At night we camped a little east by north from the South Pass, and two men in my hundred died. It devolved on me to bury them. This I did before breakfast. The effluvia from these corpses were horrible, and it is small matter for wonder that after performing the last sad offices for them I was taken sick and vomited fearfully. Many said my 'time' had come, and I was myself afraid that such was the cue, but by the blessing of God I got over it and lived." John continued: "Near South Pass we found more brethren from the Valley, with several quarters of good fat beef hanging frozen on the limbs of the trees where they were encamped. These quarters of beef were to us the handsomest pictures we ever saw. The statues of Michelangelo, or the paintings of the ancient masters, would have been to us nothing in comparison to these life-giving pictures."[16]

From October 26 to October 30, the Willie Company made their way to the Green River. Although deaths continued to occur during this time, the general health of the company improved.

Martin Company
Red Buttes
October 23–27, 1856

On October 23, as the Willie Company was ascending Rocky Ridge, the Martin Company traveled five miles, reaching Red Buttes, where they camped for the night. Josiah Rogerson noted: "Captain Martin must have taken an inventory of the physical condition of his company, and realizing our predicament, with the snow clouds still hanging around us, he must have decided not to place any more miles between us and the fort, near the Platte bridge, and the nearest source of supplies, if perchance we should be compelled to remain here for the winter."[17]

Patience Loader recalled: "What a deplorable condition we was in at that time seven hundred miles from Salt Lake and only nine days full rations that morning the bugle sounded to call us together the captain asked us if we was willing to come on four ounces of flour a day. All answered yes. We had already been reduced to half pound per day."[18]

Of the days spent at Red Buttes, John Jaques recalled:

> The next day after crossing the Platte the company moved on slowly, about 10 miles, through the snow, and camped again near the Platte and at the point where the road left it for the Sweetwater.

> It snowed three days, and the teams and many of the people were so far given out that it was deemed advisable not to proceed further for a few days, but rather to stay in camp and recruit. It was hoped that the snow and cold would prove only a foretaste of winter and would soon pass away and the weather would moderate, but that hope proved delusive. It was expected that help from Salt Lake would soon reach the company, which cheering expectation was shortly realized. In this camp the company stayed, resting and recruiting as well as could be under the circumstances, the snow remaining on the ground and the frost being very keen at nights. Here the flour fell to four ounces per day, and again, for the third and last time. . . . This was the extremity of their privations as to food, but not the end of their sufferings, for the injurious effects of their privations told upon them during the remainder of their journey and for some time after. Indeed, with some of the company relics of these effects remain, of one sort or another, to this day. In addition to the flour ration, considerable beef was killed and served to the company, as had been the case most of the journey. But the cattle had now grown so poor that there was little flesh left on them, and that little was as lean as could be. The problem was how to cook it to advantage. Stewed meats and soups were found to be bad for diarrhea and dysentery, provocative of and aggravating those diseases, of which there was considerable in the company, and to fry lean meat without an atom of fat in it or out of it was disgusting to every cook in camp. The outlook was certainly not encouraging, but it need not be supposed that the company was in despair, notwithstanding that the situation was rather desperate. O no! A hopeful and cheerful spirit pervaded the camp, and the "songs of Zion" were frequently heard at this time, though the company was in the very depths of its privations. Though the bodies of the people were worn down, their spirits were buoyant, while at the same time they had become so accustomed to looking death in the face that they seemed to have no fear of it, nor of corpses either, the bodies of the dead having become such familiar sights as to lose their ordinary thrilling influence on beholders, and to be no more thought of with repulsive aversion, nor specially and nervously avoided, than the living.[19]

The Martin Company remained at Red Buttes for six extremely difficult days with a scarcity of food and fuel. Many deaths occurred at this time. Josiah Rogerson noted: "From the day we left Fort Laramie till we reached the Buttes, there certainly wasn't a night when our deaths were less than three to six and eight, and one evening more . . . the writer remembers eighteen adults that were buried in three graves, side by side, for I assisted in the digging and the interments. . . . I shall not depict further here our sufferings, deaths and the increasing and exceeding hunger that prevailed in the camp."[20]

In spite of the grim outlook, Samuel Openshaw recalled: "After camping here several days, and all the flour in the camp nearly used up and were not able to move and about 370 miles from [Great Salt Lake] City, and it being by far the nearest to look for succor. Yet, we did not despair. We look forward for support with gleaming hope upon [our] countenances."[21]

Parkinson Family

John and Ellen Smalley Parkinson were among the first to be baptized in England in 1837. John was one of the first elders ordained by Heber C. Kimball. The Parkinsons emigrated in 1856 on board the *Horizon*. They had nine children: eighteen-year-old Samuel, sixteen-year-old Joseph, eleven-year-old Jane, nine-year-old Margaret, seven-year-old John, five-year-old Ellen, three-year-old Mary, two-year-old Esther, and their infant son, William. While in Iowa, William died. Five days later on July 25, Mary died. Although the dates were not officially documented, Esther and Joseph and parents John and Ellen also died. While at Red Buttes, Samuel left the company and returned to England, leaving Jane, Margaret, John, and Ellen as orphans.[22]

Pucell Family

Samuel and Margaret Perren Pucell were among the first to hear the gospel preached by Heber C. Kimball in England. They were also among the first to be baptized in the River Ribble in 1837. The Pucells were traveling to the valley with their four children, a daughter-in-law, and a grandson. Along the way, Margaret became ill and rode in the handcart. With the lack of food and the additional burdens he was called upon to bear, Samuel became very weak. During the river crossing, he slipped and fell, and three days later, on October 22, he died. Margaret was grief stricken and felt as though she also would die shortly. With great concern for the welfare of her children, she asked Mary Rogerson if she would care for them. Josiah Rogerson noted, "No words of mother could cheer her up, or dispel her conclusion." On October 27, five days after the death of Samuel, fifty-three-year-old Margaret died.[23]

McBride Family

Following the death of Robert McBride, the family endured unspeakable trials and challenges as they valiantly fought to survive. Sixteen-year-old Janetta took over responsibility of the family. Peter later recalled: "My mother was sick all the way over, and my sister Janetta had the worry of us children. She carried water from the river to do the cooking. Her shoes gave out, and she walked through the snow barefoot, actually leaving bloody tracks in the snow." With food rations nearly depleted, Heber wrote: "I don't know how many days we had to lay over. The snow was so deep that we could not pull our handcarts through, and there we were in a starving condition, and the oxen that pulled the wagons began dying but every one that died was devoured very quickly, and us little boys would get strips of rawhide and try and eat it. All that we could do anything with it was to crisp it in the fire and then draw a string of it through our teeth and get some of the burnt scales of[f] that way and then crisp it again and repeat the operation until we would get tired." The McBrides had early on accepted the gospel of Jesus Christ. They were poor and worked diligently for nineteen years in hopes to have enough to realize their greatest desire, joining with the Saints in the Salt Lake Valley. They willingly gave up everything for the gospel, including their reputation, their family, and their homeland, and traveled to the Salt Lake Valley under the most humble of circumstances, pulling their meager belongings in a handcart. They suffered greatly while laboring valiantly with faith and fortitude to ensure their survival. Through their courage, service, sacrifice, and love for each other, they brought the highest of honors to the family name. This in stark contrast to the comments made by Margaret's father prior to their departure of the disgrace they brought upon the family name for joining the Church.[24]

Elizabeth Horrocks Jackson

During these desperate days snowbound at Red Buttes, many members of the Martin Company were blessed with heaven-sent hope of their future rescue. Elizabeth Horrocks Jackson recalled:

> A few days after the death of my husband, the male members of the company had become reduced in number by death; and those who remained were so weak and emaciated by sickness, that on reaching the camping place at night, there were not sufficient men with strength enough to raise the poles and pitch the tents. The result was that we camped out with nothing but the vault of Heaven for a roof, and the stars for companions. The snow lay several inches deep upon the ground. The nights were bitterly cold. I sat down on a rock with one child in my lap and one on each side of me. In that condition I remained until morning. . . . It will be readily perceived that under such adverse circumstances I had become despondent. I was six or seven thousand miles from my native land, in a wild, rocky, mountain country, in a destitute condition, the ground covered with snow, the waters covered with ice, and I with three fatherless children with scarcely nothing to protect them from the merciless storms. When I retired to bed that night, being the 27th of Oct., I had a stunning revelation. In my dream, my husband stood by me and said—"Cheer up, Elizabeth, deliverance is at hand."[25]

Fifty-five-year-old John Rodwell shared with the company the dream he had: "I dreamed that it was Tuesday or Wednesday, and about noontide, as near as I could judge. I saw a mule, packed with blankets and cooking utensils, come right in the middle of our camp, as we are now followed by three Californians, wearing blue soldier overcoats, riding mules or horses. They stopped and told us of teams and relief from the valley, after which we started again on our journey." John declared with great conviction to members of the company that they all would see the dream come true.[26]

Rescue Companies
October 25–27, 1856

After assisting the Willie Company at Rock Creek Hollow, Redick N. Allred returned to South Pass with instructions from Captain George D. Grant to remain ready to assist the Martin Company when they were brought through. On October 25, two men went to the Salt Lake Valley to bring news of the condition of the Willie Company. The rest of the Rescue Company pushed on with all possible speed in search of the Martin, Hunt, and Hodgett Companies. As noted by Captain George D. Grant: "Previous to this time we had sent on an express to ascertain, if possible, the situation and whereabouts of the company yet back, and report to me. Not thinking it safe for them to go farther than Independence Rock. I advised them to wait there. When we overtook them they had heard nothing from the rear companies, and we had traveled through the snow from eight to twelve inches deep all the way from Willow Creek to this place."[27]

Devil's Gate

By Sunday, October 26, the Main Rescue Company met up with the Express Company at Devil's Gate. They had traveled more than 320 miles in nineteen days under adverse weather conditions. Robert T. Burton recorded the Main Rescue Company "found the express that had been sent on at this place, waiting further orders. Had heard nothing from the company behind."[28]

Completely exhausted, the men of this Rescue Company called upon the heavens for direction through fasting and prayer. Daniel W. Jones wrote: "Having seen the sufferings of Brother Willie's company, we more fully realized the danger the others were in. The Elders who had just returned from England having many dear friends with these companies, suffered great anxiety, some of them feeling more or less the responsibility resting upon them for allowing these people to start so late in the season across the plains. At first we were at a loss what to do for we did not expect to have to go further than Devil's Gate. We decided to make camp and send on an express to find where the people were and not to return until they were found."[29]

Solomon F. Kimball later documented:

> The boys felt no particular uneasiness concerning the Willie company, as it was in good hands and had the South Pass provisions to draw from until other arrangements could be made; but they felt alarmed concerning the other companies that had not been heard from since they were passed on the plains by the Richards' party, more than six weeks before. What a tremendous responsibility rested

> upon the shoulders of these young men, and what a picture of discouragement was here presented! Here they were, three hundred and thirteen miles from home, hemmed in on all sides by the drifting snows of an early winter, with instructions from President Brigham Young not to return until every emigrant on the plains was accounted for. They had already endured hardships greater than the ordinary individual could endure; but it was a matter of small moment compared with the work yet to be accomplished. Many trying experiences the boys had passed through during the early day settlement of Utah, but their burden, on this occasion, seemed greater to them than they could bear.[30]

The following day, on October 27, Captain George D. Grant sent an express rescue team consisting of Joseph A. Young, Abel Garr, and Daniel W. Jones ahead with instructions not to return until the companies were found. Captain George D. Grant noted: "Not having much feed for our horses, they were running down very fast, and not hearing from the companies, I did not know but what they had taken up quarters for the winter, consequently we sent on another express to the Platte bridge." Daniel W. Jones recorded: "With picked saddle horses and a pack mule we started out." The Express Team rode hard all day. The Main Rescue Company remained at Devil's Gate.[31]

Redick N. Allred's Station South Pass

Back at South Pass, Redick N. Allred's group was receiving reinforcements from the Salt Lake Valley. At the arrival of John Van Cott and Claudeus Spencer, they learned that no word had been received from the Martin, Hunt, and Hodgett Companies. Both John and Claudeus determined it was unwise to remain at South Pass under such adverse conditions and decided to return to the Salt Lake Valley. Unfortunately, they took with them several wagons filled with life-sustaining supplies. Along their return trip, they met seventy-seven wagons, all of which they persuaded to turn back to the valley as well. Redick wrote:

> Bro. Spencer tried to induce me to break up camp and return to the city. I declined his proposition, and he said he would return. I advised him to stay, for the lives of the company depended upon us

> & he then said that he moved that as I was president of the station they center their faith in me that I could get the word of the Lord to know what we must do. To this I objected as he had already said what he would do. They returned next day. I sent a letter by them to the companies on the road for them to come on as fast as the condition of their teams would allow, but [he failing to present the letter] all the companies turned back with them until they got to "Bridger" where Lewis Robinson prevailed on them to stop until he could send a messenger to President Young, the result of which was to turn them all back again with instructions to go until they met Capt. Geo. Grant.[32]

Ephraim Hanks
Salt Lake Valley

After returning to the Salt Lake Valley from delivering mail to the East, on October 25, Ephraim Hanks, one of the premier frontiersmen of the day, made his way to Utah Lake: "Hanks had contracted a load of fish for the Salt Lake market. He had driven to Utah Lake, thirty miles south, where fish were plentiful, and was staying at the home of Gerney Brown." Ephraim recalls: "This night I was down near Utah Lake where I had gone to fish. . . . I was after a load that time, not just a string for supper. Well, I was staying at Gerney Brown's place, and though the bed was comfortable enough, I could not sleep." No matter what he did or where he went, he couldn't forget about the Martin Company and kept wondering how they were getting on. Finally he did drop off to sleep

> but no sooner that I'd done it I was waked up again. Somebody said, "Ephraim," . . . so I said "Yes?" But it wasn't Gerney that was speaking. No one was in that room. Then my name was spoken again. My heart was like to pound right out of my body, but I couldn't see anything. The third time the voice said "Ephraim," seemed like it was sort of sharp and out of patience. I said, "Yes, yes. Is there something I can do for you?" Then the voice said clear as if I'd been face to face with a neighbor, "Ephraim, that handcart company is in trouble, will you help them out?" I got right out of bed. Gerney, he got my team hooked up and Sister Brown fixed me a bite and some food to carry along. I got to Salt Lake about daylight, and what should happen but I met a messenger from brother Brigham, on his

> way to fetch me. . . . I now hastened to Salt Lake City, and arrived there on the Saturday, preceding the Sunday on which the call was made for volunteers to go out and help the last handcart companies in. When some of the brethren responded by explaining that they could get ready to start in a few days, I spoke at once saying, "I am ready now!" The next day I was wending my way eastward over the mountains with a light wagon all alone.[33]

Express Rescue Team Searching For The Martin Company

On October 28, the Express Rescue Team did not begin their day's ride until around noon.

> The first night we camped, our horses followed a band of buffaloes several miles; it was near noon the next day when we returned with them. We determined to get even with them so [we] rode at full gallop wherever the road would permit. After riding about twelve miles we saw a white man's shoe track in the road. Brother Young called out, 'Here they are.' We put our animals to their utmost speed and soon came in sight of the camp at Red Bluff. This was Brother Edward Martin's handcart company and Ben Horgett's wagon company. There was still another wagon company down near the Platte Crossing.[34]

Martin Company Red Buttes to Avenue Hill October 28–30, 1856

"At last, some of the Company gave up and decided they could go no further. We all gathered around and held a meeting, praying God to help us, as we knew it was He alone who could deliver us from death. We were happy and willing to die for a just cause. The Lord knew our desperate condition, and sent us deliverance. A 'hurrah!' burst from the camp as three messengers came riding in," wrote sixteen-year-old Louisa Mellor.[35]

Of the arrival of the Express Rescue Team in camp, sixteen-year-old Albert Jones recalled:

> It was at this place that Joseph A. Young arrived as the leader of

> the relief party sent from the valleys by President Brigham Young. He rode a white mule down a snow-covered hill or dugway. The white mule was lost sight of on the white background of snow, and Joseph A. with his big blue soldiers' overcoat, its large cape capacious skirts rising and falling with the motion of the mule, gave the appearance of a blue-winged angel flying to our rescue. The scene that presented itself on his arrival I shall never forget: women and men surrounded him, weeping, and crying aloud; on their knees, holding to the skirts of his coat, as though afraid he would escape from their grasp and fly away. Joseph stood in their midst drawn up to his full height and gazed upon their upturned faces, his eyes full of tears. I a boy as I was, prayed "God bless him."

Albert's description contains many details of the fulfillment of John Rodwell's dream.[36]

These men the company had long prayed for were truly angels sent from heaven. Josiah Rogerson wrote: "They had traveled through the snow and storms, day and night, nearly [350] miles, regardless of exposure and their lives. Who shall ever write and record the meed of praise due these three brave men?"[37]

John Jaques recalled: "The 28th day of October was the red letter day to this handcart expedition. . . . All was now animation and bustle in the handcart camp, and everybody was busy at once in making preparations for a renewed start in the morning. The revived spirits of the company were still further exhilarated by an increased ration of flour that day, three quarters of a pound I believe. With cheered hearts and renewed hopes the emigrants retired to their beds that night."[38]

The Express Rescue Team found the Martin Company sixteen miles above the Platte bridge in desperate and deplorable conditions. On October 28, James Bleak recorded fifty-six members of their company had been lost. John Jaques described how the once strong and robust men of the company were now "worn down by the labors and fatigues of the journey, and pinched by hunger and cold, the manliness of tall, healthy, strong men would gradually disappear, until, they would grow fretful, peevish, childish, and puerile, acting sometimes as if they were scarcely accountable beings."[39]

Daniel W. Jones recalled the following of the rescuers' arrival in the Martin camp:

> This company was in almost as bad a condition as the first one. They had nearly given up hope. Their provisions were about exhausted, and many of them worn out and sick. When we rode in, there was a general rush to shake hands. I took no part in the ceremony. Many declared we were angels from heaven. I told them I thought we were better than angels, for this occasion, as we were good strong men come to help them into the valley, and that our company, and wagons loaded with provisions, were not far away. I thought this the best consolation under the circumstances. Brother Young told the people to gather 'up', and move on at once, as the only salvation was to travel a little every day. This was right, and no doubt saved many lives, for we, among so many, (some twelve hundred) could do but little, and there was danger of starvation before help could arrive unless the people made some headway toward the valley.[40]

Although this Express Rescue Team had insufficient supplies to bring relief to so many in need, they did bring with them encouraging news that rescuers were stationed some fifty miles west at Devil's Gate. The Express Team continued on at full gallop in search of the wagon companies and found them twelve miles further,

> almost out of provisions, and their cattle dying for want of food. The majority of them had become so discouraged that they knew not what to do. We explained to them how impossible it was for us to give them substantial aid, as we had but nine loads of provisions left, which amounted to very little where there were so many to feed. We urged them to move on towards the Valley, every day, no matter what the sacrifice might be. We gave them to understand that the authorities at Salt Lake City had no idea that they were so far from home, and had made no arrangements to meet such conditions. The clouds were gathering for another storm, and just as we were leaving, it commenced to snow quite hard.[41]

On the morning of Wednesday, October 29, the Martin company "summoned all our efforts and strength, impulsed with the prospect of deliverance, we again started on our journey." Patience Loader recalled: "We was all glad to make a move from this place, it seemed that if God our Father had not sent help to us that we must all have perished and died in a short time for at that time we had only very little provisions left and at the request of Brother Martin we had come on four ounces of flour a day for each one to make the flour last us as long he could I don't know how long we could have lived and pulled our handcart on this small quantity of food."[42]

Joseph A. Young traveled to the Platte Bridge, while Daniel W. Jones and Abel Garr remained with the Hunt Company to offer assistance in getting them started for the day. The rescuers noted the spirit of apathy found within the company:

> The clouds were gathering thickly for storm, and just as we were about to start it commenced snowing very hard. The heavens were obscured by clouds, excepting a small place about the shape of the gable end of a house. This opening was in the direction of the valley, and the sun seemed to shine through with great brightness. We mounted our mules, Brother Garr, pointing to the bright spot in the heavens, said, "Do you see that hole? You had better get out of here before that closes up, for it is your opening to the valley. We are going." The people, I believe, took, this for a warning, and soon started for their cattle. [The] next morning they moved on.[43]

John Jaques wrote: "Early on the morning of the 29th the handcart company left the Platte and struck across the country for the Sweetwater. Joseph A. Young and his companions, returning from [John] Hunt's company, overtook [Edward] Martin's company before night and camped with it at Rock Avenue, about thirty-six miles east of Devil's Gate."[44]

Daniel W. Jones recorded:

> We continued on, overtaking the handcart company, ascending a long, muddy hill. A condition of distress here met my eyes that I never saw before or since. The train was strung out for three or four miles. There were old men pulling and tugging their carts; sometimes loaded with a sick wife or children—women pulling along sick husbands, little children six to eight years old struggling through the mud and snow. As night came on the mud would freeze on their clothes and feet. There were two of us, and hundreds needing help. What could we do? We gathered on to some of the most helpless with our lariats tied to the carts, and helped as many as we could into camp on Avenue hill. This was a bitter, cold night and we had no fuel except very small sagebrush. Several died that night.[45]

After getting the Martin Company into the camp on Avenue Hill, the Express Rescue Team, consisting of Joseph A. Young, Abel Garr, and Daniel W. Jones, returned to the main rescue camp stationed at Devil's Gate. They apprised Captain Grant of the whereabouts, and of the condition of the Martin, Hunt, and Hodgett Companies. "All were rejoiced to get the news that we had found the emigrants."[46]

Harvey H. Cluff noted: "On the following day, every team but one, and all the men but ten started out on force march for to meet the companies. . . . The one team and ten men immediately began hauling from the hills the cedar and the pine wood to the stockade and clearing the snow off so the emigrants could be comfortable when they arrived. For several days we made every effort possible to get things in good shape."[47]

19

TRAVEL ON, THERE IS HELP FOR YOU

SALT LAKE VALLEY,
GREEN RIVER TO FORT BRIDGER,
GREASEWOOD CREEK TO DEVIL'S GATE

SALT LAKE VALLEY
OCTOBER 30, 1856

On October 30, in the Salt Lake Valley, President Brigham Young wrote a letter to Orson Pratt, President of the British Mission, informing him that the last two companies had not yet arrived. He expressed his concern with the snow in the mountains and on the plains and informed him that rescue teams were sent out with supplies to aid their suffering. President Young counseled Orson not to permit any company to leave the Missouri River later than the first of August preferring them to leave early in May or June, declaring it a great mistake to start the companies across the plains so late.[1]

WILLIE COMPANY
GREEN RIVER, WYOMING
OCTOBER 30, 1856

That same day, the Willie Company traveled eleven miles, forded the Green River, and camped on its banks. They were now 167 miles from the Salt Lake Valley. Crossing the Green River was difficult during any time of the year, but during this early blast of winter, in their weakened condition, it was especially difficult. George Cunningham wrote:

> Our Captain showed us all a noble example. He was furnished a mule to ride on our start from Iowa City, but he said, "I will never get on its back, I shall show the example, you follow it." He did so and the captains of hundreds followed him. They would crowd on ahead to be the first into the streams to help the women and children across. After getting the last one across, they would crowd on ahead to be the first. They waded every stream, and I might say, a dozen times between Iowa City and Green River, with the exception of the Missouri River, by this time they were completely exhausted and had to be hauled the balance of the way. Some of them not being able to stand on their feet. Their names were: James Willie, Millen Atwood, Levi Savage, William Woodward, and the fifth was a Danish brother whose name I can't recall [John Ahmanson].[2]

Oborn Family

It was late before they arrived in camp that evening, and many were sick. Millen Atwood, William Woodward, and Neils Christiansen remained behind to urge on the sick. Two deaths occurred in the company, fifty-nine-year-old Mary Gurdlestone and forty-four-year-old Joseph Oborn. Joseph was emigrating with his wife, Maria Stradling, and son, twelve-year-old John. Joseph and Maria joined the Church in England around 1843. In 1856, they left two of their children, Eliza and Henry, and relatives and friends to join with the Saints in the Salt Lake Valley. Of his father's death on October 30, John wrote: "Privation and starvation were taking their toll. A day or two later my own father closed his eyes, never to wake again. He, too, had given his life cheerfully and without hesitation, for the cause that he espoused. We buried him in a lonely grave, its spot unmarked, not far from Green River, Wyoming, he was only forty five. During these terrible times it seemed only a matter of days before all would perish."[3]

Smith & Bain Family

By the time the Willie Company reached the Green River, all who remained physically capable were expected to continue to walk, because wagons were already filled to capacity with those who needed the greatest assistance. Thirteen-year-old Elizabeth "Betsey" Smith recalled:

> About three miles on this side of Green River, as I was walking ahead of the train, leading my little brother of six, and encouraging him along by telling him stories of what he would get when we arrived at the Valley, he said, "When we get to that creek, I wish we could see our brother Rob." I said "Come along, maybe we will, when we get to the top of the bank." When we arrived at the top of the bank and looked down we saw a wagon with just one yoke of oxen on. We had never seen the like before, so we waited on the summit until they should pass. The man stared at us, and as his team came beside us, he yelled, "Whoa" to the oxen. It was then we knew him. He jumped off the wagon and caught his sisters in his arms as they came up with the cart. How we all wept with joy! The cart was then tied behind the wagon. Little Alex climbed into the wagon as happy as a prince instead of a poor tired child. The next question from Rob was, "Where is Mother and sister Mary?" "They are behind somewhere, Robby. You will find them by the road." Mother was still sick, and when she stopped to rest she had to lie down; she could not sit up. Some had died that way. They would go to sleep and never awaken. Mary was afraid that Mother would do likewise, and tried to arouse her by telling her about a team coming with only one yoke of cattle on. Mother replied, "Well, never mind, Mary. Don't bother me. I am so tired." "Well, Mother, the man is running this way. It surely is Robert." "Oh, no, Mary. That would be too good to be true!" Well, she was soon convinced, as Robert took her in his arms and helped her into the wagon. As he did so, mother exclaimed, 'I couldn't be more thankful to get into the Kingdom of Heaven than I am to see you, and lie here and rest. Explanations followed. Robert stated that he had suffered from a mountain fever, and was just recovering when he received a letter that we were coming. He then borrowed and hired an outfit to come and meet us. None too soon![4]

Martin Company
Greasewood Creek to Devil's Gate
October 31–November 1, 1856

While struggling through the difficulties of travel on October 31, Patience Loader described the heaven-sent hope she received: "Some time in the afternoon a strange man appeared to me as we was resting as we got up the hill he came and looked in my face. He said, 'are you Patience?' I said, 'Yes.' He said again 'I thought it was you. Travel on, there is help for you. You will come to a good place, there is plenty.' With this he was gone. He disappeared. I looked but never saw where he went. This seemed very strange to me. I took this as someone sent to encourage us and give us strength."[5]

John Jaques described the events of the day as follows:

> In the afternoon of the last day of October, the company met C. H. Wheelock, Daniel W. Jones, and David Garr, who were going to meet the various companies. About dark the company arrived at Greasewood Creek, between thirty and forty miles from the last crossing of the Platte. At Greasewood creek were found George D. Grant, R. T. Burton, Charles Decker, C. G. Webb, and others, with six wagons laden with flour and other things, from Salt Lake, who had come to the assistance of the belated emigrants. This was another time of rejoicing. Some of the relief party had met the emigrants a mile or two away from camp and had helped to pull some of the carts along. Here some stockings, boots and other clothing were distributed among the emigrants, also a few onions, which were highly prized, and a pound of flour ration was served out. . . . This was the beginning of better days as to food and assistance, but the cold grew more severe, and was intense much of the way.[6]

Patience Loader continued:

> We traveled on and got into camp. There five or six brethren with their wagons camped there. They had been and got quantities of wood and they already made a dozen big fires for us. And there was plenty of lovely spring water. That was a great treat to us for the last water we had seen was when we crossed the Platt River. We had nothing but snow water and that did not taste very good as we had to melt it over the camp fire and it tasted of sage brush, and sometimes of cedar wood smoke. We felt very thankful to our brethren for making us these good fires and supplying us with wood so abundantly.[7]

On Saturday, November 1, members of the Rescue Company spent the morning in preparation to get the Martin Company moving again. Captain George D. Grant noted: "After stowing our wagons full of the sick, the children and the infirm, with a good amount of luggage, started homeward about noon. The snow began to fall very fast and continued until late at night. It is now about 8 inches deep here, and the weather is very cold."[8]

John Jaques recalled:

> On the evening of November 1st, the handcart company camped at the Sweetwater bridge, on this side of the river, about five miles on the other side of Devil's Gate, arriving there about dark. There was a foot or eighteen inches of snow on the ground. As there were but one or two spades in camp, the emigrants had to shovel it away with their frying pans, or tin plates, or anything they could use for that purpose, before they could pitch their tents, and then the ground was frozen so hard that it was almost impossible to drive the tent pegs into it. Some of the men were so weak that it took them an hour or two to clear the places for their tents and set them up.[9]

Griffiths Family

Sixteen-year-old Margaret Griffiths recorded the sacrifices her family made at this time: "It almost seemed that we would perish. In fact, many of our company froze to death, my twelve-year-old brother among them, and we buried him there in the desolate wilderness fifty miles the other side of Devil's Gate. . . . At Independence my other brother, six years old, died from cold and exposure and my only sister had her feet so badly frozen that she lost the two first joints of her big toes." Along the way, John struggled terribly with rheumatism, and at one point his health became so bad that he was allowed to ride in one of the provision wagons. For a short time, he felt he had regained his strength and set out walking again. Shortly thereafter, however, he realized he couldn't keep up and took hold of the end of the last wagon. When one of the teamsters saw John, "he tried to rouse him by using his whip, but the sick man fell to the ground and could not get up." That night when the last wagon reached camp and John was nowhere to be found, sixteen-year-old

Margaret walked back along the trail three miles, frantically searching for him to no avail. After John was whipped, unable to get back up on his own strength, he crawled on his hands and knees in the deep snow following the tracks of an independent wagon company. Miraculously, he made it into their camp, and two men took him to the Martin Company.[10]

Express Team—Salt Lake Valley
October 31–November 2, 1856

The Express Team, sent to the Salt Lake Valley on October 25, reached their destination on October 31. They brought a much-anticipated report of the Willie Company but had no word of the Martin, Hunt, and Hodgett Companies. In the Valley, criticism began to swell regarding the handcart plan and why these companies were allowed to continue so late in the season. Brigham Young and Heber C. Kimball addressed the issue while speaking to the Saints in the Old Tabernacle on November 2. When Brigham Young spoke, he shared his deep concern for the companies still out on the plains:

> We can return home and sit down and warm our feet before the fire, and can eat our bread and butter, etc., but my mind is yonder in the snow, where those immigrating Saints are, and my mind has been with them ever since I had the report of their start from Winter Quarters on the 3rd of September. I cannot talk about anything, I cannot go out or come in, but what in every minute or two minutes my mind reverts to them; and the questions—whereabouts are my brethren and sisters who are on the plains, and what is their condition, force themselves upon me and annoy my feelings all the time.

When Jedediah Grant spoke, he spoke of the rescue effort well underway and shared that two hundred wagons had already been dispatched, but the reality was, it simply wasn't enough: "We have now some two hundred teams out to meet them, and some were only prepared with seven days' forage for animals. It will be necessary for more teams to go to their relief with grain and hay enough to sustain the animals already out, or they will die."[11]

Weeks earlier, on October 13, Brigham Young attempted to

join in the rescue efforts himself: "He wanted to know first hand how they were getting along." He asked Arza Hinckley to drive his carriage. By the time they reached Canyon Creek, President Young was cramping with severe stomach pains and was vomiting. It was decided to return Brigham Young and his company back to the Salt Lake Valley. Of this experience, Arza recorded Brigham Young's words:

> I can realize more fully how the handcart people are suffering, even more than I have. . . . Their small children, babies and elderly people must be freezing. They should not have left so late in the season, they should have waited until spring. . . . some times our anxiety gets the best of our judgment. We venture and rely upon our faith rather than combining faith with wisdom. We also neglect calling upon our Heavenly Father for directions. God expects us to use our resources to sustain us, then when necessary he comes to our aid. I am sure that the handcart folks are now praying for help from their Heavenly Father and we hope that our relief wagons will find them without delay.

Once back in the Salt Lake Valley, Daniel Wells requested the help of Arza in the rescue efforts. Arza and Dan Johnson were soon off, each driving east a four-mule wagon loaded with supplies.[12]

Willie Company
Fort Bridger
November 2, 1856

On November 2, the Willie Company camped a half mile west of Fort Bridger, located 113 miles from the Salt Lake Valley. Earlier that morning, Ephraim Hanks passed the Willie Camp near Fort Bridger, bringing news that many teams from the valley were on their way. Ephraim continued east in search of the Martin Company. He would not reach them until nine days later, on November 11.[13]

Throughout the day, Captain James G. Willie, William Woodward, and Niels Christiansen worked tirelessly to assist the sick and weakened members of the company as "we had not teams enough to haul the feeble that were left behind." After expending all of his energy in efforts to help others, "Bro. Willie's feet were in such a bad condition from frost that he was unable to walk to the Camp; a wagon was sent for him." John Chislett noted: "At Fort Bridger we found a great many teams that had come to our help. The noble fellows who came to our assistance invariably received us joyfully, and did all in their power to alleviate our sufferings. May they never need similar relief!" From this point on, all members of the company were able to ride in the wagons.[14]

When rescuers Arza Hinckley and Dan Johnson reached Fort Bridger, they were delayed a few days by a blizzard. Soon they were back on the trail and met two rescue companies that were returning to Salt Lake City. They mentioned they had traveled as far as Pacific Spring and heard word that the Willie Company had been found but decided the Martin Company must have perished. After listening to the explanation for returning home, Arza made a proposition with the returning companies. "There is a good place to camp just a short distance from here. You go on and camp and wait until you hear about the carts, and Dan and I will go and find the handcarts." Arza was determined, regardless of the difficulties, to find the company's members remaining on the plains or give his life trying.[15]

Arza's family history noted: "After Arza and Dan left Ephraim was troubled, he could not stop thinking about what the voice said to him at Brother Browns and Arza and Dan's determination to find the handcart people. He decided to follow and began to gather the things he was in need of when one of the relief men asked him what he was doing? He said, 'I am preparing to leave camp and follow Arza and Dan, I am sure that I can catch up with them in a short time as I can travel much faster than they can with loaded wagons.'" Ephraim reached Arza and Dan at the Green River. Because of the death of one of Brigham Young's mules and the remaining three wearing down fast, it was decided Ephraim would hitch his horses to Arza's wagon, and Dan would return to Fort Bridger with the mules.[16]

Martin Company
Independence Rock to Devil's Gate
November 2, 1856

On November 2, the Martin Company passed Independence Rock and traveled on through to Devil's Gate, the Willie Company having passed it nineteen days earlier. It was a very difficult day's travel through deep snow. Located a short distance from Devil's Gate was Seminoe's Fort, which was composed of nine structures—a trading post, a blacksmith shop, store rooms, and living quarters. The fort was abandoned in 1855 because of trouble with the Sioux Indians, and it had remained unoccupied through the 1856 emigrant season.[17]

Of the arrival of the Martin Company at the fort, Harvey H. Cluff wrote:

> It was a Sunday evening when the handcart veterans pulled into the quarters provided for them. Every room nook and corner was taken. Wagons and tents were filled to their utmost capacity, to protect the people from the northern blizzard then raging. Every possible assistance from the boys from Utah was freely given. And these young hardy men from the Rockies were a mighty force and power in the salvation of that people. No more efficient help could have been furnished. They had crossed the dreary plains, new what hunger, thirst, starvation, weary, traveling, with sore feet ment; hence with the subsequent experience in the vallies gave them the vim to endure and they did endure and they worked valiantly for the poor emigrants. But oh! What a sight to see. Aged men, women, children, and young maidens plodding along through the snow several inches deep, with icicles dangling to their skirts and pants as they walked along pushing and pulling their handcarts, the wheels of which were burdened with snow. The roaring fires of cedar and pitch pine wood soon cheered the weary souls and the youthful of both sexes were singing the songs of Zion around the campfires.[18]

Patience Loader described:

> We came to Devil's gate that night to camp; the snow was terrible cold freezing. When we got to camp we found several big fires there and several log huts and several brethren from the valley was camping there. Brother Joel Parrish was cooking supper for the rest of the brethren. We was all so hungry and cold, many ran to get to the fire to warm but the brethren asked for all to be as

> patient as possible and we should have some wood to make us fires so we could get warm. Brother George Grant was there. He told us all to stand back for he was going to knock down one of those log huts to make fires for us. He said, "You are not going to freeze tonight." . . . He raised his ax and with one blow knocked in the whole front of the building, took each log and split in four pieces and gave each family one piece. Oh! Such crowding for wood. . . . [Brother Grant] said, "There is one sister standing back waiting very patiently and she must have some." I called out, "Yes, Brother Grant, my name is Patience and I have waited with patience." He laughed and said, "Give that sister some wood and let her go and make a fire." I was very thankful to get wood. I had waited so long that my clothing was stiff and my old stockings and shoes seemed frozen on my feet and legs.[19]

Daniel W. Jones wrote: "The winter storms had now set in, in all their severity. The provisions we took amounted to almost nothing among so many people, many of them now on very short rations, some almost starving. Many were dying daily from exposure and want of food. We were at a loss to know why others had not come on to our assistance." It became a question that night, whether the Martin Company should camp at Devil's Gate for the winter, or go forward to the Salt Lake Valley. Rescuers knew it would be impossible to winter these companies in this area of Wyoming; they simply did not have the resources. Yet it also seemed physically impossible to continue moving the companies forward on their own strength with 327 miles to go to reach the Valley.[20]

20

WE GO ON DOING ALL WE CAN, NOT DOUBTING NOR DESPAIRING

MUDDY CREEK
DEVIL'S GATE TO MARTIN'S COVE

WILLIE COMPANY
MUDDY CREEK
NOVEMBER 3–4, 1856

On November 3, the Willie Company crossed the Basin Rim, forded Muddy Creek, and camped on its banks near a Rescue Company made up of ten wagons on their way to meet the Martin, Hunt, and Hodgett Companies. The Willie Company was less than a week away from arriving in the Salt Lake Valley. William H. Kimball went ahead as an Express to apprise Brigham Young of their impending arrival. The condition of the company remained desperate, with deaths continuing to occur daily. On Tuesday, November 4, the Willie Company again met up with several Rescue teams from the Valley, who distributed potatoes, onions, and clothing.[1]

MARTIN COMPANY
DEVIL'S GATE TO MARTIN'S COVE
NOVEMBER 3–4, 1856

On the morning of November 3, Captain George D. Grant sent Joseph A. Young and Abel Garr as an express to the Salt Lake Valley to report on the condition of the Martin, Hunt, and Hodgett

Companies and to request additional help in the rescue efforts. Before leaving, Joseph A. Young "put on three or four pairs of woolen socks, a pair of moccasins, and a pair of buffalo hide over-shoes with the wool on, and then remarked, 'There, if my feet freeze with those on, they must stay frozen till I get to Salt Lake.'"[2]

Captain Grant sent with the express team a letter to President Brigham Young:

> It is not much use for me to attempt to give a description of the situation of these people, for this you will learn from your son, Joseph A., and from Br. Garr, who are the bearers of this express; but you can imagine between 500 and 600 hundred men, women and children, worn down by drawing carts through snow and mud; fainting by the wayside; children crying, their limbs stiffened by the cold, their feet bleeding, and some of them bare to snow and frost. The sight is too much for the stoutest of us, but we go on doing all we can, not doubting, nor despairing. Our company is too small to help much; it is only a drop to a bucket, as it were, in comparison to what is needed. I think that not over one-third of br. Martin's company is able to walk. This you may think is extravagant, but it is nevertheless true. Some of them have good courage and are in good spirits, but a great many of them are like children, and do not help themselves much more, nor realize what is before them. I never felt so much interest in any mission that I have been sent on, and all the brethren who came out with me feel the same. We have prayed without ceasing, and the blessing of God has been with us. Br. Charles Decker has now traveled this road the 49th time, and he says he has never before seen so much snow on the Sweetwater at any season of the year. . . . We will move every day toward the valley, if we shovel snow to do it, the Lord helping us. I have never seen such energy and faith among the "boys," nor so good a spirit as is among those who came out with me. We realize that we have your prayers for us continually, also those of all the Saints in the Valley.[3]

The Martin Company remained at Devil's Gate on November 3, and the weather continued to be severe. There were six to eight inches of snow on the ground, the wind blew furiously, and the temperature plummeted to six degrees below zero. Charles Decker suggested the company move to a horseshoe-shaped ravine or cove three miles west that could offer better protection from the winter blast and a more plentiful source of firewood, where they could wait out the storm. Josiah Rogerson noted: "It is not exactly a ravine, but a recess or opening in the mountains, which here ran along near to the river." It was decided at this time to relieve the company from the labors of pulling the handcarts, everything not absolutely essential to sustain life was stowed away in the log cabins and wagons located near Devil's Gate. Of the handcarts that continued west, only the best were selected and they were heavily loaded with essential items."[4]

On November 4, the Martin Company "started from Devil's Gate westward and about three miles away crossed the Sweetwater to the north side. The creek here was at least two rods wide, and from two to three feet deep, with plenty of ice and snow, so as to carve the recollection forever in the minds of all that waded that stream." John Jaques records:

> The passage of the Sweetwater at this point was a severe operation to many of the company. . . . It was the worst river crossing of the expedition. It was the last ford that the emigrants waded over. The water was not less than two feet deep, perhaps a little more in the deepest parts, but it was intensely cold. The ice was three or four inches thick, and the bottom of the river muddy or sandy. I forget exactly how wide the stream was there, but I think thirty or forty yards. It seemed a good deal wider than that to those who pulled their handcarts through it. Before the crossing was completed, the shades of evening were closing around, and as everybody knows, that is the coldest hour of the twenty-four, or at least it seemed to be so, in a frosty time, and it seemed so then, for cold enough it was.[5]

Patience Loader, describing her feelings when she saw the river that had to be crossed, wrote,

> It was reported around camp that we would not have to pull our handcarts any further, that we would leave them at Devil's Gate and that we would all be able to ride in the wagons. This was delightful news to us to think we would not have to pull the carts any more. I felt I could still walk if I did not have the cart to pull. But, oh, what a disappointment the next morning we found it was only those could ride that was too sick and weak to pull their carts and so we girls all pretty well in health we had to start out with our cart again. . . . I was feeling somewhat bad that morning and when I saw this stream of water we had to go through. I felt weak and I

> could not keep my tears back. I felt ashamed to let those brethren see me shedding tears, I pulled my old bonnet over my face so they should not see my tears.[6]

On this day at the Sweetwater River crossing, countless members of the Martin Company were overcome with emotion at the thought of crossing this river. During these desperate hours prayers were answered through the actions of valiant and noble men. With great fortitude seventeen-year-old David P. Kimball, seventeen-year-old George W. Grant, twenty-two-year-old Stephen W. Taylor, and twenty-five-year-old C. Allen Huntington spent the day carrying women, children, and some of the weak and weary men across the river choked with ice.[7]

John Jaques recorded:

> In that rear part of the company two men were pulling one of the handcarts, assisted by two or three women, for the women pulled as well as the men all the way, so long as the handcarts lasted. When the cart arrived at the bank of the river, one of these men, who was much worn down, asked, in a plaintive tone, "Have we got to go across there?" On being answered yes, he was so much affected that he was completely overcome. That was the last straw. His fortitude and manhood gave way. He exclaimed, "Oh dear! I can't go through that," and burst into tears. His wife, who was by his side, had the stouter heart of the two at that juncture, and she said soothingly, "Don't cry, Jimmy. I'll pull the handcart for you," a noble and generous offer, which, however, was not carried out. Jimmy besought one of the "boys" from "the valley," who was in the water, to carry him over. . . . The "boy" urged that the women and children had the first claim, but finally consented to carry him across. Jimmy got on the back of the "boy" to ride over, and the "boy" started with him. This little episode, however, ended badly for Jimmy, for, before he was carried entirely across, the "boy" slipped and fell with Jimmy into the water, very wet water it was too, and very cold, freezingly cold, enough to congeal anything. The women with the handcart were carried over safe, and the cart remained with the one man to pull it through. He rolled up his pants as he could, pulled off his stockings and boots which he happened to receive at Greasewood creek, put on a pair of old shoes he carried with him, and all alone went into the river with naked legs and with his cart laden with pots and kettles. . . . When in the water the narrow felloes of the cart wheels

> cut into the soft bottom of the river bed, and he soon got stalled. Two of the "boys" in the water went to his help. . . . So hard was the tugging, that it required the utmost combined strength of the three to take the vehicle through safe dry land. While in the river the sharp cake of floating ice below the surface of the water struck against the bare shins of the emigrant, inflicting wounds which never healed until he arrived in Salt Lake, and the dark scars of which he bears to this day. When the river was forded, he found that Jimmy and the women assigned to help pull the cart were all gone on to the camp at the base of the mountains, from half a mile to a mile distant. The way to camp was over rising ground, covered with sage brush, and with about a foot of snow on the surface. . . . All alone he pulled his heavy laden cart over the snow and clumps of brush, for road there was none, till he reached the camp. . . . When he arrived at the camp, he had to climb the mountain to cut some cedar for firewood. The "boys" of the relief party had cut some wood for the camp, but was all appropriated before he arrived in camp. So he went on the mountain, and the mountains there are little else than rocks, and he took his little hatchet, for axes were few in the camp. Green cedar was of little use. Nothing but dry cedar was really serviceable for fuel, and the dry cedar was almost as hard as iron, while his hatchet had not been ground since he left the Missouri, if it had since he left Iowa City. So I will leave you to imagine how long he was that night before he succeeded in getting fuel for those depending on him.[8]

Josiah Rogerson wrote: "We reached the cove or ravine in time to get our tents pitched before dark, and found plenty of good, dry cedar and pine, close by on the rocks and ledges. The night was as cold as nearly any we had at the Devil's Gate, and the snow so frozen to the ground that many were not able to clear it out of the tents, so they threw down their buffalo robes and blankets and lay down exhausted. We remained here the evening of Tuesday, November 5, 6, 7, and 8—five nights and four days."[9]

Isaac Wardle

Isaac Wardle was born in England in 1835 and did not have the privilege of attending much school because of his family's financial circumstances. At age seven, he worked in a rope factory, and by age nine, he was working in the coal mines, where he spent the next ten years. At age eighteen, Isaac was baptized, and three years later, in

1856, he emigrated alone. In Iowa, Isaac traveled with the Bailey family. When their eighteen-year-old son, Langley, became deathly sick, Isaac and Langley's fifteen-year-old brother, John, pulled him in the handcart until rescuers arrived. Shortly after his arrival ,in the cove, Isaac recorded: "At one time I became so weary and overcome with cold that I fell down and was forced to lay there for some time." Isaac's descendants relate that upon arrival in the cove, he was so exhausted that he was ready to give up and die. A member of the Rescue Company noticed Isaac had become despondent, and he would have no part of him giving up. The rescuer assigned him to get some wood over a little hill. Obediently, Isaac got up and set out to accomplish his assignment. He cut down three trees before returning. Later, he attributed fulfilling that assignment to saving his life. While searching for the exact location of Martin's Cove over one hundred and thirty years later, a granddaughter of Isaac's located three old tree stumps that could have been the very ones Isaac cut down on that frigid evening in November.[10]

21

NOTHING BUT THE POWER OF A MERCIFUL GOD KEPT THEM FROM PERISHING

ECHO CANYON TO LITTLE MOUNTAIN, MARTIN'S COVE

WILLIE COMPANY ECHO CANYON TO LITTLE MOUNTAIN NOVEMBER 5–8, 1856

On November 5, the Willie Company reached Echo Canyon. Two deaths occurred that day: sixty-two-year-old Peder Madsen from Denmark and thirty-three-year-old Susannah Osborn of England. Peder had served as clerk of the company, faithfully keeping daily records until September 8. Peder's journal entries are part of the invaluable records documenting the travels of the Willie Company.[1]

MCPHAIL FAMILY

Toward evening on November 5, it began to storm, and the temperature once again plummeted. Thirty-nine-year-old Archibald McPhail of Scotland was near death. On his journey to the valley, Archibald had served as captain of a group of twenty assigned to his tent. Upon reaching camp one evening, after a difficult day's travel through a blizzard, Archibald discovered a woman was missing and he went back to look for her. Archibald found her on the opposite side of a creek and pled with her to continue forward. She refused, saying she was going to remain there and die. No amount of convincing could encourage her to cross. Determined not to let her die, Archibald crossed the frozen creek, picked her up, and proceeded to cross back over to return to camp. With the additional weight of this woman on his back, Archibald broke through the ice soaking him to the waist in the chilling water. Archibald's clothing quickly froze to his body, and by the time he reached camp, he was chilled through to the bone. Without anything to eat or drink, Archibald went to bed with a covering from a handcart pitched over the top of him for a tent. The wind blew fiercely throughout the night, blowing the makeshift tent over three times; finally, it was just left down. His daughter Henrietta remained by his side and brushed the snow from his face. Archibald never regained his strength and was placed in a wagon. As death was nigh at hand, his wife, Jane, sat up with him. Jane's descendants recorded the following tender experience of his death: "She was sitting in the wagon in the night with her sick husband's head on her lap watching him as she knew he could not live. Having a small piece of tallow candle, she prayed that the candle might last until her husband should pass away; her prayer was answered for the light of the candle and the life of her husband went out at the same time."[2]

On November 6, the storm raged most of the day, making traveling down Echo Canyon and fording the Weber River difficult. The following day, three deaths occurred. On November 8, the Willie Company ascended Big Mountain and camped about a mile from Little Mountain. William H. Kimball returned from the Valley and brought a load of provisions. Arrangements were made to ensure each person would have a place to stay upon their arrival in the Salt Lake Valley the following day.[3]

Martin Company
Martin's Cove
November 5–8, 1856

As the Willie Company was nearing the Salt Lake Valley, the Martin Company remained in the area now known as Martin's Cove to wait out the raging blizzards, the temperature ranging from six to eleven degrees below zero. James Bleak wrote, "Our ration of flour was reduced to 4 oz. and 2 oz. for the children, making 1 lb. a day for the 6 of us. Through the blessing of our Father we felt as contented, as when we had 1 lb. per head." As a result of the severe weather and lack of food, a great many deaths, including that of the cattle, occurred at this campsite.[4]

Thirteen-year-old Heber McBride recalled: "[We] camped in a little cove in the mountains where the wind would not get such a sweep at us. . . . Then was the time to hear the children crying for something to eat. Nearly all of them would cry themselves to sleep every night. My two little brothers would get the sack that had flour in it and turn it wrong side out and suck and lick the flour dust off it."[5]

Elizabeth Horrocks Jackson noted:

> We camped for several days in a deep gulch called "Martin's Ravine." It was a fearful time and place. It was so cold that some of the company came near freezing to death. The sufferings of the people were fearful, and nothing but the power of a merciful God kept them from perishing. The storms continued unabated for some days. . . . When the snow at length ceased falling, it lay thick on the ground, and so deep that for many days it was impossible to move the wagons through. I and my children with hundreds of others were locked up in those fearful weather-bound mountains.[6]

Of the time spent at Martin's Cove, Josiah Rogerson wrote:

> Our losses daily and nightly in this ravine were as great as at the Red Buttes, because of the intensely cold weather and our rations of four ounces of flour for adults and two ounces for children. Here nearly all the balance of our oxen died. . . . This cove, or ravine, was indeed our Valley Forge or graveyard, and though some have censured Captain Martin for taking us there, yet if we had stayed at the Devil's Gate fort it would have been more fatal, on account of the full sweep the bitter cold winds had on us there, and one day or night with the thermometer 11 degrees below zero. Here we had plenty of good cedar wood and shelter on three sides.[7]

Rescuer Harvey H. Cluff noted how critical their situation became at times:

> Camp was made, tents set, supper over and the people retired for the night when a snow storm accompanied by a raging wind from the north, came over the mountain and with a terrific whirl around the cove, leveled every tent to the ground. Here again the Utah boys found that their services very much needed. To rescue the people from beneath their tents and re-set the tents in the dark hours of the night was a very trying ordeal for the boys and also the people, but marvelous as it may seem, not a single person was seriously injured. Now again the blizzard set in with increased fury, the snow covering the grass compelling the cattle and horses to forage upon the willows along the river bottoms. Cattle died daily. The situation was, indeed, very critical. No power could save the people from death but that of God. To our rescue O Lord God Almighty seemed the fervent prayer constantly offered to our Heavenly Father. The carcasses of dead cattle were preserved in a frozen state from wolves, for food for the people in case we should be winter bound; which really seemed inevitable. Over four hundred miles of mountainous country lay between the emigrants and their destined home in Utah where snow in winter frequently falls to a depth that stops all travel by teams. The only glimmer of hope that seemed to reconcile our feeling and that was the utmost confidence in President Brigham Young's inspiration that he would keep companies coming out to meet us and thereby keep the road opened.[8]

Six-year-old Peter McBride recalled his experiences in the cove: "The next day we had nothing to eat but some bark from trees. Later we had a terrible cold spell; the wind drifted so much I knew I would die. The wind blew the tent down. They all crawled out but me. The snow fell on it. I went to sleep and slept warm all night. In the morning I heard someone say, 'How many are dead in this tent?' . . . So they jerked the tent loose, sent it scurring over the snow. My hair was frozen to the tent. I picked myself up and came out quite alive, to their surprise."[9]

John Jaques recorded:

> One afternoon Captain Martin and two or three other men started to go from the camp to Devil's Gate, but a snow storm came on and they mistook their bearings and lost their way. After wandering about for several hours, they came near perishing. In their exigency they endeavored to make a fire to warm themselves. They gathered some cedar twigs and struck match after match to light

> them, but in vain. At length, with their last match and the aid of portions of their body linen, they succeeded in starting a fire. This was seen from the handcart camp. From which, after all their anxious and weary wanderings, they were only about half a mile distant. Help soon came to the benighted wanderers and the "boys" carried Captain [Edward] Martin who was nearly exhausted, back to camp.[10]

During these desperate hours, Heavenly Father truly heard and answered the heartfelt prayers of the Saints who had been called upon to endure so much. Patience Loader wrote:

> I can testify that our Heavenly Father heard and answered our prayers and we was blessed with health and strength day by day to endure the severe trials we had to pass through on that terrible journey before we got to Salt Lake City we know that if God had not been with us that our strength would have failed us and our bodies would have been left on the plains as hundreds of our poor brothers and sisters was. I can truthfully say that we never felt to murmur at the hardships we was passing through. I can say we put our trust in God and he heard and answered our prayers and brought us through to the valleys.[11]

While the Martin Company was camped in the cove, the rescuers spent their days stowing the freight and readying themselves to continue with the journey as soon as the weather broke. In the evenings, they gathered to petition the heavens to temper the elements that they might have a chance at rescuing these faithful Saints from death.

Josiah Rogerson noted:

> Every morning and evening prayer meetings were called, at which addresses were made by the members of the rescuing and relief party, at one of which, a night or two before we left, Elder Cyrus H. Wheelock, who had just returned from a three-year mission to the British Isles, during which period he had become greatly attached to scores in our camp and company, offered a very remarkable prayer. His heart and soul was filled with sorrow at our condition, as we had several in our camp yet that had to a certain extent lost their minds—since crossing the North Platte river, at least they became like children and impersonal. Raising his hands to heaven in a very impressive and appealing manner, his voice nearly stifled with emotion and grief, he prayed to the Father that if for any fault or weakness

> that he might have done or committed in his life and ministry the progress of members of our company that he loved dearer than his own life was impeded; that if through anything he had done or left undone he had caused or helped to cause, or bring about our present plight, that He would instantly remove him out of the way by death, and let the company go on without further loss, to the valleys of the mountains. It was touching and deep in its humility.[12]

Daniel W. Jones described the difficult decisions faced by the Rescue Company during this time:

> Many suggestions were offered as to what should be done, some efforts being made to cache the imperishable goods and go on with the rest. Accordingly pits were dug, boxes opened and the hardware, etc., put in one, while clothing, etc., were put in another. Often these boxes belonged to different persons. An attempt was made by Brother Cantwell, to keep an account of these changes. This caching soon proved to be a failure for the pits would fill up with drifting snow as fast as the dirt was thrown out, so no caches were made. The goods were never replaced. Each evening the Elders would meet in council. . . . What to do was all that could be talked about. Five or six days had passed and nothing determined upon.[13]

Daniel W. Jones's account continued:

> Steve Taylor, Al Huntington and I were together when the question, 'Why doesn't Captain Grant leave all the goods here with someone to watch, and move on?' was asked. We agreed to make this proposal to him. It was near the time appointed for the meeting. As soon as we were together, Capt. Grant asked if anyone had thought of a plan. We presented ours. Capt. Grant replied, 'I have thought of this, but there are no provisions to leave and it would be asking too much of anyone to stay here and starve for the sake of these goods; besides, where is there a man who would stay if called upon.' I answered, 'Any of us would.' I had no idea I would be selected, as it was acknowledged I was the best cook in camp and Captain Grant had often spoken as though he could not spare me. That a proper understanding may be had, I will say that these goods were the luggage of a season's emigration that these two wagon trains had contracted to freight, and it was being taken through as well as the luggage of the people present. Leaving these goods meant to abandon all that many poor families had upon earth. So it was different from common merchandise. There was a move made at once to adopt this

> suggestion. Accordingly, next morning store rooms in the fort were cleared and some two hundred wagons run in and unloaded. No one was allowed to keep out anything but a change of clothing, some bedding and light cooking utensils. Hauling provisions was not a weighty question. This unloading occupied three days. The hand-cart people were notified to abandon most of their carts. Teams were hitched up and the sick and feeble loaded in with such light weight as was allowed. All became common property.[14]

By November 8, the weather improved enough that the rescuers were confident they could make another attempt toward the valley on the morrow. Daniel W. Jones recorded:

> When everything was ready Brother Burton said to me, 'Now Brother Jones we want you to pick two men from the valley to stay with you. We have notified Captains Hunt and Horgett to detail seventeen men from their companies to stay with you. We will move on in the morning. Get your company together and such provisions as you can find in the hands of those who may have anything to spare. You know ours is about out. Will you do it?' I said, 'Yes.' 'Well, take your choice from our company. You are acquainted with the boys and whoever you want will stay.' I had a great mind to tell him I wanted Captains Grant and Burton. There was not money enough on earth to have hired me to stay. . . . I had left home for only a few days and was not prepared to remain so long away; but I remembered my assertion that any of us would stay if called upon. I could not back out, so I selected Thomas Alexander and Ben Hampton. I am satisfied that two more faithful men to stand under all hardships could not have been found.[15]

Daniel W. Jones continued:

> That night we were called together and organized as a branch. Dan W. Jones, Thomas Alexander and Ben Hampton were chosen to preside, with J. Laty as clerk. The rest of the company was composed of the following names: John Cooper, John Hardcastle, John Shorton, John Chapel, John Galbraith, John Ellis, John Whitaker, William Handy, William Laty, Edwin Summers, Rossiter Jenkins, Elisha Manning, Henry Jakeman, George Watt, George Watts and _____. Captain Grant asked about our provisions. I told him they were scant, but as many were suffering and some dying, all we asked was an equal chance with the rest. He told us there would be a lot

> of worn out cattle left; to gather them up and try to save them. They consisted mostly of yearlings and two-year-old heifers, someone was taking through.[16]

Those remaining behind were men of integrity, and great trust was placed in them for the safekeeping of the luggage throughout the winter. Captain Grant counseled there was to be no grumbling or faultfinding. He wanted the men to agree together and be obedient to those called to preside over them. They were counseled to remember to call on the Lord mightily that they might be blessed, to be vigilant in protecting the luggage, and to keep everything in good repair. Finally, they were promised that word would be sent from the Salt Lake Valley before the spring. Daniel W. Jones was specifically counseled by President Grant to "maintain the dignity of his calling and not joke too much or suffer himself to be joked with those under him so sure was he to lose his influence."[17]

22

HEARTS MOVED WITH GREAT COMPASSION

ARRIVAL IN SALT LAKE VALLEY, DEPARTURE FROM MARTIN'S COVE, SOUTH PASS TO SIXTH CROSSING

WILLIE COMPANY ARRIVAL IN THE SALT LAKE VALLEY NOVEMBER 9, 1856

OAKEY FAMILY

Early in the morning of Sunday, November 9, eleven-year-old Rhoda Rebecca Oakey of England died. She was the final death in the Willie Handcart Company before reaching the Salt Lake Valley. Rhoda was traveling with her parents, Thomas and Ann Collett, and her siblings, twenty-three-year-old Ann, eighteen-year-old Charles, sixteen-year-old Jane, fourteen-year-old Heber Thomas, twelve-year-old Joseph Lorenzo, eight-year-old Reuben Hyrum, and four-year-old Sarah Ann. Wilford Woodruff introduced the gospel to her parents in 1840, and they were among the first six hundred he converted. The Oakeys worked earnestly for sixteen years to save enough money to join with the Saints in the Salt Lake Valley, but it never was enough. It was only through the blessings of the Perpetual Emigration Fund that they finally recognized their dreams. In Florence, following the discussion whether to winter there or continue on to the valley that season, twelve-year-old Joseph disagreed with the notion of continuing forward and left camp. After a frantic search, he was not found. Ann was given a priesthood blessing promising her she would one day see her son. With much sorrow, the Oakey family traveled on. Soon after leaving Florence, Thomas became ill. His illness grew much worse after Rocky Ridge, at which time eleven-year-old Rhoda also became deathly ill. Sarah later recorded, "Father's health began to fail and sometimes he would fall down and have to be helped. He would sit down to rest. When he felt better we would go on and catch up with the rest of the company again. . . . There were many people in camp who died but we fared fairly well until we reached the deep snow in Wyoming. Our father froze his feet and hands and his toenails came off. Though the family suffered many hardships we always held our family prayer." For sixteen days, Thomas and Rhoda struggled near death. Throughout the evening and into the morning of November 9, Ann stayed up attending to the needs of Thomas. "When she went to wake the children in the morning she discovered that Rhoda had died. She was so close to Zion. This was the long-awaited day that the company would finally reach the Valley of their dreams, but Thomas was gravely ill, rendering him unable to travel. He was left to mourn alone with Rhoda's body. Ann continued with the company and the rest of the children into the valley where she settled them at the home of her brother, Daniel Collett, and then returned for her husband and Rhoda's body." Rhoda was buried in the Salt Lake City Cemetery. Her sister Sarah later wrote: "Rhoda Rebecca had a sweet soprano voice and many evenings after the camp had been set up and supper eaten she would sing the hymn "Come, Come, Ye Saints, which helped lift the weary travelers in camp."

Years later, Thomas and Ann spoke with Charles C. Rich, a member of the Quorum of the Twelve Apostles, who was going east on business. They asked if he would place advertisements in Nebraska asking for any knowledge of their son. In 1876, twenty years after their arrival in the Salt Lake Valley, the family was reunited with Joseph, his wife, and children, who were then living in Kansas. Joseph later shared that he left the company because he was discouraged, tired, and hungry. He sought refuge in one of the homes in the area; when his parents came searching at the home, Joseph hid. The family raised him as their own son. Throughout their lives, Thomas and Ann Oakey remained poor, but they continued to make payments to the Perpetual Emigration Fund until their debt was forgiven in 1880 by President John Taylor.[1]

As the Willie Company was nearing the Salt Lake Valley, Captain James G. Willie's eight-year-old son, William, who had not seen his father for four years, "was so anxious to see his father that he walked to the mouth of Emigration Canyon. There he met him. James was delighted to see his son and lifted him into the wagon so that he could ride back with him. James' feet and legs were wrapped in burlap sacks because his shoes had worn out. Both feet had been badly frozen when he went to find the rescue party. It was feared they would have to be amputated." James's wife, Elizabeth, often shared with relatives, "there was nothing but his faith and the power of the priesthood and administration that saved his legs."[2]

"About noon on the 9th of November, William H. Kimball halted his sixty wagon loads of suffering humanity in front of the Old Tithing Office building, where Hotel Utah now stands. The company was greeted by hundreds of Salt Lake citizens who were anxiously awaiting their coming. The scene that followed would be hard to describe. In less than an hour from the time that ill-fated company reached its destination, every man, woman and child that belonged to it, was being tenderly cared for in a manner that brought tears of joy to their bloodshot eyes."[3]

James G. Willie wrote: "On our arrival there the bishops of the different wards took every person who was not provided with a home to comfortable quarters. Some had their hands and feet badly frozen; but everything which could be done to alleviate their sufferings was done, and no want was left unadministered to. Hundreds of citizens flocked around the wagons on our way through the city, cordially welcoming their brethren and sisters to their new home in the mountains."[4]

John Chislett recorded: "President Young had arranged with the bishops of the different wards and settlements to take care of the poor emigrants who had no friends to receive them, and their kindness in this respect cannot be too highly praised."[5]

JOSEPH B. ELDER

Of his arrival in the Salt Lake Valley, twenty-one-year-old Joseph B. Elder, who had given up his educational pursuits to assist the immigrating Saints, wrote: "At last we emerged from amongst the mountains, and the beautiful valley with all its loveliness spread itself out before our view. My heart was filled with joy and gratitude. The lovely city of G. S. Lake lay about 5 miles distant in full view. We entered it. The houses at first looked odd being built of adobes or sun dried brick. Truly it is unlike anything I ever before had seen. The journey was over at last and the people were soon distributed amongst the several wards, and I put up with my old friend Wm. Kimball." Joseph remained in the Salt Lake Valley only for a short time before attending a meeting on November 23, where a call for volunteers was issued to help bring in the last handcart company. That evening, Joseph set out to help rescue the Martin Company.[6]

REEDER & HURREN FAMILIES

Upon the arrival of the Reeder/Hurren families in the Salt Lake Valley, little seven-year-old Mary Hurren was in terrible condition: "When we arrived in Salt Lake City, we camped in the old tithing office lot where the Hotel Utah now stands. We were met by Uncle George Reeder. When he saw what a pitiful condition we were in, he went for medical aid. Two doctors came back with him. In the meantime my mother had warmed some water and was engaged in soaking the rags from off my frozen legs and feet. One of the doctors remarked, 'She'll never get over this. There's nothing we can do here.' He did not expect that I would live more than a day or two at the most." The doctor returned the following morning and stated: "I will take her feet off; one above the knee and one below—then she will live for a little while. That is all I can do with feet frozen as black as that." Mary continued: "My father objected to this and said that his little girl had not walked for a thousand miles across the plains to have her legs cut off." Mary's mother then "stood up straight and firm and said the memorable words that have been printed, like a crest, on my heart: 'If she dies, she dies with her feet on.'" The family went to Brigham City where they met a nurse who "looked at the limbs and recommended trying fresh raw-beefsteak on them. Fresh meet was not obtainable at Box Elder so her father walked to Ogden and obtained some round stake." Mary writes of her parents' selfless sacrifices to care for her: "The flesh fell away from the calves of my legs, so that it was necessary to grow new flesh. My mother put sweet oil on my legs. I remember that on several occasions after coming to Brigham City that father walked [20 miles] to Ogden to secure fresh beef to bind on my legs. It was three long years before I was able to walk." Mary would later boldly testify: "If I had my life to live over again I would not want to avoid any of the hardships that I have passed through. I would not want it any different."[7]

JAMES G. WILLIE

It is written of James G. Willie:

> He loved these saints, who in their native lands responded to the numerous calls for church donations as well as met the personal needs of the elders, he among them, out of their scanty earnings and in their poverty. Now, without means to come by wagon train, they were emigrating to Zion by the humblest method, a handcart, showing their full dedication to the Lord. James was a grateful man; he could not forget their kindnesses nor their willingness to obey. His heart was moved with great compassion. He not only struggled with his might to assist them, but he invoked the blessings of heaven in their behalf. Sacred accounts of these saints testify those prayers were heard, the heavens were moved, and there was divine intervention.[8]

Less than a month after the arrival of the Willie Company in the valley, on December 27, 1856, James G. Willie was ordained as bishop of a ward in Salt Lake City, and he would continue to serve faithfully in numerous callings throughout the remainder of his life. Of his death, Jim S. Willie wrote: "James Gray Willie passed away September 9, 1895, at the age of eighty. . . . The whole town went to his funeral. The funeral was held in the Mendon Ward and everyone was there whether they were church members or not. . . . I remember the casket was taken out of the bedroom window and let down because they couldn't get it out the door."[9]

Martin Company Departure from Martin's Cove

November 9, 1856

On the same day that the Willie Company arrived in the Salt Lake Valley, on Sunday, November 9, the Martin Company made preparations to once again resume their 327-mile journey to the Salt Lake Valley. Daniel W. Jones wrote: "The storm had now ceased to rage and great hopes were felt for a successful move. We were daily expecting more help and often wondered why it did not come."[10]

John Jaques recorded:

> It was a trying time that day in leaving the ravine. One perplexing difficulty was to determine who should ride, for many must still walk, though, so far as I recollect, and certainly for most of the company, the cart pulling occupation was gone. There was considerable crying of women and children, and perhaps of a few of the men, whom the wagons could not accommodate with a ride. One of the relief party remarked that in all the mobbings and drivings of the "Mormons," he had seen nothing like it. Cyrus H. Wheelock could scarcely refrain from shedding tears, and he declared that he would willingly give his own life if that would save the lives of the emigrants.[11]

Eighteen-year-old Langley Bailey, who had been seriously ill since Iowa, wrote: "On leaving this morning, my bro. John saw the wolves devouring the bodies he had helped to bury the day before. He tried to drive them away. He had to run for his life."

Langley's account continued:

> That morning in starting I was placed in a wagon on top of frozen tents. A very [few] oxen was left to haul or pull the few wagons. Made about 4 miles. When the company stopp[ed] that evening, mother came around the wagons calling 'Langley.' I could hear her calling. She could not hear me answer. When she found me,

> lifted me out of the wagon, my legs & arms was stiff like a frozed shirt. An ox was about to die, he was killed. Mother got some of the meat, boiled it, gave me some of the broth. It run through me like going through a funnel. "

Langely later wrote: "The 'half will never be told' of what we suffered before we reached great Salt Lake City, our promised land. On that memorable November day, the Martin Company left behind sacred ground, made hallowed by the suffering and sacrifice endured by so many faithful Saints."[12]

Of her experience in leaving the cove, Thisbe Read recorded: "So the company moved slowly—not all together as they had at first, but strung out in a long line that made a needle and a trailing black line in the snow. No one sang, no one talked. Folks just pushed along at their own pace and tried not to think of how the days might stretch into weeks and months before the last of them found a long sleep in a trench of snow."[13]

James Bleak wrote of his experiences that day: "We traveled 5 miles. I have suffered very much today with my feet, which are frost-bitten." James's feet became so badly frozen that the flesh dropped off his heels and he could no longer walk. His wife, Elizabeth, was among the few to continue to pull a handcart at this time. She pulled James along with her children, six-year-old Richard, four-year-old Thomas, two-year-old James Jr., and eleven-month-old Mary. As James's condition worsened, he begged Elizabeth to leave him and continue forward with the children. Elizabeth wrapped James in a blanket and laid him alongside the trail. In camp later on, Elizabeth told her friend Maria Jackson Normington, that at the request of James, he had been left behind. Maria replied, "No, it can't be," and told her she should not have permitted him to be left because of the promise he had been given in England that he "shall see the angel of death laying waste on his right and on his left, on his front and on his rearward, yet he and his family shall gather to Zion in safety, and not one of them shall fall by the way." Maria and her brothers took their handcart and went back on the trail until they found James. They brought him back into camp and cared for him until his health was restored.[14]

Daniel W. Jones Company
Devil's Gate
November 9, 1856

After getting the camp regulated at Devil's Gate and offering instruction to the men remaining, Daniel W. Jones rode out to see how the Martin Company was moving along. After riding a few miles, he came upon twenty-nine-year-old Mary Linforth of the Hunt Company sitting alone on the side of the road, weeping bitterly. He noticed the elegant way she was dressed and that she appeared to be strong and in good health. Daniel asked her what was wrong, to which Mary replied: "This is too much for me. I have always had plenty, and have never known hardships; we had a good team and wagon; my husband, if let alone, could have taken me on in comfort. Now I am turned out to walk in this wind and snow. I am determined not to go on but will stay here and die. My husband has gone on and left me, but I will not go another step." Daniel persuaded her to go on, and she returned to the Martin Company. Upon returning back to Devil's Gate, Daniel called his company together and told them "that if there was a man in camp who could not help eat the last poor animal left with us, hides and all, suffer all manner of privations, almost starve to death, that he could go with me the next day and overtake the trains. No one wanted to go. All voted to take their chances." Taking stock of their provisions, Daniel W. Jones noted: "Twenty day's rations. No salt or bread excepting a few crackers. There was at least five months of winter before us and nothing much to eat but a few perishing cattle and what game we might chance to kill. The game was not very certain, as the severe storms had driven everything away. The first move was to fix up the fort." Their nearest potential sources of supply were over 50 miles to the east at the Platte Bridge and 215 miles to the west at Fort Bridger, though neither was a real possibility.[15]

Rescuers
South Pass to Sixth Crossing

Ephraim Hanks noted:

> The terrific storm which caused the immigrants so much suffering and loss overtook me near the South Pass, where I stopped about

three days with Redick N. Allred, who had come out with provisions for the immigrants. The storm during these three days was simply awful. In all my travels in the Rocky Mountains both before and afterwards, I have seen no worse. When at length the snow ceased falling, it lay on the ground so deep that for many days it was impossible to move wagons through it. Being deeply concerned about the possible fate of the immigrants, and feeling anxious to learn of their condition, I determined to start out on horseback to meet them; and for this purpose I secured a pack-saddle and two animals (one to ride and one to pack), from Brother Allred, and began to make my way slowly through the snow alone. After traveling for some time I met Joseph A. Young and one of the Garr boys, two of the relief company which had been sent from Salt Lake City to help the companies. They had met the immigrants and were now returning with important dispatches from the camps to the headquarters of the Church, reporting the awful condition of the companies. In the meantime I continued my lonely journey, and the night after meeting Elders Young and Garr, I camped in the snow in the mountains. As I was preparing to make a bed in the snow with the few articles that my pack animal carried for me, I thought how comfortable a buffalo robe would be on such an occasion and how I could relish a little buffalo meat for supper, and before lying down for the night I was instinctively led to ask the Lord to send me a buffalo. Now, I am a firm believer in the efficacy of prayer, for I have on many different occasions asked the Lord for blessings, which He in His mercy has bestowed on me. But when I, after praying as I did on that lonely night in the South Pass, looked around me and spied a buffalo bull within fifty yards of my camp, my surprise was complete; I had not expected so immediate an answer to my prayer. However, I soon collected myself and was not at a loss to know what to do. Taking deliberate aim at the animal, my first shot brought him down; he made a few jumps only, and then rolled down into the very hollow where I was encamped. . . . After this I enjoyed a refreshing night's sleep, while my horses were browsing on the sage brush. Early the next morning I was on my way again, and soon reached what is known as the Ice Springs Bench. There I happened upon a herd of buffalo, and killed a nice cow. I was impressed to do this, although I did not know why until a few hours later, but the thought occurred to my mind that the hand of the Lord was in it, as it was a rare thing to find buffalo herds around that place at this late part of the season.[16]

Ephraim Hanks continued:

> Thereupon I resumed my journey, and traveled on till towards evening. I think the sun was about an hour high in the west when I spied something in the distance that looked like a black streak in the snow. As I got near to it, I perceived it moved; then I was satisfied that this was the long looked for hand-cart company, led by Captain Edward Martin. I reached the ill-fated train just as the immigrants were camping for the night. . . . The sight that met my gaze as I entered their camp can never be erased from my memory. The starved forms and haggard countenances of the poor sufferers, as they moved about slowly, shivering with cold, to prepare their scanty evening meal was enough to touch the stoutest heart. When they saw me coming, they hailed me with joy inexpressible, and when they further beheld the supply of fresh meat I brought into camp, their gratitude knew no bounds. . . . At first I tried to wait on and handed out the meat as they called for it; but finally I told them to help themselves. Five minutes later the meat was all gone, and the next few hours found the people in the camp busily engaged in cooking and eating it, with thankful hearts.[17]

In a blessing given to Ephraim Hanks at the hands of Patriarch John Smith on February 11, 1848, Ephraim was promised: "Thou shalt have faith to feed the great multitude in the wilderness. In a day of hunger and thirst, the springs shall break forth at thy command." Ephraim was also promised: "Thou shall be able to do miracles that ever was done by man, when it is necessary to forward the cause of Zion, or for the salvation of the children of men."[18]

For a short time, Ephraim Hanks conversed with the Read family, to whom he had been introduced two weeks earlier when joining with the Martin Company while on assignment to deliver mail to the east. He shared the following with them:

> No matter what I did or where I went I couldn't forget you folks. I kept wondering how you were getting on, what with the early snows and everything. . . . Seems since I was a boy that the Lord has always been willing to keep in touch with me if I'd keep in touch with Him. . . . This is the way I have it figured. . . . The Lord isn't going to fool around with any gifts just to impress folks. I don't hold for goings on in meetings like I've seen in some sects. I do know when a body needs the Lord—needs something the Lord can do for him so

> bad that there isn't any other way out—that is the time that the Lord will show His face or His voice and there'll be healings and tongues and prophesy and all the rest. . . . Yes, the Lord does do strange things, but I notice He always counts on human folks to help Him out. Now I've traveled this road time and time again and at this time of year I wouldn't ever have expected to meet a buffalo. But you folks needed meat and he was put in my way. Now, if I hadn't been there, or if I couldn't have brought him down—well, the way I figure, the Lord wouldn't have bothered to have him there, that's all.[19]

About ten o'clock that evening Arza Hinckley's family history notes that Ephraim Hanks returned to the place where he and Arza were going to camp for the night with news that he had found the Martin Handcart Company. Early the next morning both men arrived in the Martin camp and began caring for members of the company. [20]

Ephraim and Arza found many lives were endangered because of the effects of frostbite. Ephraim recalled: "Many of the immigrants whose extremities were frozen lost their limbs, either whole or in part. Many such I washed with water and castile soap, until the frozen parts would fall off, after which I would sever the shreds of flesh from the remaining portions of the limbs with my scissors. Some of the emigrants lost toes, others fingers, and again others whole hands and feet." Before amputating, Ephraim offered priesthood blessings petitioning the heavens that the Saints would not feel any pain; many testified they indeed did not experience pain during the rough frontier surgery.[21]

Ephraim and Arza spent the greater portion of their time going from tent to tent administering to and caring for those in greatest need. Ephraim related: "Truly the Lord was with me and others of his servants who labored faithfully together with me in that day of trial and suffering. The result of this our labor of love certainly redounded to the honor and glory of a kind and merciful God. In scores of instances when we administered to the sick, and rebuked the diseases in the name of the Lord Jesus Christ, the sufferers would rally at once; they were healed almost instantly."[22]

In his personal account, Arza Hinckley mentioned only a few short lines about his experience in taking part in the rescue efforts of the Martin Company: "We met the handcart folks at Ice Springs on the Sweetwater River, from there in to Salt Lake City. Ephraim Hanks, one of my battalion chums, spent much of our time while in camp administering to the sick. Ephraim was a man of great faith." Josiah Rogerson paid the following tribute to Ephraim Hanks: "Very few men—or members of the rescuing party, if any, surpassed Ephraim Hanks in the services and assistance that he rendered our company, day and night, until the last one of us reached Salt Lake, and from that day till this we have been crowning him with thanks and blessings." Arza also was a man of great faith and was revered by many members of the Martin Company for his heaven-sent service. James Bleak "was so grateful to Arza Hinckley that whenever he saw him, he put his arms around him and said, 'My Savior.'"[23]

Arza Hinckley

Throughout Arza's life, he endured countless difficulties, beginning with the death of his father when he was only five years old. The difficulties increased with his acceptance of the gospel, as he endured the trials associated with the Saints in Missouri and Illinois. These experiences prepared him for all that he would endure while serving in the Mormon Battalion and the difficulties experienced in establishing the Salt Lake Valley. Arza's life had been one of constant exposure, privation, and hard work, and it was these experiences that qualified him and countless others to serve as rescuers of the Martin and Willie Handcart Companies.[24]

David Blair

On the evening that David Blair of the Martin Company lay near death, his wife, Deborah, went to Daniel Tyler and asked him to administer to her husband. When Daniel arrived at the Blair tent and saw the condition of David, he reportedly commented: "I cannot administer to a dead man." Daniel then asked Ephraim Hanks to prepare the body for burial. With great compassion, Ephraim turned to a few men gathered nearby and asked:

> "Will you boys do just as I tell you?" The answer was in the affirmative. We then went to work and built a fire near the tent which

> I and Elder Tyler had just visited; next we warmed some water and washed the dying man, whose name was Blair, from head to foot. I then anointed him with consecrated oil over his whole body, after which we laid hands on him and commanded him in the name of Jesus Christ to breathe and live. The effect was instantaneous. The man who was dead to all appearances immediately began to breathe, sat up in his bed and commenced to sing a hymn. His wife, unable to control her feelings of joy and thankfulness, ran through the camp exclaiming: "My husband was dead, but now he is alive. Praised be the name of God. The man who brought the buffalo meat has healed him."

David reportedly lived another two weeks and then he, along with his six-month-old son, David, passed away. David and his wife, Deborah, were introduced to the gospel in 1842 in London. David served as a branch president until he emigrated in 1856 with his wife and three children. Patience Loader recalled the following about the Blairs:

> I remember well poor Brother Blair, he was a fine tall man and had been one of Queen Victoria's life guards in London. He had a wife and four small children. He made a cover for his cart and he put his four children on the cart. He pulled his cart alone, his wife helped by pushing behind the cart. Poor man, he was so weak and worn down that he fell down several times that day but still he kept his dear little children on the cart all day. This poor man had so much love for his wife and children that instead of eating his morsel of food himself he would give it to his children. Poor man, he pulled the cart as long as he could then he died and his poor wife and children had to do the best they could without him to help them. The poor children got frozen some parts of their bodies was all sores.[25]

23

VAGUE CONCLUSIONS

FORT BRIDGER TO SALT LAKE VALLEY, SIXTH CROSSING TO THREE CROSSINGS, DEVIL'S GATE TO SALT LAKE VALLEY

EXPRESS TEAM SENT FROM FORT BRIDGER SALT LAKE VALLEY
NOVEMBER 11, 1856

On November 11, the Express Team sent from Fort Bridger to the Salt Lake Valley arrived to apprise Brigham Young of the relief teams' return. Hosea Stout noted: "This news was very unexpected as the Hand Cart Company was in a suffering condition being beyond the South pass and destitute of clothing and provisions. Immediately upon receiving the news the president sent W. H. Kimball, Joseph Simmons, James Furgeson and myself as an express to go and turn the teams East again and for us to find where the Hand Cart company was."[1]

Redick N. Allred wrote: "President Young told Wm. Kimble that he did not care if he turned some so quick that it would snap their neck." Many of the returning teams made it all the way to Little Mountain before they were turned around again."[2]

On November 12, this Rescue Company met up with John Van Cott and the returning relief teams just after they had crossed the top of Big Mountain. Hosea Stout recorded he felt justified in returning because he had not obtained any information of the whereabouts of the companies and had "concluded they had returned to the states, or stopped at Laramie, been killed by the Indians. . . . So on these vague conclusions he had not only turned back but had caused all the rest of the teams to return and thus leave the poor suffering Hand carters to their fate." John Van Cott was severely reprimanded, and he and the other returning relief teams began eastward again.[3]

Later that evening, this company neared the Weber River and met up with Joseph A. Young and Abel Garr, whom Captain George D. Grant had sent from Devil's Gate eight days earlier. Upon receiving the report on the condition of the remaining companies, this rescue company pressed forward with the utmost urgency.[4]

Daniel W. Jones

Daniel W. Jones followed the Martin Company to their second encampment and traveled with them the next day. He recorded on November 12:

> There was much suffering, deaths occurring often. Eph Hanks arrived in camp from the valley and word that some of the teams that had reached South Pass and should have met us here, had turned back towards home and tried to persuade Redick Allred, who was left there with a load of flour, to go back with them. The men who did this might have felt justified; they said it was no use going further, that we had doubtless all perished. I will not mention their names for it was always looked upon by the company as cowardly in the extreme. If this had not occurred, it was the intention of Capt. Grant to have sent someone down to us with a load of flour. As it was, by the time any was received, the people were in a starving condition, and could not spare it.[5]

The Martin Company sent an express to South Pass, and they returned with four teams and some flour. Rations were increased to eight ounces for adults and four ounces for children. The company camped above Three Crossings. John Ollerton died and was buried with Brother Bridge and thirteen others the next morning. The rescuers would spend their days and nights caring tirelessly for the members of the Martin Company.[6]

Ollerton Family

John Ollerton and his wife, Alice, were among the first converts baptized by Heber C. Kimball. The Ollertons were traveling to the valley with their four children and a son-in-law. Their granddaughter was born and subsequently passed away on board the ship *Horizon*. John Ollerton passed away November 12, and Alice followed eight days later, on November 20. Their nineteen-year-old daughter, Alice, suffered terribly from the effects of frostbite, her feet being badly frozen, and "she was brought into Salt Lake more dead than alive, expiring the next day and buried Dec 3."[7]

Express Team Sent from Devil's Gate to Salt Lake Valley

After traveling 327 miles in ten days of hard riding, over almost impassable roads, Joseph A. Young and Abel Garr arrived in the Salt Lake Valley on November 13. Along their return trip, this Express Team turned around many rescue teams who had made the decision to return to the valley before reaching the stranded companies. Immediately upon the arrival of Joseph and Abel in the valley, they reported to President Brigham Young the condition of the Martin, Hunt, and Hodgett Companies.[8]

24

INTENSITY INCREASED

ROCKY RIDGE TO GREEN RIVER

MARTIN COMPANY ROCKY RIDGE TO GREEN RIVER NOVEMBER 16–21, 1856

Twenty-five days behind the Willie Company, the Martin Company reached Rocky Ridge on November 16. They were in a dreadful condition when they were met by a company of rescuers led by Anson Call, who recalled the following: "We found them starving and freezing and dying, and the most suffering that I ever saw among human beings."[1]

SERMON FAMILY

The recently widowed Elizabeth Sermon was suffering beyond imagination. Elizabeth was traveling to the valley with her fifty-three-year-old husband and her young children: nine-year-old John, seven-year-old Henry, five-year-old Robert, and three-year-old Marian. Their oldest son, Charles, did not want to emigrate and remained in England with grandparents. Following Elizabeth's baptism in 1852, she was determined to gather with the Saints in the Salt Lake Valley. Although her husband, Joseph, did not join the Church, he agreed to emigrate with the family. The Sermons sold both of their homes in the suburbs of London and sailed on the ship *Caravan*, arriving in Iowa with plans to travel in a wagon company. Elizabeth noted: "After much discussion and counsel from the Elders, we were convinced (at least I was) that it was God's will that the [wagon] be sold and we buy handcarts so that more Saints could make the journey to Zion." Joseph determined to go no further, feeling as if pulling the handcarts was demeaning. Elizabeth finally persuaded Joseph to continue, and the family left Iowa with the Martin Company. As the Sermon family traveled, Joseph and John became ill. Elizabeth recorded Joseph's words: "What have you brought us to, you, yourself in the shafts, drawing like a beast of burden, your children hungry and almost naked, myself will soon be gone, and My God, what will become of you and the children. You will find out how true all I have told you is, when it is too late." Joseph made it to Devil's Gate, was carried over the Sweetwater River by David Kimball, and died in Martin's Cove. Of Joseph's death, Elizabeth recalled, "I stood like a statue, bewildered—in tears—the cold chills, even now as I write, creep over my body, and it seems I can still hear and see the wolves watching for their bodies, as they would come down to camp before we were very far away."

The suffering continued for Elizabeth and her children. Elizabeth wrote:

> When we got into camp, I would clear the snow away with a tin plate, gather my wood, get my bed clothes from the wagons, I was too weak to haul much, get my allowance of flour then pack the children to the fire, make their beds on the ground. The tent was frozen and the ground so hard we could not set it up. . . . We went to bed without supper in order to get a little better breakfast. I found it some help to toast the raw hide on the coals and chew it; it helped to keep the hunger away, for, I assure you, I was feeling it rather keenly now. I had to take a portion of poor Robert's feet off which pierced my very soul. I had to sever the leaders with a pair of scissors. Little did I think when I bought them in old England, that they would be used for such a purpose. Every day some portion was decaying until the poor boy's feet were nearly all gone. Then John's began to freeze; then after a while my own.[2]

The Martin Company had 259 miles of the most difficult terrain still ahead of them. John Jaques recalled:

> As the emigrants proceeded on their terrible journey, there was no appreciable mitigation of the piercing wintry cold, but its intensity rather increased. The Rocky Ridge and the South Pass were crossed on the 18th of November, a bitterly cold day. The snow fell fast and the wind blew piercingly from the north. For several days company had been meeting more relief teams, which had been urged on by the Joseph A. Young express, and as the company was crossing the south pass, there was a sufficiency of wagons, for the first time, to carry all the people, and thence forth the traveling was more rapid.[3]

Peter McBride recalled: "No one but a person having gone through what we had suffered can imagine what a happy moment it was for this 'belated handcart company.' Men, women, and children knelt down and thanked the Almighty God for our delivery from certain death. It put new life into all the Saints. The next day several more teams arrived, and there was room for all to ride."[4]

On November 18, the Martin Company reached Redick Allred's station at South Pass. Redick had been left in charge of this relief station by Captain Grant on October 17 and had remained steadfast at his post in spite of others' encouragement to return home. All the while Redick suffered terribly from the effects of pleurisy, a condition that made even breathing severely painful and at times he felt as if it would take his life. One can only imagine the inexpressible joy Redick felt as he was greeted by Captain George D. Grant, who expressed his gratitude for Redick staying: "Hurrah for the Bulldog. Good for hanging on."[5]

The Martin Company was also met by William H. Kimball, James Ferguson, Joseph Simmons, Hosea Stout, and others who had been sent out again by Brigham Young on November 11. They had traveled just over 230 miles in seven days. Hosea Stout wrote:

> When traveling on fastly we arrived at the Station on Sweet Water just before night, the rest of the teams coming in shortly afterward. Here we met the advance of the Hand Cart Company who informed us that the company would be here to night. Several teams were dispatched to meet them and help them in. Soon they began to come in some in wagons, some on horses some on foot, while some [had] to be [led] or carried on the backs of men. This presented a sad sight to see men women & children thinly clad poor and worn out with hunger & fatigue trudging along in this dreary country facing

a severe snow storm and the wind blowing hard in their face. The wagons could not accommodate the half of those not able to walk. Many were sick and many frosted and some severely.

The following day Hosea Stout noted: "This evening I went with Eph Hanks to visit and administer to the sick and had an opportunity of seeing the suffering and privations through which they had passed."[6]

With the additional rescue companies arriving, Redick Allred described: "The teams having all arrived we were organized into companies of tens by wagons, each ten taking up a company of 100 as they were organized in the handcarts. All could ride, although much crowded. We then set out for the City with this half starved, half frozen, almost entirely exhausted company of about 500 Saints. But from that time on they did not suffer with hunger or fatigue but all suffered more or less with cold. As well as I was provided I even lost my toenails from frost."[7]

Rescuer Joseph Simmons wrote:

> One old lady lay dead within twenty feet of me, babies crying, some singing, some praying, &c &c, but among all this I feel to rejoice for the hand of the Lord has been continually with us. Almost every day angry storms arise very threatening and judging from their appearance one would think that we should be unable to withstand the tempest, but the prayers of the holy men of God are heard. The clouds divide to the right and left, letting the saints pass through in safety. The suffering of the camp from frozen feet and various other causes I will not attempt to describe. Suffice to say bad, bad, bad. The boys, including your humble servant, are all enjoying the blessing of health, lonely in their feelings, and doing all in their power to make the saints comfortable. We have some seventy wagons, divided into six divisions, one captain appointed over each, but all make one camp at night. We intend reaching the valley next Saturday [29 November], but this calculation is founded upon the faith of our Heavenly Father being continually with us, staying the storms as in the past, for without the help of high heaven, we should have been snow bound in the mountains long ago.[8]

On Friday, November 21, the Martin Company camped near the Green River. Jesse Haven recorded the temperature at three degrees below zero. Captain George D. Grant, William Kimball, and Hosea Stout left the Martin Company as an express team to the

Salt Lake Valley the day prior. Robert T. Burton was left in charge of the group.[9]

Robert T. Burton

Robert T. Burton's parents left England in 1817 to immigrate to America but lived in New York for only a few short years before making their way to Canada, where Robert was born in 1821. At age sixteen, Robert came in contact with two Mormon missionaries and convinced his father to listen to them. While visiting relatives in Ohio in October 1838, Robert and his family were baptized. During 1843–44, Robert served three missions, and, upon his arrival in Nauvoo, he enlisted in the Nauvoo Legion and was on duty the night of Joseph's and Hyrum's martyrdom. In 1845, Robert served a mission in Illinois and later married Maria Susan Haven. Following their expulsion from Nauvoo, Robert, Maria, and their infant daughter traveled to the Salt Lake Valley in 1848 with the Brigham Young Company (not to be confused with Brigham Young's First Company arriving in 1847). In Salt Lake City, Robert joined the local militia under the direction of Captain George D. Grant, and by 1855, he received his commission as major in the militia.[10]

25

VALIANT MEN OF GOD

FORT BRIDGER TO BIG MOUNTAIN

MARTIN COMPANY
FORT BRIDGER TO BIG MOUNTAIN
NOVEMBER 23–NOVEMBER 29, 1856

By Sunday, November 23, the Martin Company had reached Fort Bridger, twenty-one days behind the Willie Company. They were now 113 miles from the Salt Lake Valley. Robert T. Burton wrote: "Snowed again tonight. Camped at Fort Bridger." Josiah Rogerson recalled:

> The writer remembers the cold nights at Red Buttes, at the Devil's Gate and in Martin's ravine, but this was the "Black Friday" night of them all. The children cried the livelong night. It froze hard and the wind had a full sweep at us here, so much so that I could not get or keep warm in the tent, and hearing a violin start up, got out of our blankets, went to a fire a short distance away and there, sure enough, was Lewis Robinson and Eph Hanks, clapping their hands and keeping time to the fiddle, while one of the valley teamsters was "cutting the pigeon wing" on the hind endgate of a wagon box. Others of our company and more boys from the valley soon gathered, and possibly a little valley tan may have been in one or two of their ankles, which would not have been out of place at all, for around the fire we were burning on one side and freezing on the other.[1]

JAQUES FAMILY

While at Fort Bridger, Flora Loader Jaques, two-year-old daughter of John and Zilpah Jaques, died. "Flora had the measles just as we were leaving the ship. She was never thoroughly healthy afterwards. At Iowa City she had the diarrhea, which afflicted her, with more or less severity, until we arrived at Green River, where, on Nov. 22nd, her spirit returned to Him who gave it."[2]

Of his experiences at this time, Ephraim Hanks recalled:

> One evening after having gone as far as Ft. Bridger, I was requested by a sister to come and administer to her son, whose name was Thomas [Dobson]. He was very sick, indeed, and his friends expected he would die that night. When I came to the place where he lay he was moaning pitifully, and was almost too weak to turn around in his bed. I felt the power of God resting upon me and addressing the young man said, "Will you believe the words I tell you?" His response was, "Yes." I then administered to him and he was immediately healed. He got up, dressed himself and danced the hornpipe on the inboard of the wagon, which I procured for that purpose. . . . As the train moved forward in the day time I would generally leave the road in search of game; and on these expeditions killed and dressed a number of buffaloes, distributing their meat among the people. On one occasion when I was lagging behind with a killed buffalo, an English girl by the name of Griffin gave out completely, and not being able to walk any further, she lay down with her head in the snow. When I saw her disabled condition I lifted her on my saddle the horse being loaded with buffalo meat, and in this condition she rode into camp. Soon more relief companies were met and as fast as the baggage was transferred into the wagons, the hand carts were abandoned one after another, until none were left. I remained with the immigrants until the last of Captain Martin's company arrived in Salt Lake City on the thirtieth day of November, 1856.[3]

ECHO CANYON

The Martin Company camped in Echo Canyon on November 26. The day would be marked with a miracle as Sarah Squires delivered a baby girl. How Sarah survived her pregnancy during those severe conditions is truly incredible. John Jaques recalled: "one of the relief party generously contributed part of his under linen to clothe

the little stranger. The mother did quite as well as could have been expected, considering the unpropitious circumstances. The little new comer also did well, and was named Echo, in honor of the place of her nativity."[4]

Some twenty miles from the valley, the man affectionately known as "Father Waugh" died. He was described as "one of the most devoted Scottish worthies that ever came to Utah." Sixty-eight-year-old George Waugh compassionately spent the last years of his life ministering to the sick and the afflicted, the aged and the infirm. "The aged Scotch worthy had braved and weathered the storms of the Rocky mountains from the Platte bridge, and when within eighteen to twenty miles from the valley, and the Zion he worshiped, and to which he was returning after a three or four years' mission to Scotland (his native land), succumbed to the hardships of the journey, between the Big and Little mountains, and was brought into the city for internment."[5]

Big Mountain

By November 28, the first of the Martin Company were crossing Big Mountain. The terrain was nearly impassable with "four feet of fresh snow with twenty-foot drifts on the north side of the summit. With help from the tamping teams, by stomping main and side tracks and shoveling through the drifts, Burton's men brought the wagons over. A camp was made in East Canyon, to which men from the valley began to filter. Some of these hurried back to advise Brigham Young on the company's progress. By the time the immigrants camped at the head of Emigration Canyon the following evening, fresh supplies were waiting for them." Josiah Rogerson stated: "Tonight I remember my brother and I making our bed between two large quaking asp logs here, the fire at our feet, and next morning, waking up, found two chimneys of snow over our faces, through which we had breathed during the night with from eight to ten inches of snow on our blankets."[6]

As the company camped near Emigration Canyon, the Rescue Company spent the day packing the snow with their teams in order to make the roads passable for the wagons. John Bond recorded:

> The worst snowy point to cross to arrive in the valley. They are ordered to go on again and commence to ascend the mt. Five miles in four feet of snow up a heavy grade . . . on arriving half a mile from the top of the mt. The valley boys working with patience as the teams were taking a rest, ready for the heavy pull for the horses, and they had not rested long when "Hurrah! Hurrah!" Is heard from the mt. top and as such is heard from the boys below gave three cheers Hurrah! Hurrah! and a Tiger. When on the top of the mt. they were enjoying a hearty shaking of hands and God blessings. They were volunteer valley boys as snow shovelers. On the top of the mt. the snow had drifted on the east side approximately twenty feet deep and Brigham Young had teams driven backwards and forwards until the snow was well packed so as the "Valley boys" could drive the teams and wagons over with the saints with comfort. The men worked valiantly and I will not forget their manly courage while mortality endures.[7]

John Bond continued: "On arriving at the top of the mt. encounter very deep snow. When all have arrived at the top of the mt. have a magnificent view of the snow covered mts. On to the east and west. We now see the long looked for Salt Lake Valley though an opening of the gigantic mts. In the valley below. This brought many smiles as well as tears to the faces of the saints what had been so far now so near to where every heart wished to see and be."[8]

Though not every heroic effort of the rescuers dispatched on this "Heaven sent mission" was documented for future generations to read, it is safe to say that all of these valiant rescuers should be hailed for their willingness, at the peril of their own lives, to save the members of the Willie and Martin Handcart Companies and the Hunt and Hodgett Wagon Companies. Their actions are forever etched in the hearts of those they served as well as in the hearts of all who become familiar with their accounts.

26

LABOR OF LOVE

SALT LAKE VALLEY

MARTIN COMPANY
ARRIVAL IN THE SALT LAKE VALLEY
NOVEMBER 30–DECEMBER 31, 1856

On Sunday morning, November 30, the Saints in the Salt Lake Valley gathered in the Old Tabernacle. Brigham Young stood before the congregation and addressed them as follows:

> We expect that the last hand-cart company, br. Martin's, will soon be in the streets by the Council House. . . . When those persons arrive I do not want to see them put into houses by themselves; I want to have them distributed in this city among the families that have good and comfortable houses; and I wish the sisters now before me, and all who know how and can, to nurse and wait upon the comers and prudently administer medicine and food to them. To speak upon these things is a part of my religion, for it pertains to taking care of the Saints. . . . We have quite a task upon us this season, for when the last hand-cart company arrives and is comfortable disposed of, we still have about 400 more brethren and sisters who are yet beyond Fort Bridger, probably near Green river. They are those that came out with teams, or the independent companies. . . . I can say the great majority of the brethren here, so far as we have called on them to assist this year's immigration, have freely and nobly manifested their faith by their works. True, some that went out have

been imprudent, though I think it will all come out right and I can feel to bless them, notwithstanding they have been imprudent and foolish. . . . As soon as this meeting is dismissed I want the brethren and sisters to repair to their homes, where their Bishops will call on them to take in some of this company; the Bishops will distribute them as the people can receive them. . . . The afternoon meeting will be omitted, for I wish the sisters to go home and prepare to give those who have just arrived a mouthful of something to eat, and to wash them and nurse them up. You know that I would give more for a dish of pudding and milk, or a baked potato and salt, were I in the situation of those persons who have just come in, than I would for all your prayers, though you were to stay here all the afternoon and pray. Prayer is good, but when baked potatoes and pudding and milk are needed, prayer will not supply their place on this occasion; give every duty its proper time and place. This is what I can say truly, with the rest of your counselors and directors, that no man or woman, that we have any knowledge of in the church, has refused to do as requested, with regard to this immigration; they have run by day and night. Our messengers have been traveling from here to the Platte, and back and forth between Bridger, Green river and the Sweetwater; and scores of men have been riding by day and night, without having enjoyed an undisturbed night's rest during the last two months, only occasionally snatching a little sleep when sitting by the camp fire. They have been riding by day and night, hurrying to and fro and laboring with their might, and have not refused to do what we have required of them; this is to their praise. Works have been most noble when they were needed; we put works to our faith, and in this case we realize that our faith alone would have been perfectly dead and useless would have been of no avail, in saving our brethren that were in the snow, but by putting works with faith we have been already blest in receiving many and bringing them to where we can now do them more good. Some of you will find with their feet frozen to their ankles; some are frozen to their knees and some have their hands frosted. They want good nursing, and if you do not know how to treat frozen flesh, let me inform you that the same treatment is needed as in a burn, and by pursuing that method you can heal them. . . . I want you to understand that we desire this people to nurse them up; we want you to receive them as your own children, and to have the same feeling for them. We are their temporal saviors, for we have saved them from death. Br. Chislett, who has just been addressing you, would have been dead long before this,

> had it not been for the assistance of br. George D. Grant and those who went back with him. The rear companies would never have got over the Rocky Ridge, or seen the upper crossing of the Sweetwater, had they not been helped from here. Now that most of them are here we will continue our labors of love, until they are able to take care of themselves, and we will receive the blessing. You need not be distrustful about that, for the Lord will bless this people; and I can feel to bless them all the time, and this I continually try to carry out in my life.[1]

The arrival of the Martin Company was a solemn occasion, as many were met by friends and relatives. John Jaques wrote:

> On Sunday the 30th passed down the latter canyon and arrived in this city about noon, driving into East Temple street as the congregation was leaving the old adobie tabernacle in the southwest corner of Temple block. The meeting of the emigrants with relatives, acquaintances, and friends was not very joyous. Indeed it was very solemnly impressive. Some were so affected that they could scarcely speak, but would look at each other until the sympathetic tears would force their unforbidden way. In a short time, however, the emigrants were taken into the houses of their friends and made as comfortable as circumstances would permit them to be while they thawed the frost out of their limbs and recruited their health and strength.[2]

Of the Martin Company's arrival in the valley Robert T. Burton recorded: "Here (South Pass) General Grant and Col. Kimball left me in charge of the company which finally arrived in Salt Lake on the last day of Nov. with 104 wagons and teams winding their way over the Big mountain. This indeed was a grand sight to us as we looked back upon the hardships and sufferings of this most critical campaign of my life. The hardships and sufferings of this company of people can never be told."[3]

Although their condition was extremely grave, the Martin Company entered the Salt Lake Valley triumphantly after having endured a journey to the Salt Lake Valley unlike any other. This journey transformed these Saints into different people as they traveled through the most indescribable suffering and hardship than any handcart company. Harvey H. Cluff wrote: "How inadequate is language to depict, or pen to write, the soul stirring pleasure, and gratitude to the allwise Creator for our safe arrival home."[4]

Redick Newton Allred led one group, and Robert T. Burton led the other, as they traveled up the street in two lines. They passed the temple block around noon and stopped at the tithing yard, where they were received with open arms. Redick wrote: "Thus ended one of the hardest and most successful missions I have ever performed, for although the mission with the Mormon Battalion was long, hard, tedious and therefore very severe, yet this was short and sharp in the extreme."[5]

Solomon F. Kimball later wrote:

> Probably no greater act of heroism was ever recorded in the annals of history than that performed by the twenty-seven young men who, on the morning of October 7, 1856, went from the city of the Great Salt Lake to the relief of the 1,550 belated emigrants, who were caught in the early snows of a severe winter, hundreds of miles from human habitation, without food and without shelter. By their indefatigable labors these brave mountain boys were instruments in the hands of the Lord in saving 1,300 of that number. Had it not been for their heroic efforts, not enough emigrants would have been left to tell the dreadful tale.[6]

Josiah Rogerson recorded:

> What a contrast in crossing the plains of America then with a hand-cart. . . . Well may a few of the great-grand daughters of the revolutionary fathers, and the not too many sons and daughters still living in Salt Lake of the pioneers of 1847 take an interest in the perpetuation of their memories and the preservation of their records; but the future historian will say that none the less mead of praise is due, and none the more worthy of record, that ever crossed the plains, or demonstrated their firmness of faith and adherence to Mormonism than the members of the handcart companies of 1856.[7]

For members of the Willie and Martin Handcart Companies and their rescuers, their arrival in the Salt Lake Valley did not mark the end of their trials and challenges. In spite of their already countless difficulties, they went forward with great faith, patiently enduring and overcoming the physical and emotional pains attributed to their most remarkable journey to Zion. They settled new areas, fulfilled missions, and labored to make ends meet. Very few ever spoke a word of complaint or regret regarding their journey to the Salt Lake Valley.

Mellor Family

Sixteen-year-old Louisa Mellor had been such a pillar of strength to her mother, who delivered twins just prior to boarding the ship *Horizon*. She recalled:

> Brother Wheelock and Brother Goddard were in the crowd to meet us when we arrived. They asked for James Mellor. When they saw him they were stunned! A man 38 years of age with hair as white as the driven snow! Indeed, the trials and tribulations, the hardships and the deprivations they had suffered from England to Salt Lake Valley had taken its toll. They took him in their arms and wept! They also greeted my mother, to whom they had promised life and that she would live to see Zion. We were received by the saints, some with tears in their eyes and some with joy. We were a pitiful sight to see, and for weeks this company was not allowed to eat much nor to see themselves in a mirror. President Young met us and when he saw us he was so melted down with grief at sight of our condition he had to go home sick, but he blessed us first.[8]

Ashton Family

After losing their newborn sister, eleven-year-old sister, and mother Sarah Ann, and then being abandoned by their father at Fort Laramie, seven-year-old Sarah and four-year-old Mary were left in the care of the Martin Company for the remainder of their journey to the Salt Lake Valley. As a result of exposure to the elements, Sarah became blind in one eye. Upon arriving in the valley, they went to the home of the Hatfields. At age fifteen, Sarah married Thomas W. Beckstead, and Mary later married Isaac Wardle, who was employed by Thomas Beckstead's father. Mary lived only a few short hours after the birth of her firstborn son, William Ashton Wardle. William was named after Mary's father, whom she must have forgiven. While living in Idaho, Sarah received a copy of an article printed in the *Millennial Star* that contained an inquiry about relatives of William Ashton. Recognizing the writer as her father, Sarah sent correspondence in answer to the inquiry and eventually sent money for his passage from England to America. She lovingly cared for her father until his death. Sarah lived a long life, dying at age ninety-two.[9]

GRIFFITHS FAMILY

Of the arrival of the Griffiths family, sixteen-year-old Margaret recalled: "We reached the valley of Salt Lake on the 30th day of November, 1856 after two months of the most indescribable suffering and hardships, the worst we thought of any company of men, women and children was ever called upon to endure."

Margaret's eight-year-old sister, Jane, wrote:

> When we arrived in Salt Lake we were taken to the assembly room and the people were asked to take as many into their homes as they could take care of. My father and mother were taken to one place, my sister and I each to another. I did not see my father again. He died the next day. . . . We were six in a family when we started, father, two brothers, my stepmother, a sister 16 years old and myself. It seems strange that more men and boys died than women and girls. My two brothers died on the way and my father the day after we arrived in Salt Lake.

Jane's account continued:

> Brother Samuel Mulliner took my father and step-mother to his home. My father died the next morning at five o'clock. I was so sick that they did not tell me about it for some weeks. My sister went with Bro. and sister Montague. She was very sick and her heels were badly frozen. Mr. and Mrs. Horne took me to their home, my toes were very badly frozen. . . . I stayed three weeks at the place where I was taken, then Brother Mullener, the one who had taken Father to his home, heard that I was to be sent to the poor house in Provo and he said, "Never as long as I have a home." So he brought a wheel barrow with some quilts and pillows in and took me to his home where I stayed all winter, being in bed all the time. I did not stand on my feet until the 6th of March. I lost the first joint of six of my toes. My stepmother then carried me the 12 blocks to a man's home who had been a friend of father's. He said he would keep me. I went there on my 9th birthday. Mother could carry me as far as she could then put me down in the snow and we would cry a while and then go on."

Margaret wrote, "I was terribly frozen up myself, I was laid up nine weeks in Salt Lake, because my feet had been so badly frozen. (After I was placed into the wagons and the frost left my feet, large bags of water formed at my heels.)"[10]

Pucell Family

Both Samuel and Margaret Pucell were buried along the trail on their journey to the Salt Lake Valley, leaving ten-year-old Ellen "Nellie" and fourteen-year-old Maggie orphans. They were left in the care of Mary Rogerson. Many died and many others suffered from frozen limbs, among them the Pucell girls, all having badly frozen feet and legs. William Palmer later wrote:

> Nellie's parents were among those who died and were laid to rest in snow banks. Poor little Nellie, nothing could be done to save her feet. When they took off her shoes and stockings the skin with pieces of flesh came off too. The doctor said her feet must be taken off to save her life. They strapped her to a board and without an anesthetic the surgery was performed. With a butcher knife and a carpenter's saw they cut the blackened limbs off. It was poor surgery, too, for the flesh was not brought over to cushion the ends. The bones stuck out through the ends of the stumps and in pain she waddled through the rest of her life on her knees. In poverty and pain she reared a family of six children but never asked for favors of pity or charity because of her tragic handicap. William was a poor man and unable to provide fully for his family; so Nellie did all she could for herself. She took in washings. Kneeling by a tub on the floor she scrubbed the clothes to whiteness on the washboard. She knit stockings to sell, carded wool and crocheted table pieces. She seldom accepted gifts or charity from friends or neighbors unless she could do a bundle of darning or mending to repay the kindness. The bishop and the Relief Society sometimes gave a little assistance which Nellie gratefully accepted, but once a year, to even the score, she took her children and cleaned the meeting house. The boy carried water, the girls washed the windows and Nellie, on her knees, scrubbed the floor. This heroic woman gave to William Unthank a posterity to perpetuate his name in the earth and he gave her a home and a family to give comfort and care in her old age. In memory I recall her wrinkled forehead, her soft dark eyes that told of toil and pain and suffering, and the deep grooves that encircled the corners of her strong mouth. But in that face there was no trace of bitterness or railings at her fate. There

> was patience and serenity for in spite of her handicap she had earned her keep and justified her existence. She had given more to family, friends and to the world than she had received.[11]

EDWARD MARTIN

Edward Martin heard the missionaries preach in England and was baptized at the hands of Orson Hyde on October 14, 1837. He and his wife immigrated to America in 1841. They gathered with the Saints in Nauvoo, where they buried their daughter Lucy Ann. The Martins endured unspeakable horrors during their expulsion by the mobs. Edward volunteered to serve in the Mormon Battalion, leaving behind his pregnant wife and three-year-old daughter, Mary Ellen. During his absence, his wife gave birth to a son who lived only five months. Two weeks after arriving in the Salt Lake Valley, the Martins buried yet another child, a daughter born while traveling to the valley in the Heber C. Kimball Company. Edward accepted the call to serve a mission to England from 1852–56. In 1856, Edward spent the last few months of his four-year mission in Liverpool, overseeing the emigration of 4,395 Saints. He also led a handcart company that would be forever remembered by his namesake. Following this journey to the Salt Lake Valley, Edward returned home to his wife, Alice, and twelve-year-old daughter, Mary Ellen. Throughout his life, Edward continued to experience great difficulties. He lived to age sixty-four. His wife and fourteen of his twenty-one children preceded him in death.[12]

Rescuers December 2, 1856

On December 2, 1856, two days after the Martin Company arrived in the Salt Lake Valley, another sixty relief teams started east to help the Hunt and Hodgett Companies. John Jaques recorded:

> Isaac Bullock and all the men at Fort Supply, on Green River, went to the assistance of the wagon companies, taking all the oxen, down to the 2-year-olds, in the settlement. On the 2nd of December, sixty horse and mule teams, mostly two span, with provisions and forage, left the city to fetch in the wagon companies, which

> arrived here by detachments. It has been stated that they were all in, excepting a few persons who tarried at Fort Supply, by the 16th of December. Perhaps most of them were, but individuals who were there affirm that some of the wagons were arriving during most of the remainder of the month.

With all but Daniel W. Jones and his company, who remained at Devil's Gate, the immigration season of 1856 was officially closed. During the years 1856 to 1860, ten handcart companies consisting of approximately 3,000 Saints journeyed to Utah.[13]

27

A MOST REMARKABLE SACRIFICE

DEVIL'S GATE TO SALT LAKE VALLEY

DANIEL W. JONES COMPANY
DEVIL'S GATE
NOVEMBER 9, 1856–JUNE 11, 1857

For Daniel W. Jones and the men remaining with him at Devil's Gate with the charge of keeping the luggage safe throughout the winter, enduring the winter season would be their most difficult and trying experience. In the fort vicinity, over two hundred head of cattle had perished, and the remaining cattle were very poor. Wolves came in droves to the camp; it became nearly impossible for the men to keep them away. Within the first week, wolves killed at least twenty-five cattle, and, at risk of losing them all to the wolves, the remaining fifty were killed. What little meat they were able to obtain was dressed and hung. Before long, the flour supply was depleted, and by January all of the meat had been consumed.

Near Christmastime, while Daniel W. Jones and several others were out on a hunting expedition, the company received unexpected visitors: Ephraim Hanks and Feramorz Little. They were traveling east with the mail and had arrived at the fort to deliver a letter from Brigham Young. It stated that help would come as early as possible in the spring, but might not reach them until May. Daniel was disappointed to learn Ephraim had continued east without seeing him, and by the contents of the letter, he was also disappointed to learn that Brigham Young had no idea about their dire situation. Daniel wrote: "From this letter it is plain to see that Brother Brigham was not apprised of our condition. He afterwards said if he had known our situation he would have relieved us if it had taken half the men in the valley. I never felt to complain. The brethren who left us knew but little about what was left to provision us. The supposition was that the cattle would have furnished us in case game could not be killed. . . . Game soon became so scarce that we could kill nothing. We ate all the poor meat; one would get hungry eating it."

It was under these circumstances that the men resorted to eating the hides, which made them sick.

> Things looked dark, for nothing remained but the poor raw hides taken from starved cattle. We asked the Lord to direct us what to do. The brethren did not murmur, but felt to trust in God. . . . We had cooked the hide, after soaking and scraping the hair off until it was soft and then ate it, glue and all. This made it rather inclined to stay with us longer then we desired. Finally I was impressed how to fix the stuff and gave the company advice, telling them how to cook it; for them to scorch and scrape the hair off; this had a tendency to kill and purify the bad taste that scalding gave it. After scraping, boil one hour in plenty of water, throwing the water away which had extracted all the glue, then wash and scrape the hide thoroughly, washing in cold water, then boil to a jelly and let it get cold, and then eat with a little sugar sprinkled on it. This was considerable trouble, but we had little else to do and it was better than starving. We asked the Lord to bless our stomachs and adapt them to this food. We hadn't the faith to ask him to bless the rawhide. For it was "hard stock." On eating now, all seemed to relish the feast. We were three days without eating before this second attempt was made. We enjoyed this sumptuous fare for about six weeks, and never had the gout.[1]

By February, the men were "out of everything, having not only eaten the hides taken from the cattle killed, but had eaten the wrappings from the wagon-tongues, old moccasin-soles were eaten also, and a piece of buffalo hide that had been used for a foot mat for two months." The men gathered one evening to fast and pray: "During the meeting we became impressed that there were some wrongs existing among the brethren in camp that should be corrected, and that if we would make a general cleaning up, and present our case before the Lord, He would take care of us, for we were there on His business." Daniel learned that hunger was getting the best of some of the men. They were secretly cutting steaks from the carcasses of cattle that had died months earlier, and it had made them quite sick. Other men were tempted by the frozen wolf carcasses and frozen offal, or the parts of the butchered cattle that are considered inedible.

Many asked Daniel for his opinion on eating the carcasses and offal. Daniel told them: "If they would all do as I advised we would have a good clean supper of healthy food; that these carcasses were unclean; that we were on the Lord's service, and did not believe He wanted us to suffer so much, if we only had faith to trust Him and ask for better. We all became united in this feeling." They disposed of the carcasses and then "went and washed out our store-house and presented it before the Lord empty, but clean." No one seemed disheartened about their present situation. Later in the evening, the Magraw Party, led by Jesse Jones, arrived at the fort. By ten o'clock that same evening, members of the Daniel W. Jones Company sat down with the Magraw Party for supper. The next day, they again found themselves without any food. Daniel noted: "Some may ask why we did not leave. There was no time during the winter but what the attempt would have been certain death to some of us. The company at no time was strong enough to make the trip to Platte bridge, neither did we wish to abandon our trust that we had accepted with our eyes wide open to the perils around us." Again their prayers were answered when an Indian they had befriended provided them with a buffalo he had killed with his bow.[2]

By early March, nothing was left to eat. All that remained was a set of harnesses and an old packsaddle covered with rawhide. As it was being prepared for cooking, Daniel and a few others went out to hunt game. After traveling through the snow for several miles, they spotted a drove of mountain sheep, but by the time Daniel readied himself for a shot, he looked up and they were gone. Daniel wrote: "My heart almost failed me, and I could have cried like a child, for I knew that nothing was in camp when we left and our comrades expected us to bring something for supper." As the men were returning back to the Fort, Daniel decided he would set out on foot the following morning for the Platte Bridge to obtain some provisions. It would be a dangerous four-day journey through snow eighteen inches to three feet deep, yet Daniel was determined to do whatever it took to save the lives of his men. Upon returning to the fort that afternoon empty handed, "A shout of joy rang out from our crowd that made the hills ring." Members of the Y. X. Express had arrived on their way east carrying mail. The mail company the day before "had killed a large buffalo and packed the whole of it into our camp." When the Y.X. Express left the Fort, Daniel decided to accompany them to the Platte Bridge and along the way they met up with "some men from the Platte bringing us some beef. They had heard in some way that we were still alive. I think the Indians must have passed the word. They could not get buffalo meat, so had killed some cattle and were bringing them to us. They had been four days on the road, tramping snow and working through drifts, expecting to find us starving. I often think of these old pioneers, who were always so ready to help a fellowman in need."[3]

From time to time, small bands of Indians camped around the fort, and when it became known to them that the company was short of provisions, they traded freely until game became so scarce that the Indians had to move out or starve. "We were a little uneasy to have all these hungry Indians come upon us at once; the greatest care had to be taken to avoid trouble. . . . This naturally made us feel a little uneasy. We had some two hundred wagon loads of valuable goods under our charge, and only twenty men, the greater portion of them with no frontier experience."[4]

In early May, a company of men from the valley arrived, bringing nearly a ton of flour and other provisions as well as news they were sent to strengthen the Devil's Gate post. They had received specific information about a large group of approximately fifty apostate men who "had become dissatisfied with 'Mormonism' and were going back to the states. As their goods had not arrived in Salt Lake City, they demanded that they should be delivered at Devil's Gate. . . . Quite a number settled their freight bills and brought orders for their goods and received them all right. Others refused to settle, but threatened that if the goods were not given up they would take them by force." When the apostate company arrived, one man presented a claim for a lot of goods, which proved not genuine and was refused. This refusal angered the apostates even further, and they demanded the goods be given up or "they would tear down the fort or have them." Daniel's instructions "were to deliver no goods to anyone unless they presented an order from the right parties." When the threats escalated into possible action, Daniel declared to the apostates: "We have been here all winter eating poor beef and rawhide to take care of these goods. We have had but little fun, and would just as soon have some now as not; in fact would like a little now. If you think you can take the fort, just try it. But I don't think you can take me to commence with; and the first one that offers any violence to me is a dead man. Now I dare you to get past me towards the fort. This seemed to take them back. I meant what I said." Tom Williams, the leader of the apostates, responded, "For your family's sake I will spare you, for I think you fool enough to die before you would give up the goods." The men departed without further incident.[5]

As wagons from the Salt Lake Valley began to arrive to transport the goods to the valley, Daniel awaited a letter, supposedly en route from Brigham Young that contained specific instructions regarding how to arrange the transportation of the freight.

> There were over two hundred teams now on the ground, many of the owners beginning to get impatient at the delay. I was at a loss what to do, so I went out after night and asked the Lord to help me out. I told Him I desired to do exactly what was best, but did not know a thing about it, and made this proposition that I would take my clerk with me in the morning, and when a question was asked me by any one what to do, I would tell the clerk to write down just what first came to my mind. And if that was right to please remove the spirit of oppression that I was laboring under and allow me to go back to the fort and enjoy myself with my friends. My mind was entirely relieved. I went and passed a pleasant evening. Next morning without saying anything about the lack of instructions we commenced business. Soon someone asked whose teams were to be loaded first, I dictated to my clerk.

They continued this process for four days before the teams were on their way to the valley.[6]

Daniel left Devil's Gate with orders that he would return once again to take charge of the Y. X. Express Station, newly established there. When Daniel arrived in the Salt Lake Valley, he went directly to Brigham's Young office. During this meeting, Daniel wrote that President Young was very glad to see him: "expressing much sympathy and saying that if he had known of our suffering in time he would have sent us supplies at any cost." Brigham then asked Daniel if he followed the instructions sent. Daniel notes: "I acted a little stiff for I did not know whether my management of the last business would be approved or not, but I was determined to defend my actions, for I knew I had done the best I could." Daniel responded that he did not receive the instructions and handed Brigham the report from his clerk detailing all that was done to organize the goods to transport them to the valley. At this time, it was discovered the letter from Brigham was mistakenly never sent. After Brigham read Daniel's report, he determined it agreed with all of the instructions as contained in the letter. Daniel wrote: "This confirmed me more than ever in my faith in inspiration. Also in the honesty of Brigham Young and his counseling, for if his instructions had not been honest I would never have been inspired to anticipate them." Brigham then "countermanded the order [to return to the Y. X. Express Station], saying that I had had enough of Devil's Gate for one man." Brigham then asked Daniel to help deliver the goods to their owners.[7]

The following day, Daniel traveled to Provo to see his family, and he learned of the wild accusations being circulated against him about stealing and hiding away thousands of dollars worth of goods. So strong was the belief in his guilt that one man traveled to Daniel's house and proceeded to tell his wife she ought to leave Daniel and marry a good man. Daniel's wife held her ground and stood up to the character assault on her husband. At one time, an entire family came to search Daniel's home for the stolen goods. Daniel wrote: "My wife treated them with perfect civility; no doubt they were ashamed of themselves and are to this day when they think of the indignity. While delivering their goods I was often accused of having robbed people."[8]

On June 11, 1857, President Brigham Young sent a letter out to all of the bishops in Utah exonerating Daniel W. Jones of these accusations. The letter stated: "The men who find fault with the labors of Brother Jones the past winter, we wish their names sent to this office, and when the Lord presents an opportunity we will try them and see if they will do any better."[9]

Throughout the next few months, Daniel recorded: "There was so much rascality brought to light that winter that it was no wonder that nearly everyone except my wife and family thought I was guilty." Several of the accusers eventually filed a formal complaint, and Brigham Young personally asked Daniel to attend a hearing at his office. At this request, Daniel replied: "Yes, sir, I am both willing and glad of the opportunity." He then gave President Young names of some he wished to be witnesses. Upon his return to Provo, Daniel was so hurt by these allegations, he was tempted at times to leave the country, for it seemed to him he had no friends. After prayerfully considering this, the Spirit whispered to Daniel that the prophet would be able to discern the truth.[10]

Upon his arrival at the hearing, Daniel immediately noticed there were no witnesses to testify on his behalf. Brigham Young assured him that they would be sent for when they were needed. The hearing began by Brigham Young asking Daniel to give an account of all of the expenditures incurred throughout the winter at Devil's Gate. "Among the charges brought against him was one which said that he must have doctored the accounts he turned in to Brigham, in which he had charged up the keep of twenty men all winter at seventy-five cents a week. He was obviously a liar in presenting so ridiculously small a bill, and therefore must be a liar in his account of what had happened to the freight. So Dan itemized the winter's expenses for them." Daniel stated:

> "I then made the statement that we had killed and eaten forty head of cattle that were so poor they were dying; we had lived on the meat and hides some two months; that we had not credited to the owners anything for them, as we thought it was worth the cattle to eat them. That we had killed some game at various times. That was ours, no credit allowed; had lived on two weeks on thistles dug from the frozen ground, no credit; one week on native garlic; three days on minnows caught with a dip-net, fish too small to clean, rather bitter in taste, no credit; several meals on prickly pear leaves roasted,

> no credit; some five days without anything much but water to drink, no credit; some five months mostly on short rations without bread or salt. These were about all the reasons for the price being so low. The seventy-five cents per week covered all the meats bought of Indians or anyone else. All groceries, soap, candles, in fact everything used belonging to the companies, including some leather owned by F. D. Richards, who remarked to me that he was glad it was there for me to use. Brothers Jas. Ferguson and W. C. Dunbar also made the same remark about some groceries used of theirs. Not so with some others. They grieved very much over what stuff had been used of theirs.[11]

Upon the completion of his accounting, Brigham spoke each man's name, asking them one at a time if they believed what I had said. "All replied in the affirmative. He asked each one if they believed I had been honest, and taken good care of their goods. All answered, 'Yes.'" Brother Young then stood up and chastised the men present and "commenced to pronounce a curse upon those who had spoken falsely about me. I asked him to stop before he had finished the words, and told him I could bear their accusations better than they could bear his curse. He then blessed me, saying they would be cursed if they did not cease their talk." President Young then said "if we had set fire to the whole outfit and run off by the light of it he would never have found fault." At the request of Daniel, on August 25, 1857, Brigham signed a recommend testifying of Daniel's character.[12]

28

ABSOLUTE KNOWLEDGE THAT GOD LIVES

SALT LAKE VALLEY

FRANCIS WEBSTER

Years after the arrival of the Martin and Willie Handcart Companies in the Salt Lake Valley, a man named William R. Palmer wrote of an experience hearing the testimony of a member of the Martin Company. William writes:

> I heard a testimony once that made me tingle to the roots of my hair. It was in an adult Sunday School class of over fifty men and women. Nathan T. Porter, then Principal of the Branch Normal School, was the teacher and the subject under discussion was the ill fated hand cart company that suffered so terribly in the snow in 1856. Some sharp criticism of the church and its leaders was being indulged in for permitting any company of converts to venture across the Plains with no more supplies or protection than a hand cart caravan afforded. One old man in the corner sat silent and listened as long as he could stand it then he arose and said things that no person who heard him will ever forget. His face was white with emotion yet he spoke calmly, deliberately, but with great earnestness and sincerity. He said in substance, "I ask you to stop this criticism. You are discussing a matter you know nothing about. Cold historic facts mean nothing here for they give no proper interpretation of the questions involved. Mistake to send the Hand Cart Company out so late in the season? Yes. But I was in that Company and my wife was in it and

> Sister Nellie Unthank whom you have sited was there too. We suffered beyond anything you can imagine and many died of exposure and starvation, but did you ever hear a survivor of that Company utter a word of criticism? Not one of that Company ever apostatized or left the church because every one of us came through with the absolute knowledge that God lives for we became acquainted with him in our extremities. I have pulled my hand cart when I was so weak and weary from illness and lack of food that I could hardly put one foot ahead of the other. I have looked ahead and seen a patch of sand or a hill slope and I have said I can go only that far and there I must give up for I cannot pull the load through it. I have gone on to that sand and when I reached it the cart began pushing me. I have looked back many times to see who was pushing my cart but my eyes saw no one. I knew then that the Angels of God were there. Was I sorry that I chose to come by hand cart? No. Neither then nor any minute of my life since. The price we paid to become acquainted with God was a privilege to pay and I am thankful that I was privileged to come in the Martin Hand Cart Company."[1]

"The speaker was Francis Webster and when he sat down there was not a dry eye in the room. We were a subdued and chastened lot. Charles H. Mabey who later became Governor of Utah, arose and voiced the sentiment of all when he said, 'I would gladly pay the same price for the same assurance of the eternal verities that Brother Webster has.'"[2]

Francis was emigrating to the Salt Lake Valley with his pregnant wife, Elizabeth Ann; Ann's mother and stepfather, William; and Amy Parsons Middleton; and her step-brother, fifteen-year-old John Middleton. They had the means to travel by wagon but instead opted to travel by handcart, making it possible for nine others to emigrate. Francis was ill from Iowa to Florence, and through the power of the priesthood, he was blessed with the ability to continue forward with renewed vigor. Francis and Ann's daughter, Amy Elizabeth, was born on September 27 at Wolf Creek on the Platte; she was only a few weeks old when the terrible storms and suffering began. When rations became scarce, Francis willingly gave his portion to his wife and her mother so they could survive. Although Francis's feet were terribly frozen, he and his family arrived safely in the Salt Lake Valley.[3]

CONCLUSION

During one of the darkest periods in Church history, when many of the strongest fell from the faith and joined hands with the mobs, faithful missionaries embarked on a most remarkable journey—bringing the message of the restored gospel of Jesus Christ to the European nations.

As the men went to serve missions, many families were left in desperate and destitute circumstances and faced all manner of adversity and unspeakable hardships. Though not called on formal missions, women also became involved in missionary work as they firmly placed the gospel in the hearts of their children and others they came in contact with. Their testimonies played an important role in preparing the way and making ready the hearts of converts not only in America but also in the European nations. The youth also played an important missionary role. They were hungry for the truth and readily accepted the gospel and helped to convert their families and friends.

In both the American and European nations, missionaries and converts experienced great opposition. Abuse was heaped upon them with an unsparing hand, dealing cruel blows such as no human work could hope to withstand. In spite of the tireless efforts of those who opposed, missionary work moved forward with great majesty and power.

The afflictions experienced by these early Saints built the great strength of their character, increased their spirituality, and prepared them for even greater trials and responsibilities ahead. Regardless of the difficulties, they stood firm amid so much uncertainty, remaining meek, humble, faithful, and committed to the cause. They were true instruments in the hands of God in order to fulfill His mighty purposes.

These tremendous examples can become a compelling motivation for us in carrying forth the missionary work in our day. President Gordon B. Hinckley has reminded us of the "great mandate given by the Lord to all who desire to be known as his disciples. It is a mandate we cannot dodge, and one from which we cannot shrink. That mandate is to teach the gospel to the nations and peoples of the earth." President Hinckley continued:

> Truly we are engaged in a marvelous work and a wonder . . . now even greater challenges lie ahead for the future. One cannot think of the hundreds of millions who have never heard of this work without wondering how our charge to teach all mankind can ever be accomplished. There are nations where we presently cannot legally go. We honor and obey the laws of these nations. But if we will be both alert and patient, the Lord will open the way in the appropriate season. His is the timetable. Meanwhile, there is much to be done with those immediately around us. As we put forth our effort and pray humbly for inspiration, we will be blessed in our desires to share the gospel with our families, friends, neighbors, and acquaintances. The progress of the Church in our day is truly astounding. The God of heaven has brought to pass this latter-day miracle, and what we have seen is but a foretaste of greater things yet to come. The work will be accomplished by humble men and women, young and old, who will do it because they believe in the word of the Lord when he said: "And any man that shall go and preach this gospel of the kingdom, and fail not to continue faithful in all things, shall not be weary in mind, neither darkened, neither in body, limb, nor joint; and a hair of his head shall not fall to the ground unnoticed. And they shall not go hungry, neither athirst." The work will succeed because it is the Lord who has promised: "And whoso receiveth you, there I will be also, for I will go before your face. I will be on your right hand and on your left, and my Spirit shall be in your hearts, and mine angels round about you, to bear you up." . . . This is God's

> work that we do, and with his blessing we shall not fail" for in the words of the Prophet Joseph Smith: "The Standard of Truth has been erected; no unhallowed hand can stop the work from progressing; persecutions may rage, mobs may combine, armies may assemble, calumny may defame, but the truth of God will go forth boldly, nobly, and independent, till it has penetrated every continent, visited every clime, swept every country, and sounded in every ear, till the purposes of God shall be accomplished, and the Great Jehovah shall say the work is done."[1]

Once hunted and persecuted from city to city, the early Saints in America withstood cruel and unjust treatment and endured great suffering for a cause that they loved more than life itself. Though for some time they were denied the rights as bequeathed to them by God, the desire for these freedoms nonetheless remained sacred and dear to them. For they understood the founding of the United States and reverenced the great fundamentals established under divine inspiration at the hands of wise men.

In 1846, righteous and noble men accepted the call to serve the country that had ignored the atrocities perpetrated against them.

> Though unjust, insulting, and cruel, it was a call from our native or adopted country. The common rights of man, bequeathed him by God and nature, were assailed. Though its benefits had been denied us, the Constitution was still sacred and dear to us, and a death-blow was aimed at its principles. With hell raging in mad fury behind, and the threatening statutes based on perfidious treaties before us, our camps exposed and defenseless, the past, with all its loud wrongs, was buried deep in our tortured memories. The flag—that flag which in whatever country, or on whatever ocean, I see it now, no matter how crushed and desolate my circumstances, gleams, like the sunbeam through the black storm, full of hope and promise of a future tranquility—that flag, bespattered and still dripping with the blood of our murdered Prophets, was unfurled once more. The call was answered, and five hundred bleeding hearts were offered for immolation to defend its honour.[2]

The sacrifices made by these valiant men serving in the Mormon Battalion, under such difficult circumstances, led Brigham Young to testify that they were the salvation of the Church. Their service transformed them into frontiersmen and prepared them for even greater responsibilities: establishing the Salt Lake Valley and gathering the Saints to it.

President Ezra Taft Benson has reminded us of our responsibilities in our day:

> Our Father in Heaven planned the coming forth of the Founding Fathers and their form of government as the necessary great prologue leading to the restoration of the gospel. . . . Unfortunately, we as a nation have apostatized in various degrees from different Constitutional principles as proclaimed by the inspired founders. We are fast approaching that moment prophesied by Joseph Smith when he said: "Even this nation will be on the very verge of crumbling to pieces and tumbling to the ground, and when the Constitution is upon the brink of ruin, this people will be the staff upon which the nation shall lean, and they shall bear the Constitution away from the very verge of destruction."

President Benson continued: "For centuries our forefathers suffered and sacrificed that we might be the recipients of the blessings of freedom. If they were willing to sacrifice so much to establish us as a free people, should we not be willing to do the same to maintain that freedom for ourselves and for future generations? Only in this foreordained land, under its God-inspired Constitution and the resulting environment of freedom, was it possible to have established the restored Church. It is our responsibility to see that this freedom is perpetuated so that the Church may more easily flourish in the future."[3]

When the American nation was being founded, under the direction of the wise and inspired Founding Fathers, they understood the importance of building a moral and virtuous society. They understood that only virtuous people were capable of freedom. With that knowledge, a return to virtue was ushered in, allowing the foundation of freedom to take hold in this choice land. Samuel Adams, one of our Founding Fathers, stated the following regarding virtue: "I thank God that I have lived to see my country independent and free. She may long enjoy her independence and freedom if she will. It depends upon her virtue."[4]

With this newfound independence and freedom, the time was then right to usher in the restoration of the gospel of Jesus Christ.

This book is full of virtuous examples from our pioneer forefathers. From a young age, these pioneer children learned the value of sacrifice and hard work, many having been born under extremely difficult conditions. They worked long hours in mines, factories, and farms to help support their families. Many of these children would later write of their experiences, testifying they would not want to avoid the hardships they had passed through. These trials and challenges weaned them from the world, and the hard work helped shape their character.

Once they were converted to the gospel, friends shunned and deserted them; families disowned them, and mobs tormented and attacked them. They were falsely accused, arrested, and thrown out of their employment. They accepted the gospel at a great personal cost, that of nearly everything they had. Regardless of the sacrifice, they held fast to the restored gospel of Jesus Christ, and their only desires were to be with the Saints under the banner of hope and freedom that America was founded upon. For many, their dreams of gathering required great patience and long-suffering.

The journey to the Salt Lake Valley during the 1856 emigration season was unique; it was a special gathering of longtime members of the Church in Europe. The gathering happened during a time of great financial difficulty, when all the possible means that had been gathered just wasn't enough, thus prompting the implementation of the handcart plan. Those with sufficient means already scheduled to travel with the wagon companies were counseled to join with those in the handcart companies and donate their extra money. It was through this generosity of a few that the way was made open for many more to emigrate. The generosity prompted the need for additional ships to be chartered, though late in the season.

Once arriving on the American shores, the Saints had so long dreamed of, though discouraged upon learning sufficient preparations were not made for their travels, they rolled up their sleeves and went to work to build the handcarts and sew the tents. They were mocked and derided on every occasion, enduring every form of inducement to leave the handcart companies. Remaining true to their noble characters, the stalwart members were not ashamed to be counted among the Willie and Martin Handcart Companies.

As this most remarkable journey continued, in spite of the likely dangers ahead, they were called upon to endure even greater trials. As the difficulties intensified, they sacrificed for each other with the most heartfelt and tender examples of devotion, many giving their last strength. No tongue or pen could adequately express what they passed through. They showed the greatest form of love, even laying down their lives in the service of others.

Through the difficulties, the stalwart and courageous Saints testified that the hand of God was over them and that He became their source of strength as He fit the back for the burden every day. At their greatest hour of trial, these Saints were blessed with the absolute knowledge that God lives.

What amazing and tender examples of virtue. Bishop H. David Burton has testified:

> Virtuous traits form the foundation of a Christian life and are the outward manifestation of the inner man. . . . We need only look around us to see what is taking place in our communities to realize that personal traits of virtue are in a steep decline. . . . Brothers and sisters, we need not be a part of the virtue malaise that is penetrating and infecting society. If we follow the world in abandoning Christian-centered virtues, the consequences may be disastrous. . . . We need to stand tall and be firmly fixed in perpetuating Christlike virtues. . . . Now is the time for us to join in rescuing and preserving that which is "virtuous, lovely, or of good report or praiseworthy." As we allow virtue to garnish our thoughts unceasingly and we cultivate virtuous traits in our personal lives, our communities and institutions will be improved, our children and families will be strengthened, and faith and integrity will bless individual lives.[5]

In the words of President Gordon B. Hinckley: "The tide of evil flows. Today it has become a veritable flood. Most of us, living somewhat sheltered lives, have little idea of the vast dimensions of it. . . . God give us the strength, the wisdom, the faith, the courage as citizens to stand in opposition to these and to let our voices be heard in defense of those virtues which, when practiced in the past, made men and nations strong, and which, when neglected, brought them to decay."[6]

A return to virtue begins with us! We can no longer carelessly drift along in life indifferently, as quoted by John Jaques: "No matter the circumstance, though they be actually in some degree compromising, no matter who is the tempter nor what is the temptation, your virtue is worth more than them all, it is the pearl of great price. It is beyond all price. It should be perfectly invincible. No offer involved it is worth a moment's consideration. The unfailing motto should be, 'Never surrender.'"[7]

With great reverence, I pay honor to those who have gone before, who believed in a cause much greater than themselves. They were a people who willingly gave their all, even their lives, for the gospel of Jesus Christ. This priceless inheritance is a great and lasting legacy of their noble and courageous examples. May their legacy serve as a reminder to all that God consecrated the afflictions of those who have gone before us for our benefit—that they may serve as a valuable source of strength, comfort, inspiration, and guidance as we continue the great and marvelous work today. For we have embarked on the most remarkable and important journey. As prophesied by President Ezra Taft Benson, "We face some difficult days, the like of which we have never experienced in our lives. And those days are going to require faith and testimony and family unity, the like of which we have never had." But if we are prepared we shall not fear, and our faith shall sustain us in this work. In the words of Joseph Smith, "The work which has to be accomplished in the last days is one of vast importance, and will call into action the energy, skill, talent, and ability of the Saints, so that it may roll forth with that glory and majesty described by the Prophet; and will consequently require the concentration of the Saints, to accomplish works of such magnitude and grandeur."[8]

NOTES

† Kingsford, *Leaves from the Life of Elizabeth Horrocks Jackson Kingsford.*
‡ Hinckley, "True to the Faith," 65.

AUTHOR'S NOTE

1. Hinckley, "True to the Faith," 65.
2. Hinckley, "The Faith of the Pioneers," 3.
3. *The Mormon*, Apr. 26, 1856; Journal of Peder Madsen, July 9, 1856; Mary Ann James Dangerfield, as quoted in Carter, *Our Pioneer Heritage*, 293; *Millennial Star*, Mar. 1, 1856, 139.
4. Stegner, *The Gathering of Zion: The Story of the Mormon Trail*, 221.
5. *For the Strength of Youth.*

CHAPTER 1

1. Whitney, *Life of Heber C. Kimball*, 104–6.
2. *Autobiography of Parley P. Pratt*, 143; Cowley, *Wilford Woodruff, History of His Life and Labors*, 67; "History of Brigham Young," *Deseret News*, Feb. 10, 1858, 386.
3. Whitney, *Life of Heber C. Kimball*, 104–5; Thompson, *Journal of Heber C. Kimball*, 10.
4. Whitney, *Life of Heber C. Kimball*, 105.

5. Thompson, *Journal of Heber C. Kimball*, v–vi; "History of Joseph Smith," *Millennial Star*, July 12, 1856, 434–38; "Mission to England, or the First Foreign Mission of the Latter-day Saints," *Millennial Star*, April 1841, 289–96.
6. Thompson, *Journal of Heber C. Kimball*, 15; Whitney, *Life of Heber C. Kimball*, 119.
7. Thompson, *Journal of Heber C. Kimball*, 16; *Millennial Star*, July 12, 1856, 434–38; Whitney, *Life of Heber C. Kimball*, 119, 121.
8. Thompson, *Journal of Heber C. Kimball, 16; Millennial Star*, July 12, 1856, 434; Whitney, *Life of Heber C. Kimball*, 121–22; *Millennial Star*, Apr. 1841, 290.
9. *Millennial Star*, July 12, 1856, 434–38; Whitney, *Life of Heber C. Kimball*, 124, 128; *Millennial Star*, Apr. 1841, 289–96.
10. *Millennial Star*, July 12, 1856, 434–38; *Millennial Star*, Apr. 1841, 289–96.
11. *Millennial Star*, July 12, 1856, 434–38; *Millennial Star*, Apr. 1841, 289–96; Whitney, *Life of Heber C. Kimball*, 128.
12. Whitney, *Life of Heber C. Kimball*, 130–31.
13. Ibid., 131–32.
14. Ibid., 135.
15. Josiah Rogerson, *Salt Lake Herald*, Nov. 24, 1907, 8; John Jaques, Diary and Reminiscences, in Bell, *Life History and Writings of John Jaques*, 84.
16. Peter Howard McBride, in Carter, *Our Pioneer Heritage*, 360.
17. Thompson, *Journal of Heber C. Kimball*, 25.
18. Ibid., 31.
19. Thompson, *Journal of Heber C. Kimball*, 32–33; Whitney, *Life of Heber C. Kimball*, 179–80.
20. Thompson, *Journal of Heber C. Kimball*, 33–34; Whitney, *Life of Heber C. Kimball*, 169–71.
21. Thompson, *Journal of Heber C. Kimball*, 34; Whitney, *Life of Heber C. Kimball*, 187–88.
22. Whitney, *Life of Heber C. Kimball*, 188.
23. Thompson, *Journal of Heber C. Kimball*, 35–36; Whitney, *Life of Heber C. Kimball*, 189.
24. Thompson, *Journal of Heber C. Kimball*, 35; Whitney, *Life of Heber C. Kimball*, 188–89.
25. Thompson, *Journal of Heber C. Kimball*, 36.
26. Thompson, *Journal of Heber C. Kimball*, 37–41; Whitney, *Life of Heber C. Kimball*, 190–92; *Millennial Star*, July 12, 1856, 437.
27. Thompson, *Journal of Heber C. Kimball*, 38–39; Whitney, *Life of Heber C. Kimball*, 193.

28. Thompson, *Journal of Heber C. Kimball*, 43–44; Whitney, *Life of Heber C. Kimball*, 184–85, 202–203.
29. Whitney, *Life of Heber C. Kimball*, 211.
30. Thompson, *Journal of Heber C. Kimball*, 45; Whitney, *Life of Heber C. Kimball*, 212.
31. Boggs, letter dated Oct. 27, 1838.
32. "Truth Will Prevail," *Times and Seasons*, Dec. 1, 1840, 236; Woodruff, *Leaves from My Journal*, 108–9; Whitney, *Life of Heber C. Kimball*, 229.
33. Whitney, *Life of Heber C. Kimball*, 217.
34. Ibid., 211, 217, 219, 230.
35. Roskelly, *A Sketch of the Life of Arza Erastus Hinckley.*
36. *Times and Seasons*, July 15, 1843, 260; "Communications," *Millennial Star*, June 1841, 12.
37. *Church History in the Fulness of Times*, 215, 222.
38. Woodruff, *Leaves from My Journal*, 102–3; Whitney, *Life of Heber C. Kimball*, 252–53.
39. Woodruff, *Leaves from My Journal*, 120.
40. "Communications," *Millennial Star*, June 1841, 14.
41. "History of Joseph Smith," *Millennial Star*, July 12, 1856, 434–38; Whitney, *Life of Heber C. Kimball*, 276–77; Woodruff, *Leaves from My Journal*, 132–33; *Millennial Star*, Apr. 1841, 296.
42. Jane Eleanore Griffiths Fullmer, autobiography; Margaret Ann Griffiths Clegg, autobiography; *Times and Seasons*, June 1840, 119.
43. "Elder Woodruff's Letter," *Times and Seasons*, Mar. 1, 1841, 327–29; Woodruff, *Leaves From My Journal*, 139–45.
44. Ann Jewell Rowley, autobiography; Woodruff, *Leaves from My Journal*, 147.
45. Whitney, *Life of Heber C. Kimball*, 278; *Millennial Star*, May 1840, 20, Woodruff, *Leaves from my Journal*, 147; *Times and Seasons*, Mar. 1, 1841, 331.
46. *Millennial Star*, Sept. 5, 1840, 136; Whitney, *Life of Heber C. Kimball*, 283; "A Compilation of General Voyage Notes," *Britannia*.
47. *Millennial Star*, Apr. 1841, 310–11; West, *Life of Franklin D. Richards*, 74.
48. *Times and Seasons*, Mar. 1, 1841, 330.
49. Ibid., 331.
50. Whitney, *Life of Heber C. Kimball*, 299; *Millennial Star*, Apr. 1841, 312.
51. *Millennial Star*, Apr. 1841, 301–302, 309–312; Whitney, *Life of Heber C. Kimball*, 307–309; *Times and Seasons*, 1841, 259.
52. *History of the Church*, 4:390–91.

CHAPTER 2

1. "Life in Nauvoo the Beautiful," *Church History in the Fulness of Times*, 240–44; "Communications," *Millennial Star*, Sept. 1841, 77.
2. Taylor, *Witness to the Martyrdom*, 23, 28.
3. Taylor, *Witness to the Martyrdom*, 82; Letter of Dan Jones to Thomas Bullock, 20 Jan. 1855.
4. Taylor, *Witness to the Martyrdom*, 82; Letter of Dan Jones to Thomas Bullock, 20 Jan. 1855.
5. Dennis, *The Call of Zion*, 1–2; Dennis, "Dan Jones, Welshman," 74.
6. "The Martyrdom," *Church History in the Fulness of Times*, 278–79; Letter of Dan Jones to Thomas Bullock, 20 Jan. 1855.
7. Dennis, *The Call of Zion*; Dennis, "Dan Jones, Welshman"; Letter of Dan Jones to Thomas Bullock, 20 Jan. 1855.
8. Taylor, *Witness to the Martyrdom*, 82–84, 151; Letter of Dan Jones to Thomas Bullock, 20 Jan. 1855.
9. "Nauvoo under Apostolic Leadership," *Church History in the Fulness of Times*, 306; Cluff, Harvey Harris, autobiography.
10. "Nauvoo under Apostolic Leadership," and "The Trek across Iowa," *Church History in the Fulness of Times*, 306–13.
11. Bigler and Bagley, *Army of Israel*, 21–22.
12. Bigler and Bagley, *Army of Israel*, 46–48; "Circular to the Mormons read by James Allen, Caption of the 1st Dragoon," *Millennial Star*, Dec. 1, 1855, 756.
13. "Edward Martin," Historic Nauvoo Land and Records Research Center; Carter, *Our Pioneer Heritage*, 356; "Roster of Company C," Mormon Battalion Records.
14. "Nauvoo under Apostolic Leadership," *Church History in the Fulness of Times*, 305; *History of the Church*, 5:85.
15. Smith, *Faithful Stewards*, 12, 17, 20–21.
16. "The Trek across Iowa," *Church History in the Fulness of Times*, 318; *The Cluff Family Journal*, 111–13.
17. "The Trek across Iowa," *Church History in the Fulness of Times*, 319; Smith, *Faithful Stewards*, 22.
18. "The Trek across Iowa," *Church History in the Fulness of Times*, 319–20.
19. "Establishing a Refuge in Deseret," *Church History in the Fulness of Times*, 339; Smith, *Faithful Stewards*, 25.
20. "Edward Martin," Historic Nauvoo Land and Records Research Center; Bigler and Bagley, *Army of Israel*, 37, 417; California Pioneer Heritage Foundation Pamphlet, Diary of Redick Newton Allred Dec. 19, 1847.

21. Lila Bringhurst, *California's Pioneer Heritage*; "Edward Martin," Nauvoo Land and Records; Hanks, *Scouting for the Mormons on the Great Frontier,* 25.
22. Carter, *Our Pioneer Heritage,* vol. 12, 356; Daniel Davis, diary, 90–101.
23. West, *Life of Franklin D. Richards,* 16–19, 29.
24. Ibid., 48–49, 54–58, 62, 66.
25. Ibid., 67–69.
26. Joseph Smith in *History of the Church*, 4:540.
27. West, *Life of Franklin D. Richards,* 75–78, 82–83.
28. West, *Life of Franklin D. Richards*, 83, 85, 89; *Millennial Star,* Mar. 1, 1848, 74.
29. West, *Life of Franklin D. Richards*, 89, 92–93; Robert Campbell, journal extracts.
30. West, *Life of Franklin D. Richards,* 120.
31. Ibid., 115.
32. "Home Correspondence," *Millennial Star,* Dec. 1, 1855, 765; West, *Life of Franklin D. Richards*, 121.
33. "Thirteenth General Epistle," *Millennial Star,* Jan. 26, 1856, 52; West, *Life of Franklin D. Richards,* 121.
34. "Minutes of Conference," *Deseret News,* Sept. 18, 1852; "Important Special Conference," *Millennial Star,* Nov. 13, 1852, 600.
35. *Millennial Star,* Apr. 12, 1841, 312.

CHAPTER 3

1. James Henry Linford, autobiography, p. 4, 6; Allphin, *Tell My Story, Too,* 70.
2. Ann Jewell Rowley, autobiography.
3. Crocheron, *Representative Women of Deseret,* 82–85.
4. Ibid.
5. Ibid.
6. Ibid.
7. Ibid.
8. Ibid.
9. Petree, *Recollections of Past Days*, 21, 40–41.
10. Ibid., 42–47, 203, note 46.
11. Ibid., 53–54.
12. Jane Eleanor Griffiths Fullmer, autobiography; Margaret Ann Clegg, autobiography; Newbold, *Margaret Ann Griffiths Clegg,* 4–5.
13. England, *Gospel Seeds in Scottish Soil,* 26.

14. "Elder Hedlock's Mission," *Millennial Star*, Oct. 1841, 92.
15. "Communications," *Millennial Star*, May 1, 1841, 11; England, *Gospel Seeds in Scottish Soil*, 26.
16. Margaret Ann McFall Caldwell Bennett, reminiscences.
17. Allphin, *Tell My Story, Too*, 82.
18. Ibid., 85.
19. Goodwin, "The Tired Mother: Pioneer Recollections"; Allphin, *Tell My Story, Too*, 131.
20. Kirkwood, *Biography: Joseph Smith Clements Kirkwood.*
21. Allphin, *Tell My Story, Too,* 129.
22. Ibid.
23. *Millennial Star*, Oct. 1840, 168; "Progress of Reformation in England," *Millennial Star*, Nov. 1840, 192; "News from the Elders," *Millennial Star*, Dec. 1840, 212; "News from the Elders," *Millennial Star*, Jan. 1841, 238–39; "Conference Minutes," *Millennial Star*, Apr. 1841, 302.
24. Dennis, *Dan Jones, Welshman*; Letter of Dan Jones to Thomas Bullock, 20 Jan. 1855, p. 10; *Millennial Star*, Jan. 1, 1846, 3, 8; Dennis, *The Call of Zion*, 2.
25. "Letter to Elder Orson Spencer," *Millennial Star*, Oct. 15, 1847, 319; "Letter from Dan Jones to President Pratt," *Millennial Star*, Feb. 1, 1849, 38–42; *Millennial Star*, Mar. 1, 1849, 71; Dennis, *The Call of Zion*, 7, 150–51.
26. "Langeland, John," *Encyclopedia of Mormonism*, 1262–63.
27. Allphin, *Tell My Story, Too*, 87.
28. Allphin, *Tell My Story, Too*, 99; Lyman, *Bishop Jens Nielson.*
29. Lyman, *Bishop Jens Nielson.*
30. Lyman *Bishop Jens Nielson;* "Foreign Correspondence," *Millennial Star*, August 4, 1855, 492–93.
31. Mortensen family history, in Harmer, *Zion Bound.*
32. Ibid.
33. Ibid.

CHAPTER 4

1. West, *Life of Franklin D. Richards*, 124; *Journal of Discourses* 7:40; "Editorial," *Millennial Star*, Nov. 24, 1855, 745–47.
2. "Editorial," *Millennial Star*, Nov. 24, 1855, 745–47.
3. Ibid.
4. "Thirteenth General Epistle," *Millennial Star*, Jan. 26, 1856, 49–52.
5. "Foreign Correspondence," *Millennial Star*, Jan. 26, 1856, 61; "Hand

Carts for the Plains," *The Mormon*, Dec. 1, 1855.

6. "Hand Carts for the Plains," *The Mormon*, Dec. 1, 1855; *Millennial Star*, Dec. 22, 1855, 810–12.
7. *Millennial Star*, Dec. 22, 1855, 810–12.

CHAPTER 5

1. West, *Life of Franklin D. Richards*, 137; "Foreign Correspondence," *Millennial Star*, Nov. 24, 1855, 749; *Millennial Star*, Dec. 8, 1855, 776.
2. "Jaques, John, 1827–1900," *LDS Biographical Encyclopedia*, 254; Bell, *Life History and Writings of John Jaques*, 17–51; Allphin, *Tell My Story, Too*, 214.
3. "Emigration by Hand-Carts," *Millennial Star*, June 14, 1856, 369.
4. Ibid.
5. Petree, *Recollections of Past Days*, 56–57.
6. "Latter-day Saints' Emigration Report," *Millennial Star*, Aug. 23, 1856, 542; "Editorial," *Millennial Star*, Feb. 2, 1856, 72–73; "Editorial," *Millennial Star*, Dec. 20, 1856, 812.
7. "Editorial," *Millennial Star*, Dec. 8, 1855, 776; *Millennial Star*, February 2, 1856, 74.
8. "Editorial," *Millennial Star*, Feb. 23, 1856, 121–25; *Millennial Star*, April 5, 1856, 218; "Correspondence," *Deseret News*, July 23, 1856, 3.
9. *Millennial Star*, Apr. 5, 1856, 218.

CHAPTER 6

1. *Millennial Star*, May 24, 1856, 330; *Millennial Star*, July 12, 1856, 443; "Foreign Correspondence," *Millennial Star*, July 26, 1856, 478–79; William Woodward, journal, May 23–24, June 10, 13, 15, 20, 29; Peter Madsen, journal, May 20, 22, 24, June 13; George Cunningham, reminiscences, 1876, fd. 2, 1–5.
2. Carter, *Our Pioneer Heritage*, vol. 14, 293; Willie Company Journal, June 10, 1856.
3. *Millennial Star*, July 26, 1856, 478–79.
4. *Millennial Star*, July 26, 1856, 478–79; Lyman, *The Willie Handcart Company*, 32; Peder Madsen, journal, June 14, 1856.
5. George Cunningham, reminiscences, 1876, fd. 2, 1–5; Chapman, "The Mormon Handcart Experiences."
6. Peder Madsen, journal, June 15–16, 1856; Willie Company Journal,

November 5, 1856.

7. *Millennial Star*, June 28, 1856, 411–13; *Millennial Star*, June 14, 1856, 377; Josiah Rogerson, "Martin's Handcart Company, 1856," *Salt Lake Herald*, October 13, 1907, 5; Jaques, "Some Reminiscences," *Salt Lake Daily Herald*, Dec. 1, 1878, 1.
8. Carter, *Our Pioneer Heritage*, vol. 13, 360.
9. Ibid., vol 17, 302–3.
10. Carter, *Our Pioneer Heritage*, vol. 17, 302–3; Gregerson, *The Mellors through the Years*; *Millennial Star*, June 28, 1856, 413.
11. *Millennial Star*, June 28, 1856, 412–13; John Jaques, "Some Reminiscences," *Salt Lake Daily Herald*, Dec. 1, 1878, 1.
12. *Millennial Star*, June 28, 1856, 413; Turner, *Emigrating Journals*, 86; "Horizon Ship Manifest Records," Ollerton Family History.
13. *Millennial Star*, 26 June 28, 1856, 411, 413; Josiah Rogerson, "Martin's Handcart Company, 1856," *Salt Lake Herald*, Oct. 13, 1907, 5.
14. Jesse Haven, journal, Dec. 5, 1852, Dec.–Apr. 1853, 14 Mar. 1853; Whittaker, *Early Mormon Imprints in South Africa*, 1–6.
15. Jesse Haven, journal, Mar. 14, 1853; Carter, *Treasures of Pioneer History*, 6:246–47.
16. John Jaques, "Some Reminiscences," *Salt Lake Daily Herald*, Jan. 19, 1879, 1; *Millennial Star*, June 28, 1856, 413; Josiah Rogerson, "Martin's Handcart Company, 1856," *Salt Lake Daily Herald*, Nov. 3, 1907, 7.
17. Samuel Openshaw, diary, June 28, 1856; Allphin, *Tell My Story, Too*, 257.
18. John Jaques, "Some Reminiscences," *Salt Lake Daily Herald*, Dec. 1, 1878, 1; Joseph Beecroft, journals 1844–1883, 29–32.

CHAPTER 7

1. "More Mormons," *New York Herald*, June 14, 1856, 1 in *Journal History*.
2. Stegner, *The Gathering of Zion*, 221.
3. Joseph Beecroft, journal, July 4, vol. 6, pp. 10–40, and vol. 7, p. 1; "Letter from President Brigham Young," *Millennial Star*, July 26, 1856, 465–66; Josiah Rogerson, *The Salt Lake Herald*, Nov. 3, 1907, 7; Jesse Haven to Brigham Young, Oct. 9, 1856, Fort Laramie, in Brigham Young, Office Files 1832–1878, box 24, fd. 21; "Editorial," *Millennial Star*, Nov. 24, 1855, 745–47; Jesse Haven, journals, 1852–1892, vols. 4–5, Oct 4–7, 30–31, 1856.
4. James Bleak, journal, Feb. 24, 1855; Allphin, *Tell My Story,Too*,

167–69; "An Item of Handcart Experience," *Juvenile Instructor,* 15 June 1902, 365–367, Scribo pseudonym of James Bleak; "Editorial," *Millennial Star*, Mar. 1, 1856, 140.

5. William Palmer, *Francis Webster*, as quoted in Van Cott and Leigh, *Generations of Webster's*, 55–56.

CHAPTER 8

1. Peder Madsen, diary, June 17, 1856.
2. Peder Madsen, diary, June 23–25, 1856; Smith, *Faithful Stewards*, 95; "Latter-day Saints' Emigration Report," *Millennial Star*, Aug. 23, 1856, 536.
3. Josiah Rogerson, "Martin's Handcart Company, 1856, no. 2," *Salt Lake Herald*, Oct. 20, 1907, 12; Samuel Openshaw, diary, July 1–3, 1856.
4. John William Southwell, autobiography, p. 9.
5. John Jaques, "Some Reminiscences," *Salt Lake Daily Herald*, Jan. 5, 1879, 1; John William Southwell, autobiography, p. 9.
6. Josiah Rogerson, "Martin's Handcart Company, 1856, no. 2," *Salt Lake Herald*, Oct. 20, 1907, 12; *Millennial Star*, Aug. 23, 1856, 536.
7. John Taylor, *The Mormon*, Apr. 26, 1856.
8. "Editorial," *Millennial Star*, Feb. 23, 1856, 121–25; *Millennial Star*, Apr. 5, 1856, 216–17; *LDS Biographical Encyclopedia*, vol. 1, 286; "Daniel Spencer/Ira Eldridge Company" Mormon Pioneer Overland Travel 1847–1868.
9. "Emigration," *The Mormon*, Apr. 26, 1856.
10. *The Mormon*, Feb. 1857; *Millennial Star,* Feb. 23, 1856, 122.
11. *The Mormon,* Apr. 26, 1856.
12. *The Mormon,* Apr. 26, 1856; *Millennial Star,* May 3, 1856, 281; *Millennial Star*, Aug. 2, 1856, 490.
13. Joseph B. Elder, journal, pp. 2–4, 15.
14. Willie Company Journal, July 1–9; Peder Madsen, journal; George Cunningham, reminiscences, pp. 1–3, 5.
15. Goodwin, "The Tired Mother."
16. Josiah Rogerson, "Martin's Handcart Company, 1856, no. 2," *Salt Lake Daily Herald*, Oct. 20, 1907, 12; Mr. Chislett's narrative, in Stenhouse, *The Rocky Mountain Saints*, chapter 37.
17. *Millennial Star*, Feb. 23, 1856, 122–24; Josiah Rogerson, "Martin's Handcart Company, 1856, no. 2," *Salt Lake Herald*, Oct. 20, 1907, 12; John Jaques, "Some Reminiscences," *Salt Lake Daily Herald*, Dec. 1, 1878, 1; Levi Savage, diary; Mr. Chislett's narrative, in Stenhouse,

The Rocky Mountain Saints, chapter 37.

18. William Woodward, journal; Mr. Chislett's narrative, in Stenhouse, *The Rocky Mountain Saints*, chapter 37; Willie Company Journal, July 12; Smith, *Faithful Stewards*, 97.
19. William Woodward, journal, July 1856; Josiah Rogerson, "Martin's Handcart Company, 1856, no. 2," *The Salt Lake Herald*, Oct. 20, 1907, 12; *Millennial Star*, June 14, 1856, 377; *Millennial Star*, Aug. 23, 1856, 542; Jesse Haven, journals, vol. 4–5, August 22; *Deseret News*, Oct. 22, 1856, 258; Smith, *Faithful Stewards*, 97.
20. William Woodward, journal, 1856; *Deseret News*, Oct. 22, 1856, 258; Smith, *Faithful Stewards*, 97.
21. *The Mormon*, April 26, 1856; Peder Madsen, journal, July 9, 1856; Carter, *Our Pioneer Heritage*, 293.

CHAPTER 9

1. Peder Madsen, journal, July 15–Aug. 11, 1856; Levi Savage, journal, July 19, 1856; Smith, *Faithful Stewards* 97; Jesse Haven, Jesse, vols. 4–5, July 19–Aug. 11, 1856; Willie Company Journal, July 15–Aug. 11, 1856; Mr. Chislett's narrative, in Stenhouse, *The Rocky Mountain Saints*, 316.
2. Levi Savage, journal, July 23–24, 1856; Mr. Chislett's narrative, in Stenhouse, *The Rocky Mountain Saints*, 316; Peder Madsen, journal, July 18, 1856.
3. William Woodward, history, July 25, 1856; Levi Savage, journal, July 20–31, 1856; Smith, *Faithful Stewards*, 97–98; Willie Company Journal, July 21, 25, 1856.
4. George Cunningham, reminiscences, 1876, fd. 2, 2–5.
5. Willie Company Journal, July 31, 1856; Smith, *Faithful Stewards*, 97; Mr. Chislett's narrative, in Stenhouse, *The Rocky Mountain Saints*.
6. Mr. Chislett's narrative, in Stenhouse, *The Rocky Mountain Saints*; Willie Company Journal, August 2, 1856; Emily Hill Woodmansee, in Crocheron, *Representative Women of Deseret*, 85–86.
7. Levi Savage, journal, August 11, 1856; William Woodward, history August 11, 1856; Willie Company Journal, August 11, 1856; *Millennial Star*, May 24, 1856, 333.
8. *Millennial Star*, October 11, 1856, 651.
9. Josiah Rogerson, *Salt Lake Herald*, Oct. 20, 1907, 12; Samuel Openshaw, diary, July 25–Aug. 1, 1856; Jesse Haven, journals, July 22–27, 1856; Camp Journal, in *Journal History of the Church*, Dec. 15, 1856, 16–37.

10. Jesse Haven, journals, July 22–August 11, 1856.
11. John William Southwell, autobiographical sketch, Sept. 28, 1912.
12. John Jaques, "Some Reminiscences," *Salt Lake Daily Herald*, Dec. 1, 1878.
13. John William Southwell, autobiographical sketch, Sept. 28, 1912.
14. Samuel Openshaw, diary, Aug. 7, 1856.
15. John Southwell, autobiographical sketch, 12; Josiah Rogerson, *The Salt Lake Herald*, Nov. 3, 1907, 7.
16. Jesse Haven, journals, Aug. 19, 22, 1856; Samuel Openshaw, diary, Aug. 22, 1856; Josiah Rogerson, "Tells Story of Trials of the Handcart Pioneers," *Salt Lake Tribune*, Nov. 30, 1913, 11; Hodgett Company camp journal, in *Journal History of the Church*, 16–37; *Millennial Star*, Oct. 25, 1856, 682.

CHAPTER 10

1. *The Mormon*, Feb. 21, 1857, 2; Powell, "James R. McGaw"; *Journal History of the Church*, Apr. 4, 1856; *Millennial Star*, May 24, 1856, 333.
2. *Millennial Star*, Oct. 4, 1856, 637–38.
3. Willie Company Journal, Aug. 11–17, 1856; *Millennial Star*, Oct. 4, 1856, 638; Peder Madsen, journal, Aug. 16, 1856.
4. Levi Savage, journal, Aug. 12, 1856; Mr. Chislett's narrative, in Stenhouse, *The Rocky Mountain Saints*.
5. Levi Savage, journal, p. 33; Bigler and Bagley, *Army of Israel*, 27, 234–38; *Millennial Star*, Sept. 8, 1855, 573–74; Mr. Chislett's narrative, in Stenhouse, *The Rocky Mountain Saints*; McMullin, "Faith and Works in a Secular World."
6. Levi Savage, journal, Aug. 13, 1856.
7. Levi Savage, journal, Aug. 13, 1856; Mr. Chislett's narrative, in Stenhouse, *The Rocky Mountain Saints*.
8. Levi Savage, journal, Aug. 13, 1856; Mr. Chislett's narrative, in Stenhouse, *The Rocky Mountain Saints*.
9. Dixon, "History of Her Ancestor William James."
10. Allphin, *Tell My Story, Too*, 102.
11. Willie Company Journal, Aug. 16, 18, 1856; *Deseret News*, Oct. 22, 1856, 258; Letter, Franklin D. Richards and Daniel Spencer to Brigham Young; Smith, *Faithful Stewards*, 99.
12. Mr. Chislett's narrative, in Stenhouse, *The Rocky Mountain Saints*.
13. Dixon, "History of Her Ancestor William James."
14. Jesse Haven, journals, Aug. 19–22, 1856.

15. John Jaques, "Some Reminiscences," *Salt Lake Daily Herald,* Dec. 1, 1878, 1.
16. *Deseret News*, Oct. 15, 1856, 252–53.
17. Josiah Rogerson, *The Salt Lake Herald,* Sunday, October 27, 1907, 11.
18. Benjamin Platt, reminiscences, pp. 2–5.
19. John Jaques, "Some Reminiscences," *Salt Lake Daily Herald*, 1 Dec. 1878, 1; Josiah Rogerson, *Salt Lake Herald,* Oct. 27, 1907, 11.
20. Josiah Rogerson, *Salt Lake Herald*, Oct. 27, 1907, 11.
21. John Jaques, "Some Reminiscences," *Salt Lake Daily Herald*, Dec. 1, 1878, 1 and Dec. 8, 1878, 1; Josiah Rogerson, *Salt Lake Herald*, October 27, 1907, 11; Franklin D. Richards and Daniel Spencer, "Journey from Florence to G.S.L. City," *Deseret News*, Oct. 22, 1856, 258; "Foreign Correspondence," *Millennial Star*, Oct. 25, 1856, 682.
22. "Foreign Correspondence," *Millennial Star*, Oct. 25, 1856, 682.
23. "News from the Emigration," *Millennial Star*, Oct. 18, 1856, 668; *Council Bluff's Bugle*, Aug. 26, 1856
24. "Foreign Correspondence," *Millennial Star*, Oct. 25, 1856, 682.

CHAPTER 11

1. Mr. Chislett's narrative, in Stenhouse, *The Rocky Mountain Saints.*
2. Sarah Emily Cowley, history.
3. Willie Company Journal, Aug. 25, 1856; Goodwin, "The Tired Mother," 775–81.
4. Margaret Ann McFall Caldwell Bennett, reminiscences, 4–5; Agnes Caldwell Southworth, autobiographical sketch; Madsen, *I Walked to Zion*, 57–58; Willie Company Journal, Aug. 30–31, 1856.
5. Willie Company Journal, Sept. 3–4, 1856; Levi Savage, journal, September 1–4, 1856; Peder Madsen, journal, Sept. 1–4, 1856; Dixon, "History of Her Ancestor William James."
6. Willie Company Journal, Sept. 3–4, 1856; William Woodward, history; Levi Savage, journal, Sept. 4, 1856; Smith, *Faithful Stewards*, 100–101.
7. Smith, *Faithful Stewards*, 101; William Woodward, history; Peder Madsen, journal, Sept. 5, 1856; Willie Company Journal, Sept. 5, 1856.
8. Willie Company Journal, Sept. 6, 1856.
9. Ibid., Sept. 7, 1856.
10. Mr. Chislett's narrative, in Stenhouse, *The Rocky Mountain Saints.*
11. Ann Jewell Rowley, autobiography.
12. George Cunningham, reminiscences, 1876, fd. 2, 2–5.

13. Robert Reeder, history, pp. 2–6; Willie Company Journal, July 28, 1856.
14. Mr. Chislett's narrative, in Stenhouse, *The Rocky Mountain Saints*; Willie Company Journal, Sept. 13, 1856.
15. George Cunningham, reminiscences, 1876, fd. 2, 2–5; Levi Savage, journal, Sept. 13, 1856; Willie Company Journal, Sept. 13, 1856.
16. Willie Company Journal, Sept. 18–29, 1856; Levi Savage, journal, Sept. 15–29, 1856.
17. Margaret Ann McFall Caldwell Bennett, reminiscences, pp. 4–5.
18. Willie Company Journal, Sept. 28, 1856; Levi Savage, journal, Sept. 28, 1856.
19. *Millennial Star*, Oct. 25, 1856, 684; Willie Company Journal, Aug. 25, 1856; Camp journal, in *Journal History of the Church*, Dec. 15, 1856, pp. 16–37, and Aug. 28, 31, 1856; *Millennial Star*, Oct. 25, 1856, 682; *Deseret News*, Oct. 22, 1856, 258.
20. Margaret Ann Clegg, autobiographical sketch.
21. Langley Allgood Bailey, reminiscences and journal, pp. 4–7; Jane Bailey, obituary; Isaac J. Wardle, biography.
22. Petree, *Recollections of Past*, 62, 210.
23. Ibid., 63.
24. Ibid.
25. Ibid., 63, 66.
26. Cluff Family Journal, 115–17.
27. Petree, *Recollections of Past Days*, 66–67.
28. Peter McBride, in Madsen, *I Walked to Zion*, 44; Samuel Openshaw, diary, Sept. 6, 24, 1856; Josiah Rogerson, *Salt Lake Herald Sunday*, Nov. 3, 1907, 7; James Godson Bleak, journal, Sept. 23, 1856.
29. *Millennial Star*, July 26, 1856, 476–78; James Godson Bleak, journal, July 20–29, 1856.
30. Josiah Rogerson, *Salt Lake Herald*, Nov. 3, 1907, 7.
31. Ibid., 12.
32. Josiah Rogerson, *Salt Lake Herald*, Nov. 3, 1907, 12; John William Southwell, autobiographical sketch, Sept. 28; James Goodson Bleak, journal, Friday, Sept. 12, 1856.
33. John William Southwell, autobiographical sketch, Sept. 28.
34. Samuel Openshaw, diary, September 1, 1856; John Jaques, "Some Reminiscences," *Salt Lake Daily Herald*, Dec. 8, 1878, 1.
35. John William Southwell, autobiographical sketch.
36. Ibid.
37. Petree, *Recollections of Past Days*, 69.
38. Jesse Haven, journals, Sept. 12–13; Samuel Openshaw, diary, Sept. 16–20, 1856.

39. Petree, *Recollections of Past Days*, 70–71.
40. Ibid., 71–72.
41. Heber Robert McBride, autobiography, pp. 9–15.
42. Louisa Mellor Clark, in Carter, *Our Pioneer Heritage*, vol. 17, 305.
43. *Deseret News*, Oct. 22, 1856, 258; Caleb Grant, report, in "Church Emigration Book" Oct. 2, 1856; minutes of a meeting at the Historian's Office, *Journal History of the Church,* Oct. 4, 1856.
44. *Millennial Star,* Dec. 13, 1856, 798.
45. Wilford Woodruff, Oct. 6, 1856, in *Journal of Discourses*, vol. 4, 95.
46. *Deseret News*, Oct. 8, 1856, 245.

CHAPTER 12

1. Allphin, *Tell My Story, Too*, 118; Robert Reeder, history, 2–6; Willie Company Journal, Oct. 1, 1856.
2. Levi Savage, journal, Sept. 29–Oct. 1, 1856; Mr. Chislett's narrative, in Stenhouse, *The Rocky Mountain Saints*; Clayton, "Emigrants' Guide" as found in *A Comprehensive History of the Church*, vol. 3, addenda.
3. Clayton, "Emigrants' Guide" as found in *A Comprehensive History of the Church*, vol. 3, addenda; Mr. Chislett's narrative, in Stenhouse, *The Rocky Mountain Saints.*
4. Levi Savage, journal, Oct. 1, 1856; Willie Company Journal, Oct. 1, 1856.
5. Agnes Caldwell Southworth, autobiographical sketch, in Madsen, *I Walked To Zion*, 58; Allphin, *Tell My Story, Too*, 82.
6. Willie Company Journal, Oct. 1, 1856; William Woodward, history.
7. *Deseret News*, Oct. 8, 1856, 245; Josiah Rogerson, *Salt Lake Herald,* Dec. 8, 1907, 14; "Historian's Office Minutes," in *Journal History of the Church*, vol. 4, Oct. 1856.
8. *Journal History of the Church,* vol. 4, Oct. 1856.
9. Levi Savage, journal, Oct. 4, 1856; Willie Company Journal, Oct. 1–4, 1856; Alfred Gadd, diary, Oct. 4, 1856.
10. Alfred Gadd, diary, Oct. 4, 1856; Samuel Gadd, biography; Carter, *Our Pioneer Heritage*, 331.
11. Josiah Rogerson, *The Salt Lake Herald,* Nov. 3, 1907, 7; Clayton, "Emigrants' Guide," in *A Comprehensive History of the Church*, vol. 3, addenda; Openshaw Journal, in *Enduring Legacy*; Samuel Openshaw, diary, Sept. 7, 8, 14, 19, 21, 23, 1856; John Jaques, "Some Reminiscences," *Salt Lake Daily Herald*, Dec. 8, 1878, 1; Allphin, *Tell My Story, Too*, 257.

CHAPTER 13

1. *Deseret News*, Oct. 15, 1856, 252.
2. Ibid.
3. Ibid.
4. Cluff, *A Reminiscent Account*.
5. *Millennial Star,* July 26, 1856, 476–78.
6. Kimball, "Belated Emigrants of 1856."
7. *Deseret News,* Dec. 3, 1856, 309.
8. *Deseret News*, Oct. 15, 1856, 256.
9. Daniel W. Jones, *40 Years Among the Indians*, 41.
10. Stegner, *Gathering of Zion,* 260–61; Jones, *40 Years Among the Indians*, 10–17, 33, 316.
11. Jones, *40 Years Among the Indians*, 42; Kimball, "Belated Emigrants of 1856," 109.
12. Kimball, "Our Pioneer Boys."
13. Ibid.
14. Ibid.
15. Ibid.
16. Kimball, "Belated Emigrants of 1856," 109.
17. Jones, *40 Years Among the Indians*, 42.
18. Ibid.

CHAPTER 14

1. Levi Savage, journal, Aug. 12, 1856.
2. Mr. Chislett's narrative, in Stenhouse, *The Rocky Mountain Saints.*
3. Levi Savage, journal, Oct. 4, 1856; Willie Company Journal, Oct. 4, 9, 1856; Alfred Gadd, diary, Oct. 9, 1856.
4. Willie Company Journal, Oct. 5–13, 1856; Levi Savage, journal, Oct. 5–13, 1856.
5. Mr. Chislett's narrative, in Stenhouse, *The Rocky Mountain Saints.*
6. Susannah Stone Lloyd, family sketches, pp. 1–2; Allphin, *Tell My Story, Too*, 137.
7. Mortensen family history, pp. 1–8.
8. Willie Company Journal, Oct. 10, 1856; Levi Savage, journal, Oct. 10, 1856; "History of Reshaws Bridge," Town of Evansville, Wyoming, http://townofevansville.org/about.html; "Mormon Ferry," City of Casper, Fort Caspar Museum, http://www.casperwy.gov.
9. "History of Reshaws Bridge," Town of Evansville, Wyoming, http://townofevansville.org/about.html; "Mormon Ferry," City of Casper,

Fort Caspar Museum, http://www.casperwy.gov; Willie Company Journal, Oct. 10, 1856; Levi Savage, journal, Oct. 10, 1856; Josiah Rogerson, *The Salt Lake Herald,* Nov. 10, 1907, 3.

10. John Jaques, "Some Reminiscences," *Salt Lake Daily Herald,* Dec. 8, 1878, 1; Josiah Rogerson, *Salt Lake Herald,* Nov. 3, 1907, 12.
11. Josiah Rogerson, *Salt Lake Herald,* Nov. 3, 1907, 12; Edward Martin Company Bashore Death List; Allphin, *Tell My Story, Too,* 153.
12. Jesse Haven, journals, Oct. 10, 1856; John Jaques, "Some Reminiscences," *Salt Lake Daily Herald,* Dec. 8, 1878, 1; Josiah Rogerson, *The Salt Lake Herald,* Nov. 10, 1907, 3; Clayton, "Emigrant Guide," in *A Comprehensive History of the Church,* vol. 3, addenda.

CHAPTER 15

1. Mr. Chislett's narrative, in Stenhouse, *The Rocky Mountain Saints*; Levi Savage, journal, Oct. 15, 1856; Claytong, "Emigrants' Guide," in *A Comprehensive History of the Church,* vol. 3, addenda; Willie Company Journal, Oct. 15, 1856.
2. Robert Reeder, history, pp. 2–6.
3. Josiah Rogerson, *Salt Lake Herald* Sunday, Nov. 24, 1907, 8.
4. John Jaques, "Some Reminiscences," *Salt Lake Daily Herald,* Dec. 8, 1878, 1.
5. Ibid.
6. Ibid.
7. Bond, *Handcarts West in '56.*
8. Ibid.
9. Bell, *Life History and Writings of John Jaques,* 143–44; John Jaques, "Some Reminiscences," *Salt Lake Daily Herald,* Dec. 8, 1878, 1.
10. John Jaques, "Some Reminiscences," *Salt Lake Daily Herald,* Dec. 8, 1878, 1; Petree *Recollections of Past Days,* 70, 86, 218, note 62.
11. John Jaques, "Some Reminiscences," *Salt Lake Daily Herald,* Dec. 8, 1878, 1.
12. Josiah Rogerson, *Salt Lake Herald,* Nov. 10, 1907, 3.
13. Mortensen Family History, pp. 1–8; Wood, "Mettie Kerstena Mortensen Rasmussen."

CHAPTER 16

1. Jones, *40 Years Among the Indians,* 42; Clayton, "Emigrants' Guide," in *A Comprehensive History of the Church,* vol. 3, addenda; "Burton,

Robert T.," in *Journal History,* Nov. 30, 1856, 54–58; Letter, George D. Grant to President Young, *Deseret News,* Nov. 11, 1856, 293.

2. Clayton, "Emigrants' Guide," in *A Comprehensive History of The Church,* vol. 3, addenda; "Burton, Robert T.," in *Journal History,* Nov. 30, 1856, 54–58; Bartholomew and Arrington, *Rescue of the 1856 Handcart Companies*, 11.
3. Redick Newton Allred, biographical sketch.

CHAPTER 17

1. Levi Savage Journal, Oct. 18, 1856; Willie Company Journal, Oct. 18–22, 1856; John Oborn, reminiscences and diary.
2. George Cunningham, reminiscences, 1876, fd. 2, 2–5.
3. Levi Savage, journal, Oct. 19, 1856; Dixon, "History of Her Ancestor William James."
4. Willie Company Journal, pp. 16–53; Ann Jewell Rowley, autobiography.
5. Levi Savage, journal; Mr. Chislett's narrative, in Stenhouse, *The Rocky Mountain Saints*; Claytong, "Emigrants' Guide," in *A Comprehensive History of the Church,* vol. 3, addenda; Willie Company Journal, Oct. 19, 1856.
6. Goodwin, "The Tired Mother," 775–81.
7. Mr. Chislett's narrative, in Stenhouse, *The Rocky Mountain Saints.*
8. John Oborn, reminiscences and diary, Part 1:4, Part 2:2.
9. Kelly, "Emily Hill Woodmansee, Poetess," 52.
10. Willie Company Journal, pp. 16–53; Letter, William Woodward to Joseph F. Smith; Mr. Chislett's narrative, in Stenhouse, *The Rocky Mountain Saints.*
11. Mr. Chislett's narrative, in Stenhouse, *The Rocky Mountain Saints,* 323.
12. Goodwin, "The Tired Mother," 775–81.
13. Willie Company Journal, Oct. 20, 1856; Levi Savage, journal, Oct. 20, 1856.
14. Mr. Chislett's narrative, in Stenhouse, *The Rocky Mountain Saints.*
15. Smith, *Faithful Stewards,* 111.
16. Mr. Chislett's narrative, in Stenhouse, *The Rocky Mountain Saints.*
17. Ibid.
18. Dixon, "History of Her Ancestor William James."
19. James Henry Linford, autobiography, pp. 4, 6, 8; account by Amasa Christian Linford, James Henry Linford, autobiography, pp. 53–55.
20. Margaret Ann McFall Caldwell Bennett, reminiscences, 4–5.

21. Agnes Caldwell Southworth, autobiographical sketch, in Madsen, *I Walked to Zion,* 57–59.
22. Cluff Family Journal, Oct. 19, 1856.
23. Harvey H. Cluff, "A Reminiscent Account."
24. Ibid.
25. Mr. Chislett's narrative, in Stenhouse, *The Rocky Mountain Saints.*
26. Ibid.
27. Harvey H. Cluff, "A Reminiscent Account."
28. Mr. Chislett's narrative, in Stenhouse, *The Rocky Mountain Saints.*
29. Smith, *Faithful Stewards,* 111; Cluff Family Journal; Willie Company Journal, Oct. 22, 1856.
30. Mr. Chislett's narrative, in Stenhouse, *The Rocky Mountain Saints*; Willie Company Journal, October 22, 1856.
31. John Jaques, "Some Reminiscences," *Salt Lake Daily Herald,* December 8, 1878, 1.
32. John Bond, *Handcarts West in '56.*
33. Peter Howard McBride, in Carter, *Our Pioneer Heritage,* 362.
34. Petree, *Recollections of Past Days,* 73–74.
35. Josiah Rogerson, *Salt Lake Herald,* Nov. 10, 1907, 3, 5.
36. Margaret Ann Griffiths Clegg, autobiographical sketch.
37. John Jaques, "Some Reminiscences," *Salt Lake Daily Herald,* Dec. 8, 1878, 1.
38. Petree, *Recollections of Past Days,* 74.
39. Ibid.
40. Ibid., 75–76.
41. *The Tempered Wind,* by Sidney Alvarus Hanks, Biography of Thisbe Read Hanks.
42. Ibid
43. Hanks, *The Tempered Wind*; Allphin, *Tell My Story, Too,* 269.
44. Elizabeth Horrocks Jackson Kingsford, reminiscences, in *"Utah Pioneer Biographies,"* 17:92–103; Kingsford, *Leaves from the Life of Elizabeth Horrocks Jackson Kingsford.*
45. Josiah Rogerson, *Salt Lake Herald,* Nov. 10, 1907, 5 and Nov. 17, 1907, 14.
46. Heber Robert McBride, autobiography, pp. 9–15.
47. Josiah Rogerson, *Salt Lake Herald,* Nov. 17, 1907, 14.
48. Samuel Openshaw, diary.

CHAPTER 18

1. Clayton, "Emigrants' Guide," in *A Comprehensive History of the*

Church, vol. 3, addenda; Willie Company Journal, pp. 16–53; Levi Savage, journal, Oct. 23, 1856.

2. Dixon, "History of Her Ancestor William James"; Dangerfield, Mary Ann James, in Carter, *Our Pioneer Heritage*, vol. 14, 294; Levi Savage, journal, Oct. 23, 1856.
3. Dixon, "History of Her Ancestor William James Dangerfield."
4. Mr. Chislett's narrative, in Stenhouse, *The Rocky Mountain Saints*, 327–29.
5. Ibid.
6. Dixon, "History of Her Acestor William James Dangerfield"; Mary Ann James, in Carter, *Our Pioneer Heritage*, vol. 14, 294.
7. Mr. Chislett's narrative, in Stenhouse, *The Rocky Mountain Saints*, 317; letter, Woodward to Joseph F. Smith; Levi Savage, journal, Oct. 23, 1856.
8. Allphin, *Tell My Story, Too,* 129–30.
9. Ann Jewell Rowley, autobiography.
10. Robert Campbell Kirkwood, Kirkwood family history; Faust, "A Priceless Heritage," 84.
11. Jens Nielson, autobiography; Albert R. Lyman, *Bishop Jens Nielson*, 2; Jay P. Nielson, history; Faust, "A Priceless Heritage," 84.
12. Gadd Family History; Carter, *Our Pioneer Heritage*, vol 2; Carter, *They Came Alone*, 331.
13. Redick Newton Allred, journals, Oct. 24, 1856.
14. Mr. Chislett's narrative, in Stenhouse, *The Rocky Mountain Saints*; Willie Company Journal, Oct. 23–24, 1856.
15. Willie Company Journal, Oct. 25, 1856.
16. Mr. Chislett's narrative, in Stenhouse, *The Rocky Mountain Saints*, 330.
17. Josiah Rogerson, *Salt Lake Herald*, Nov. 17, 1907, 14.
18. Petree, *Recollections of Past Days*, 76.
19. John Jaques, "Some Reminiscences," *Salt Lake Daily Herald*, Dec. 15, 1878, 1.
20. Josiah Rogerson, *Salt Lake Herald*, Nov. 24, 1907.
21. Samuel Openshaw, diary, p. 10.
22. Josiah Rogerson, *Salt Lake Herald*, Oct. 20, 1907, 12.
23. Josiah Rogerson, *Salt Lake Herald*, Nov. 24, 1907, 8; Palmer, "She Stood Tall on Her Knees."
24. McBride, Peter Howard, in Madsen, *I Walked to Zion*, 45; Heber Robert McBride, autobiography, 9–15; McBride, Peter Howard, in Carter, *Our Pioneer Heritage*, 360–63.
25. Elizabeth Horrocks Jackson Kingsford, reminiscences, in *Utah*

Pioneer Biographies, 17:92–103

26. Josiah Rogerson, *Salt Lake Herald*, Nov. 17, 1907, 14.
27. George D. Grant, letter, dated Devil's Gate, Nov. 2; John Jaques, "Some Reminiscences," *Salt Lake Daily Herald*, Dec. 15, 1878, 1; Josiah Rogerson, *Salt Lake Herald*, Dec. 8, 1907, 14; Jones, *40 Years Among the Indians*, 43; Redick Newton Allred, journals.
28. Clayton, "Emigrants' Guide," in *A Comprehensive History of the Church,* vol. 3, addenda; Kimball, "Belated Emigrants of 1856"; "Burton, Robert T.," in *Journal History of the Church*, 30 Nov. 1856, 54–58.
29. Jones, *40 Years Among the Indians,* 44.
30. Kimball, "Belated Emigrants of 1856."
31. Jones, *40 Years Among the Indians*, 44; report, George D. Grant to Brigham Young, Nov. 2, 1856, in *Deseret News*, Nov. 19, 1856, 293; Josiah Rogerson, *Salt Lake Herald*, Nov. 17, 1907, 14.
32. Redick Newton Allred, journals, Nov. 14, 1856.
33. Hanks, *Scouting for the Mormons on the Great Frontier*, 57, 65; Hanks, *The Tempered Wind*
34. Jones, *40 Years Among the Indians,* 44.
35. Louisa Mellor Clark, in Carter, *Our Pioneer Heritage,* 305.
36. Albert Jones, reminiscences, in *Deseret Evening News*, September 1, 1906, 20.
37. Josiah Rogerson, *Salt Lake Herald,* Nov. 24, 1907, 8.
38. John Jaques, "Some Reminiscences," *Salt Lake Daily Herald*, Dec. 15, 1878, 1.
39. James Goodson Bleak, journal, Oct. 28, 1856; John Jaques, "Some Reminiscences," *Salt Lake Daily Herald*, Jan. 5, 1879, 1; *Deseret News*, Nov. 19, 1856, 292.
40. Jones, *40 Years Among the Indians,* 44–45.
41. Kimball, "Belated Emigrants of 1856"; *Deseret News,* Nov. 19, 1856, 292.
42. Samuel Openshaw, diary, pp. 3–10; Petree, *Recollections of Past Days*, 77.
43. Jones, *40 Years Among the Indians*, 46; *Deseret News*, Nov. 19, 1856, 292.
44. John Jaques, "Some Reminiscences," *Salt Lake Daily Herald*, Dec. 15, 1878, 1.
45. Jones, *40 Years Among the Indians*, 46.
46. Rescue Company Journal; Jones, *40 Years Among the Indians*, 46; *Deseret News*, Nov. 19, 1856, 292.
47. Harvey H. Cluff, "A Reminiscent Account."

CHAPTER 19

1. *Millennial Star*, Feb. 14, 1857, 97.
2. Willie Company Journal, Oct. 30, 1856; Clayton, "Emigrants' Guide," in *A Comprehensive History of the Church*, vol. 3, addenda; John Oborn, reminiscences and diary, p. 2; George Cunningham, reminiscences, 1876, fd. 2, 2–5.
3. Willie Company Journal, October 30, 1856; Clayton, "Emigrants' Guide," in *A Comprehensive History of the Church*, vol. 3, addenda; John Oborn, reminiscences and diary, p. 2; Allphin, *Tell My Story, Too*, 104.
4. Goodwin, "The Tired Mother."
5. Petree, *Recollections of Past Days*, 79.
6. John Jaques, "Some Reminiscences," *Salt Lake Daily Herald*, December 15, 1878, 1.
7. Petree, *Recollections of Past Days*, 79.
8. George D. Grant, *Deseret News*, Nov. 19, 1856, 293.
9. John Jaques, "Some Reminiscences," *Salt Lake Daily Herald*, Dec. 15, 1878, 1.
10. Margaret Ann Griffiths Clegg, autobiographical sketch, in *Wasatch Wave*.
11. *Deseret News*, Nov. 12, 1856, 282–84.
12. Stout, *On the Mormon Frontier*, 603–4; Roskelly, *Life of Arza E. Hinckley*; Paul, "The Handcart Companies of 1856 and Arza Erastus Hinckley," 8–9.
13. Clayton, "Emigrants Guide," in *A Comprehensive History of the Church*, vol. 3, addenda; Willie Company Journal, Nov. 2, 1856.
14. Willie Company Journal, Nov. 2, 1856; Mr. Chislett's narrative, in Stenhouse, *The Rocky Mountain Saints*, 330.
15. Paul, "The Handcart Companies of 1856 and Arza Erastus Hinckley," 13.
16. Paul, "The Handcart Companies of 1856 and Arza Erastus Hinckley," 15–16.
17. Wyoming State Historical Society Website; Josiah Rogerson, *Salt Lake Herald*, November 24, 1907.
18. Hafen, *Handcarts to Zion*, 235–36.
19. Petree, *Recollections of Past Days*, 81.
20. Jones, *40 Years Among The Indians*, 47; Elizabeth Horrocks Jackson Kingsford, reminiscences, in *Utah Pioneer Biographies*, 17:92–103; Clayton, "Emigrants Guide," in *A Comprehensive History of the Church*, vol. 3, addenda.

CHAPTER 20

1. Willie Company Journal, Nov. 3–4, 1856.
2. John Jaques, "Some Reminiscences" *Salt Lake Daily Herald*, Dec. 15, 1878, 1; Josiah Rogerson, *Salt Lake Herald*, Nov. 24, 1907.
3. *Deseret News*, Nov. 19, 1856, 293.
4. Jesse Haven, journals, vols. 4–5; Josiah Rogerson, *Salt Lake Herald*, November 24, 1907; John Jaques, "Some Reminiscences," *Salt Lake Daily Herald*, Dec. 15, 1878, 1.
5. John Jaques, "Some Reminiscences," *Salt Lake Daily Herald*, Dec. 15, 1878, 1; John Jaques, "Some Reminiscences," *Salt Lake Daily Herald*, Dec. 15, 1878, 1.
6. Petree, *Recollections of Past Days*, 83.
7. John Jaques, "Some Reminiscences," *Salt Lake Daily Herald*, Jan. 19, 1879, 1.
8. John Jaques, "Some Reminiscences," *Salt Lake Daily Herald*, Dec. 15, 1878, 1.
9. Josiah Rogerson, *Salt Lake Herald*, Nov. 24, 1907.
10. Isaac J. Wardle, biography; Allphin, *Tell My Story, Too*, 290.

CHAPTER 21

1. Willie Company Journal, Nov. 5, 1856; Smith, *Faithful Stewards*, 117.
2. Smith, *Faithful Stewards*, 117; James McPhail Pert, interview in *Utah Pioneer Biographies*, 23:44–45; Harper, "Life Sketch of Henrietta McPahil Eckersell."
3. Willie Company Journal, Nov. 6–8, 1856.
4. Jesse Haven, journals, Nov. 4–7, 1856; James Godson Bleak, journal.
5. Heber Robert McBride, autobiography, pp. 9–15.
6. Elizabeth Horrocks Jackson Kingsford, autobiographical sketch, n.d., pp. 2–6.
7. Josiah Rogerson, *Salt Lake Herald*, Nov. 24, 1907.
8. Hafen, *Handcarts to Zion*, 232–38.
9. Peter Howard McBride, in Madsen, *I Walked To Zion*, 46.
10. John Jaques, "Some Reminiscences," *Salt Lake Daily Herald*, Dec. 22, 1878, 1.
11. Petree, *Recollections of Past Days*, 86–87.
12. Josiah Rogerson, *Salt Lake Herald*, November 24, 1907, 8.
13. Jones, *40 Years Among the Indians*, 47–48.
14. Ibid., 48–49.
15. Josiah Rogerson, *Salt Lake Herald*, November 24, 1907, 8; Robert T.

Burton, journal; W. Jones, *40 Years Among the Indians*, 49.
16. Jones, *40 Years Among the Indians*, 49.
17. Jones, *40 Years Among the Indians*, 49; Riverton Wyoming Stake, *Remember*, 31.

CHAPTER 22

1. Willie Company Journal, p. 53; Allphin, *Tell My Story, Too*, 102–3.
2. Smith, *Faithful Stewards*, 118.
3. *Deseret News*, Nov. 26, 1856, 301; Kimball, *Belated Emigrants of 1856*.
4. Smith, *Faithful Stewards*, 117.
5. Mr. Chislett's narrative, in Stenhouse, *The Rocky Mountain Saints*.
6. Joseph Benson Elder, journal, pp. 23–24.
7. Smith, *Faithful Stewards*, 118; Wight, "If You Keep My Commandments," 571.
8. Smith, *Faithful Stewards*, 122.
9. Ibid., 179.
10. Clayton, "Emigrants Guide," in *A Comprehensive History of the Church*, vol. 3, addenda; Jones, *40 Years Among the Indians*, 49.
11. John Jaques, "Some Reminiscences," *Salt Lake Daily Herald*, Dec. 22, 1878, 1.
12. Bailey, reminiscences and journal, pp. 4–7; *Deseret Evening News*, Sept. 1, 1906, 20–21.
13. Hanks, *The Tempered Wind*, 57.
14. Games Godson Bleak, journal; Allphin, *Tell My Story, Too*, 167–69.
15. Jones, *40 Years Among the Indians*, 49–50.
16. Hanks and Hanks, *Scouting for the Mormons on the Great Frontier*, 65–67.
17. Ibid., 67–68.
18. Ephraim Knowlton Hanks, patriarchal blessing, Feb. 11, 1848.
19. Hanks, *The Tempered Wind*.
20. Roskelly, *Life of Arza E. Hinckley*; Paul, "The Handcart Companies of 1856 and Arza Erastus Hinckley," 18.
21. Hanks and Hanks, *Scouting for the Mormons on the Great Frontier*, 70.
22. Ibid.
23. Paul, "The Handcart Companies of 1856 and Arza Erastus Hinckley," 45; Josiah Rogerson, *Salt Lake Daily Herald*, Nov. 24, 1907, 8; Paul, "The Handcart Companies of 1856 and Arza Erastus Hinckley," preface, 3.
24. Roskelly, *Life of Arza E. Hinckley*.

25. Petree, *Recollections of Past Days*, 77–79; Hanks and Hanks, *Scouting for the Mormons on the Great Frontier*, 68–69; Albert Jones, "Utah Heroes Who Pulled Their All," *Deseret Evening News*, Sept. 1, 1906, 20.

CHAPTER 23

1. Brooks, *On the Mormon Frontier*, 605.
2. Redick Newton Allred, journal, Nov. 14, 1856.
3. Brooks, *On the Mormon Frontier*, 605–6.
4. Ibid., 606.
5. Jones, *40 Years Among the Indians*, 50–51.
6. Josiah Rogerson, *Salt Lake Herald,* Nov. 24, 1907, 8.
7. Ibid.
8. *Deseret News,* Nov. 19, 1856, 293.

CHAPTER 24

1. Anson Call, journal, p. 57.
2. Elizabeth Whitear Sermon Camm, Letter, San Francisco, California, to "My Dear Children" Mar. 16, 1892.
3. John Jaques, *Salt Lake Daily Herald,* Dec. 22, 1878, 1; Clayton, "Emigrants' Guide," in *A Comprehensive History of the Church*, vol. 3, addenda.
4. Peter Howard McBride, in Madsen, *I Walked to Zion*, 46.
5. Redick Newton Allred, journals, Oct. 8 and 14, 1856.
6. Robert T. Burton, journal, in *Journal History of The Church of Jesus Christ of Latter-day Saints*, Nov. 30, 1856, 54–58; Brooks, *On the Mormon Frontier*, 606–7.
7. Redick Newton Allred, journals, Nov. 18, 1856.
8. Willes, *A Brief Biography of Joseph Marcellus Simmons.*
9 Robert T.Burton, journal, in *Journal History of The Church of Jesus Christ of Latter-day Saints*, Nov. 30, 1856, 54–58, and Nov. 20–21, 1856; *Deseret News*, Nov. 26, 1856, 301; Jesse Haven, journals, Nov. 21, 1856.
10. Jensen, *LDS Biographical Encyclopedia,* vol 1; Orson F. Whitney, in *Encyclopedia of Mormonism*, vol. 4, appendix 1; Robert Taylor Burton, autobiography; Brigham Young, letter, in *Journal History of The Church of Jesus Christ of Latter-day Saints*, Aug. 20, 1848, 2; Brigham

Young to Heber C. Kimball, letter, in *Journal History of The Church of Jesus Christ of Latter-day Saints,* Aug. 28, 1848, 2–4.

CHAPTER 25

1. Robert T. Burton, journal, in *Journal History of The Church of Jesus Christ of Latter-day Saints,* Nov. 26, 30, 1856, 54–58; Josiah Rogerson, *Salt Lake Herald,* Dec. 1, 1907, 7.
2. *Millennial Star,* Apr. 18, 1857, 254–55.
3. Hanks and Hanks, *Scouting for the Mormons on the Great Frontier,* 70–71.
4. Josiah Rogerson, *Salt Lake Daily Herald,* Dec. 1, 1907, 7; John Jaques, "Some Reminiscences," *Salt Lake Daily Herald,* Dec. 22, 1878, 1.
5. Josiah Rogerson, *Salt Lake Herald,* Dec. 8, 1907, 14.
6. Ibid., 7.
7. John Bond, *Handcarts West in '56.*
8. Ibid.

CHAPTER 26

1. *Deseret News,* Dec. 10, 1856, 320.
2. John Jaques, "Some Reminiscences," *Salt Lake Daily Herald,* Dec. 22, 1878, 1.
3. Robert Taylor Burton, autobiography.
4. Hafen and Hafen, *Handcarts to Zion,* 238.
5. Redick Newton Allred, journals.
6. Kimball, "Belated Emigrants of 1856."
7. Josiah Rogerson, *Salt Lake Herald,* Nov. 3, 1907, 7.
8. Louisa Mellor Clark, in Carter, *Our Pioneer Heritage,* 306.
9. Allphin, *Tell My Story, Too,* 153–54.
10. Margaret Ann Griffiths Clegg, autobiographical sketch, in *Wasatch Wave*; Jane Griffiths Fullmer, reminiscences, in Ella Campbell, *An Early Pioneer History and Reminiscences,* 3; Jane Eleanor Griffiths Fullmer, autobiography; Margaret Ann Griffiths Clegg, autobiographical sketch.
11. Josiah Rogerson, *Salt Lake Herald,* Nov. 24, 1907, 8; Palmer, *She Stood Tall on Her Knees.*
12. *Millennial Star,* June 14, 1856, 377; Nauvoo Land and Records for Edward Martin.
13. *Deseret News,* Dec. 3, 1856, 309; Josiah Rogerson, *Salt Lake Herald,*

Dec. 8, 1907, 14; John Jaques, in *History of Utah*, vol. 2, 564; Deckker, "Some Must Push and Some Must Pull," 38–47; *Millennial Star*, Aug. 23, 1856, 542.

CHAPTER 27

1. Jones, *40 Years Among the Indians*, 52–58.
2. Ibid., 48–60.
3. Ibid., 62–64.
4. Ibid., 65–66.
5. Ibid., 78–80.
6. Ibid., 81–82.
7. Ibid., 82–83.
8. Ibid., 84.
9. Ibid., 84.
10. Ibid., 86–88.
11. Ibid., 88.
12. Ibid., 90–91.

CHAPTER 28

1. Palmer, "Pioneers of Southern Utah," *The Instructor*, May 1944, 217–18, as quoted in Van Cott and Leigh, *Generations of Webster's*, 61–62.
2. Ibid.
3. Webster, reminiscences, 1848–1881, 9, also published in Van Cott and Leigh, *Generations of Webster's*, 49, 53; William Francis Webster Palmer, privately distributed in ditto form, as quoted in Van Cott and Leigh, *Generations of Webster's*, 55–56.

CONCLUSION

1. Hinckley, "We Have a Work to Do."
2. *Millennial Star*, December 1, 1855, 756.
3. Benson, "Our Divine Constitution," 4.
4. Wells, *The Life of Samuel Adams*, 3:175.

5. Burton, "Let Virtue Garnish Your Thoughts," 76–78.
6. Hinckley, "In Opposition to Evil," 3.
7. Bell, *Life History and Writings of John Jaques*, 17.
8. *The Teachings of Ezra Taft Benson*, 106–7; *History of the Church*, 4:185–86.

BIBLIOGRAPHY

Allphin, Jolene S. *Tell My Story, Too.* Tell My Story Publishing, 2006.

Allred, Redick Newton. Journals. LDS Church Archives, Salt Lake City, Utah.

Bailey, Langley Allgood. Reminiscences and Journal, 1920–29. LDS Church Archives, Salt Lake City, Utah.

Bartholomew, Rebecca and Leonard J. Arrington. *Rescue of the 1856 Handcart Companies.* Provo, UT: Brigham Young University, 1981.

Beecroft, Joseph. Journals. LDS Church Archives, Salt Lake City, Utah.

Bell, Stella Jaques. *Life History and Writings of John Jaques.* Church Archives, 1978.

Bennett, Margaret Ann McFall Caldwell. Reminiscences. LDS Church Archives, Salt Lake City, Utah.

Benson, Ezra Taft. "Our Divine Constitution." *Ensign*, November 1987.

———. *The Teachings of Ezra Taft Benson*. Salt Lake City, UT: Bookcraft, 1988.

Bigler, David and Will Bagley. *Army of Israel: Mormon Battalion Narratives*. Logan, UT: Utah State University Press, Logan, 2000.

Bleak, James. "An Item of Handcart Experience." *Juvenile Instructor*.

———. Journal, Feb. 1854–Feb. 1860. LDS Church Archives, Salt Lake City, Utah.

Boggs, Lilburn W. Letter, dated Oct 27, 1838. Courtesy of Missouri State Archives.

Bond, John. *Handcarts West in '56*. Salt Lake City, UT: Utah State Historical Society.

Britannia. "A Compilation of General Voyage Notes." Mormon Immigration Index.

Brooks, Jaunita, ed. *On the Mormon Frontier: The Diary of Hosea Stout*. Salt Lake City: University of Utah, 1982.

Burton, H. David. "Let Virtue Garnish Your Thoughts." *Ensign*, November 2009.

Burton, Robert Taylor. Autobiography. LDS Church Archives, Salt Lake City, Utah.

Caldwell, Agnes. Autobiography. Typescript of interview conducted by Veara Southworth Fife. Daughters of Utah Pioneers.

Caldwell, Margaret Ann McFall. Reminiscences. LDS Church Archives, Salt Lake City, Utah.

"California's Pioneer Heritage: Saints, Soldiers, and Settlers." Placeville, CA: California Pioneer Heritage Foundation Pamphlet.

Call, Anson. Journal. LDS Church Archives, Salt Lake City, Utah.

Camm, Elizabeth Whitear Sermon. Letter to "My Dear Children." 1892.

Camm, Elizabeth Whittear Sermon. Reminiscence, in Joel Edward Ricks, Cache Valley Historical Material, 1955.

Campbell, Robert. Journal Extracts. June 30–October 19, 1848, in Historian Office Journal, 1844–97.

Carter, Kate B. *Our Pioneer Heritage.* Salt Lake City, UT: Daughters of Utah Pioneers. Church Archives.

———. *Treasures of Pioneer History.* Salt Lake City, UT: Daughters of Utah Pioneers.

Chapman, Glen W., comp. "The Mormon Handcart Experiences." Self-published. January 2001.

Church History in the Fulness of Times, second edition. Salt Lake City, UT: The Church of Jesus Christ of Latter-day Saints, , 1998.

Clegg, Margaret Ann Griffiths. Autobiography. LDS Church Archives. Salt Lake City, Utah.

Clegg, Margaret Ann Griffiths. Autobiographical sketch, in *Wasatch Wave*, ca. 1906.

Cluff Family Journal. Cluff Family Reunion, 1904. Rearranged 1994 by Viva Cluff Whetten.

Cluff, Harvey Harris. A Reminiscent Account 1836–1868. Brigham Young University Library.

———. Autobiography (1836–1916).

Crocheron, Augusta, comp. *Representative Women of Deseret.* N.P. 1884.

Cowley, Matthias F. *Wilford Woodruff, History of His Life and Labors.* Salt Lake City, UT: Bookcraft, 1975.

Cowley, Sarah Wall. Cowley family histories. Daughters of Utah Pioneers. Salt Lake City, Utah.

Cunningham, George. Reminiscences. LDS Church Archives. Salt Lake City, Utah.

Clayton, William, "Emigrants' Guide," as found in *A Comprehensive History of the Church*, vol. 3, addenda.

Davis, Daniel. Diary. 1846–1892.

Decker, Linda. "Some Must Push and Some Must Pull." *Ensign*, July 2006.

Dennis, Ronald D. *The Call of Zion: The Story of the First Welsh Mormon Emigration*. Provo, UT: Religious Studies Center, BYU, 1987.

———. "Dan Jones, Welshman: Taking the Gospel Home." *Ensign*, April 1987.

Dixon, Loleta Wiscombe. "Loleta Dixons History of Her Ancestor William James Dangerfield." LDS Church Archives. Salt Lake City, Utah.

Edward Martin Company. Bashore death list.

Elder, Joseph B. Journal. LDS Church Archives. Salt Lake City, Utah.

Enduring Legacy. 12 vols. Salt Lake City, UT: Daughters of Utah Pioneers, 1978–89.

England, Breck. "Gospel Seeds in Scottish Soil." *Ensign*, February 1987.

Faust, James E. "A Priceless Heritage." *Ensign*, November 1992.

For the Strength of Youth. Booklet. Salt Lake City, UT: The Church of Jesus Christ of Latter-day Saints, 2011.

Fullmer, Jane Elanor Griffiths. Autobiography. 1928.

Gadd, Alfred. Diary. LDS Church Archives. Salt Lake City, UT.

Gadd, Samuel. Biography, in "The Gadd Family History." LDS Church Archives. Salt Lake City, Utah.

Grant, Caleb. Report, in "Church Emigration Book," 1856.

Gregerson, Edna J. *The Mellors through the Years*. Springville, UT: Art City, 1963. BYU special collections.

Griffiths, Jane. Reminiscence, in Ella Campbell, "An Early Pioneer History and Reminiscences."Goodwin, Betsey Smith. "The Tired Mother: Pioneer Recollections." *Improvement Era*, 1919.

———. "Handcart Speech." *Woman's Exponent*, 1888.

Hafen, Leroy R. and Ann W. Hafen. *Handcarts to Zion: The Story of a Unique Western Migration, 1856–1860*. Bison Books, 1992.

Hanks, Ephraim Knowlton. Patriarchal blessing, February 11, 1848. Copyright 2008 Daniel C. Hanks.

Hanks, Sidney Alvarus and Ephraim K. *Scouting for the Mormons on the Great Frontier*. Orem, UT: HanksPlace Press. Originally published by Deseret Book, 1948.

———. *The Tempered Wind: The Life Story of Thisbe Read Hanks*. Salt Lake City, UT: Salt Lake Times, 1956.

Harmer, Kathryn Mortensen. *Zion Bound: The Ancestry and Descendants of Arlington Peter and Fannie Burnham Mortensen*. K.M. Harmer, 1998.

Harper, Mary Darley. "Life Sketch of Henrietta McPahil Eckersell." LDS Church Archives. Salt Lake City, Utah.

Haven, Jesse. Journal. 1852–1892, vols. 4–5. LDS Church Archives. Salt Lake City, Utah.

Hinckley, Gordon B. "In Opposition to Evil." *Ensign*, September 2004.

———. "True to the Faith." *Ensign*, May 1997.

———. "The Faith of the Pioneers." *Ensign*, July 1984.

———. "We have a Work to Do." *Ensign*, February 1988.

"History of Reshaw's Bridge." http://townofevansville.org/about.html.

Jenson, Andrew. *Latter-Day Saint Biographical Encyclopedia: a Compilation of Biographical Sketches of Prominent Men and Women in The Church of Jesus Christ of Latter-day Saints, 1827–1900.* Salt Lake City, UT: A. Jenson History, 1920.

Jones, Daniel W. *40 Years Among the Indians; Mormon Frontier Classics.* Springville, UT: Council Press. First published at the Juvenile Instructor Office, Salt Lake City, Utah, 1890.

Jones, Dan to Thomas Bullock. Letter. January 20, 1855. LDS Archives. See also *BYU Studies*, Winter 1984, 95–97.

Journal History of The Church of Jesus Christ of Latter-day Saints. 1830–1972. LDS Church Archives. Salt Lake City, Utah.

Journal of Discourses. 26 vols. London: Latter-day Saints' Depot, 1854–56. LDS Church Archives. Salt Lake City, Utah.

Kelly, Mary F. "Emily Hill Woodmansee, Poetess." *Young Women's Journal* 1, no. 2, February 1907.

Kimball, Solomon F. "Our Pioneer Boys." *Improvement Era*, 1908.

———. "Belated Emigrants of 1856." *Improvement Era*, 1913.

Kingsford, Elizabeth Horrocks Jackson. Autobiographical sketch. LDS Church Archives. Salt Lake City, Utah.

———. *Leaves from the Life of Elizabeth Horrocks Jackson Kingsford.* LDS Church Archives. Salt Lake City, Utah.

Kirkwood, Mary. *Joseph Smith Clements.* Salt Lake City, UT: Daughters of Utah Pioneers.

Kirkwood, Robert Campbell. Kirkwood family history records. Salt Lake City, UT: Daughters of Utah Pioneers.

Linford, James Henry. Autobiography. LDS Church Archives. Salt Lake City, Utah.

Lloyd, Susannah Stone. Lloyd family sketches, 1915. LDS Church Archives. Salt Lake City, Utah.

Ludlow, Daniel H., ed. *Encyclopedia of Mormonism*. 5 vols. New York: MacMilliam, 1992.

Lyman, Albert R. *Bishop Jens Nielson: A Brief Biography*. LDS Church Archives. Salt Lake City, Utah.

Lyman, Paul D. *The Willie Handcart Experience*. Provo, UT: BYU Studies, 2006.

Martin, Edward, to John Melling. Letter, April 9, 1849.

Madsen, Susan Arrington. *I Walked To Zion: True Stories of Young Pioneers on the Mormon Trail*. Salt Lake City, UT: Deseret Book, 1994.

Madsen, Peder. Journal, translated by Tove Holden Jorgensen Johnson. LDS Church Archives. Salt Lake City, Utah.

McBride, Heber Robert. LDS Church Archives. Salt Lake City, Utah.

McConkie, Bruce R. "The Coming Tests and Trials and Glory." *Ensign*, May 1980.

McMullin, Keith B. "Faith and Works in a Secular World." CES Fireside, Nov. 5, 2006. BYU.

McPhail, Archibald. Autobiography. LDS Church Archives. Salt Lake City, Utah.

Mormon Battalion records.

Mormon Immigration Index.

Mormon Pioneer Overland Travel, 1847–1868. Database. http://www.lds.org/churchhistory/library/pioneerdetails. LDS Church Archives.

Mortensen family history. LDS Church Archives. Salt Lake City, Utah.

Nauvoo Land and Records Research Center.

Newbold, Noal Clegg. *Margaret Ann Griffiths Clegg: Handcart Saint.* Sandy, UT: N.C. Newbold, 1996.

Nielson, Jens. Autobiography. LDS Church Archives. Salt Lake City, Utah.

Oborn, John. Reminiscences and diary. LDS Church Archives. Salt Lake City, Utah.

Ollerton family history. LDS Church Archives. Salt Lake City, Utah.

Openshaw, Samuel. Diary, from England to Salt Lake City, UT, May 23, 1856–November 30, 1856. LDS Church Archives. Salt Lake City, Utah.

Palmer, William. *She Stood Tall on Her Knees: Biography of Ellen "Nellie" Pucell Unthank.*

Palmer, William R. "Pioneers of Southern Utah." *The Instructor.*

Petree, Sandra Ailey. *Recollections of Past Days: The Autobiography of Patience Loader Rozsa Archer.* Logan, UT: Utah State University Press, 2006.

Pratt, Parley P. *Autobiography of Parley P. Pratt.* Salt Lake City, UT: Deseret Book, 1985.

Rasmussen, Mettie Kerstena Mortenson. LDS Church Archives. Salt Lake City, Utah.

Reeves, Pamela. *Ellis Island Gateway to the American Dream.* New York: Barnes & Noble Books, 2005.

Remember: The Willie and Martin Handcart Companies and Their Rescuers—Past and Present. Compiled by Riverton Wyoming Stake. N.P., 1997.

Reeder, Robert. History of Robert Reeder. Salt Lake City, UT: Daughters of Utah Pioneers.

Roskelly, Frances Hinckley. *A Sketch of the Life of Arza Erastus Hinckley.* Marysville, 1904.

Rowley, Ann Jewell. Autobiography, 1807–1888. Wife of William Rowley.

Savage, Levi. Journal, typescript copy, 1855 March–1858 October. LDS Church Archives. Salt Lake City, Utah.

Smith, Joseph. *History of The Church of Jesus Christ of Latter-day Saints.* Edited by B. H. Roberts. 2d ed. rev., 7 vols. Salt Lake City: The Church of Jesus Christ of Latter-day Saints, 1932–51.

Smith, Marilyn Austin, comp. *Faithful Stewards: The Life of James Gray Willie and Elizabeth Ann Pettit.* 1985.

Stegner, Wallace. *The Gathering of Zion: The Story of the Mormon Trail.* Edited by A.B. Guthrie, Jr. The American Trails Series, 1964.

Stenhouse, T. B. H. *The Rocky Mountain Saints: A Full and Complete History of the Mormons.* New York, 1873.

Southwell, John William. Autobiographical Sketch. LDS Church Archives. Salt Lake City, Utah.

Southworth, Agnes Caldwell. Autobiographical sketch. LDS Church Archives. Salt Lake City, Utah.

Taylor, Mark H. *Witness to the Martyrdom: John Taylor's Personal Account of the Last Days of the Prophet Joseph Smith.* Salt Lake City, UT: Deseret Book, 1999.

Thompson, Robert B., ed. *Journal of Heber C. Kimball.* Nauvoo, IL: Robinson and Smith, 1840.

Turner, Lynne Slater. *Emigrating Journals of the Willie and Martin Handcart Companies and the Hunt and Hodgett Wagon Trains.* L.S. Turner, 1996.

Utah Pioneer Biographies. 44 vols. 1935–1964. Family History Library. Salt Lake City, Utah.

Van Cott, Amy L. and Allen W. Leigh. *Generations of Websters.* Cedar City, Utah: Thomas Webster Family Organization, 1960. Privately distributed in ditto form.

Wardle, Isaac J. Biography. LDS Church Archives. Salt Lake City, Utah.

Wells, William. *The Life and Public Services of Samuel Adams.* Applewood Books, 2009.

West, Franklin L. *Life of Franklin D. Richards: President of the Council of the Twelve Apostles of the Church of Jesus Christ of Latter-day Saints.* Salt Lake City, UT: Deseret News Press, 1924.

Whitney, Orson F. *History of Utah.* G. Q. Cannon, 1904.

———. *Life of Heber C. Kimball,* third edition. Salt Lake City, UT. 1967.

Whittaker, David J. "Early Mormon Imprints in South Africa." *BYU Studies* 20, no. 4 (1980), 1–6.

Wight, Mary Hurren. Biography. LDS Church Archives. Salt Lake City, Utah.

Wight, La Preal. "If You Keep My Commandments." *Improvement Era*, August 1953.

Willes, Joseph Simmons. *A Brief Biography of Joseph Marcellus Simmons.* Typescript. LDS Church Archives

Willie Company Journal. LDS Church Archives. Salt Lake City, Utah.

Woodruff, Wilford. *Leaves from My Journal.* Salt Lake City, UT: Covenant Communications, 2005. Original published by Juvenile Instructor Office, 1882.

Woodward, William. History. LDS Church Archives. Salt Lake City, Utah.

Woodward, William, to Joseph F. Smith. Letter, 1907, in Utah State Historical Society Cache Valley Chapter, 1955–1956.

ABOUT THE AUTHOR

Shelli Simmons was born in Salt Lake City, Utah, and graduated with honors from a local business college. Following her marriage to her high school sweetheart, she worked in the business industry until the death of her 2½-month-old son from sudden infant death syndrome. Shelli spent the next eighteen years at home raising three beautiful children, serving in church callings, and assisting her husband with his business ventures. During her service as a stake Young Women president, Shelli had the opportunity to organize two stake pioneer handcart trek youth conferences, which began a twelve-year journey in research and intensive study of the lives of the members of the Willie and Martin Handcart Companies.

0 26575 10179 9